ROUSSEAU

BY

JOHN MORLEY

VOL. I.

London
MACMILLAN AND CO., Limited
NEW YORK: THE MACMILLAN COMPANY
1905

First printed in this form 1886
Reprinted 1888, 1891, 1896, 1900, 1905

NOTE TO THE FIRST EDITION.

THIS work differs from its companion volume in offering something more like a continuous personal history than was necessary in the case of such a man as Voltaire, the story of whose life may be found in more than one English book of repute. Of Rousseau there is, I believe, no full biographical account in our literature, and even France has nothing more complete under this head than Musset-Pathay's *Histoire de la Vie et des Ouvrages de J. J. Rousseau* (1821). This, though a meritorious piece of labour, is extremely crude and formless in composition and arrangement, and the interpreting portions are devoid of interest.

The edition of Rousseau's works to which the references have been made is that by M. Auguis, in twenty-seven volumes, published in 1825 by Dalibon. In 1865 M. Streckeisen-Moultou published from the originals, which had been deposited in the library of Neuchâtel by Du Peyrou, the letters addressed to Rousseau by various correspondents. These two interesting volumes, which are entitled *Rousseau, ses Amis et ses Ennemis,* are mostly referred to under the name of their editor.

February, 1873.

THE second edition in 1878 was revised; some portions were considerably shortened, and a few additional footnotes inserted. No further changes have been made in the present edition.

January, 1886.

CONTENTS OF VOL. I.

CHAPTER I.

PRELIMINARY.

CHAPTER II.

YOUTH.

CONTENTS.

CHAPTER III.

Savoy.

CHAPTER IV.

Theresa Le Vasseur.

CONTENTS.

CHAPTER V.

THE DISCOURSES.

CHAPTER VI.

PARIS.

CHAPTER VII.

THE HERMITAGE.

CHAPTER VIII.

MUSIC.

CHAPTER IX.

VOLTAIRE AND D'ALEMBERT.

CONTENTS.

JEAN JACQUES ROUSSEAU

Born	1712
Fled from Geneva	March, 1728
Changes religion at Turin	April, ,,
With Madame de Warens, including various intervals, until	April, 1740
Goes to Paris with musical schemes . .	1741
Secretary at Venice	Spring, 1743
Paris, first as secretary to M. Francueil, then as composer, and copyist . . .	1744 to 1756
The Hermitage	April 9, 1756
Montmorency	Dec. 15, 1757
Yverdun	June 14, 1762
Motiers-Travers	July 10, 1762
Isle of St. Peter	Sept., 1765
Strasburg	Nov., ,,
Paris	December, ,,
Arrives in England	Jan. 13, 1766
Leaves Dover	May 22, 1767
Fleury	June, ,,
Trye	July, ,,
Dauphiny	Aug., 1768
Paris	June, 1770
Death	July 2, 1778

PRINCIPAL WRITINGS.

Discourse on the Influence of Learning and Art	PUBLISHED	1750
Discourse on Inequality	,,	1754
Letter to D'Alembert	,,	1758
New Heloïsa (began 1757, finished in winter of 1759-60	,,	1761
Social Contract	,,	1762
Emilius	,,	1762
Letters from the Mountain	,,	1764
Confessions (written 1766-70) . . .	{ Pt. I. 1781 { Pt. II. 1788	

Rêveries (written 1777-78).

Comme dans les étangs assoupis sous les bois,
Dans plus d'une âme on voit deux choses à la fois :
Le ciel, qui teint les eaux à peine remuées
Avec tous ses rayons et toutes ses nuées ;
Et la vase, fond morne, affreux, sombre et dormant,
Où des reptiles noirs fourmillent vaguement.

HUGO.

ROUSSEAU.

CHAPTER I.

PRELIMINARY.

CHRISTIANITY is the name for a great variety of changes which took place during the first centuries of our era, in men's ways of thinking and feeling about their spiritual relations to unseen powers, about their moral relations to one another, about the basis and type of social union. So the Revolution is now the accepted name for a set of changes which began faintly to take a definite practical shape first in America, and then in France, towards the end of the eighteenth century; they had been directly prepared by a small number of energetic thinkers, whose speculations represented, as always, the prolongation of some old lines of thought in obedience to the impulse of new social and intellectual conditions. While one movement supplied the energy and the principles which extricated civilisation from the ruins of the Roman empire, the other supplies the energy and the principles which already once, between the Seven Years'

War and the assembly of the States General, saved
human progress in face of the political fatuity of
England and the political nullity of France ; and they
are now, amid the distraction of the various representatives of an obsolete ordering, the only forces to
be trusted at once for multiplying the achievements
of human intelligence stimulated by human sympathy,
and for diffusing their beneficent results with an
ampler hand and more far-scattering arm.   Faith in
a divine power, devout obedience to its supposed will,
hope of ecstatic, unspeakable reward, these were the
springs of the old movement.   Undivided love of
our fellows, steadfast faith in human nature, steadfast
search after justice, firm aspiration towards improvement, and generous contentment in the hope that
others may reap whatever reward may be, these are
the springs of the new.

There is no given set of practical maxims agreed
to by all members of the revolutionary schools for
achieving the work of release from the pressure of an
antiquated social condition, any more than there is
one set of doctrines and one kind of discipline accepted
by all Protestants.   Voltaire was a revolutionist in
one sense, Diderot in another, and Rousseau in
a third, just as in the practical order, Lafayette,
Danton, Robespierre, represented three different
aspirations and as many methods.   Rousseau was the
most directly revolutionary of all the speculative
precursors, and he was the first to apply his mind
boldly to those of the social conditions which the

revolution is concerned by one solution or another to modify. How far his direct influence was disastrous in consequence of a mischievous method, we shall have to examine. It was so various that no single answer can comprehend an exhaustive judgment. His writings produced that glow of enthusiastic feeling in France, which led to the all-important assistance rendered by that country to the American colonists in a struggle so momentous for mankind. It was from his writings that the Americans took the ideas and the phrases of their great charter, thus uniting the native principles of their own direct Protestantism with principles that were strictly derivative from the Protestantism of Geneva. Again, it was his work more than that of any other one man, that France arose from the deadly decay which had laid hold of her whole social and political system, and found that irresistible energy which warded off dissolution within and partition from without. We shall see, further, that besides being the first immediately revolutionary thinker in politics, he was the most stirring of reactionists in religion. His influence formed not only Robespierre and Paine, but Chateaubriand, not only Jacobinism, but the Catholicism of the Restoration. Thus he did more than any one else at once to give direction to the first episodes of revolution, and force to the first episode of reaction.

There are some teachers whose distinction is neither correct thought, nor an eye for the exigencies of practical organisation, but simply depth and fervour of the moral sentiment, bringing with it the indefinable gift of touching many hearts with love of virtue and the things of the spirit. The Christian organisations which saved western society from dissolution owe all to St. Paul, Hildebrand, Luther, Calvin; but the spiritual life of the west during all these generations has burnt with the pure flame first lighted by the sublime mystic of the Galilean hills. Aristotle acquired for men much knowledge and many instruments for gaining more; but it is Plato, his master, who moves the soul with love of truth and enthusiasm for excellence. There is peril in all such leaders of souls, inasmuch as they incline men to substitute warmth for light, and to be content with aspiration where they need direction. Yet no movement goes far which does not count one of them in the number of its chiefs. Rousseau took this place among those who prepared the first act of that revolutionary drama, whose fifth act is still dark to us.

At the heart of the Revolution, like a torrid stream flowing undiscernible amid the waters of a tumbling sea, is a new way of understanding life. The social changes desired by the various assailants of the old order are only the expression of a deeper change in moral idea, and the drift of the new moral idea is to make life simpler. This in a sense is at the bottom of all great religious and moral movements, and the Revolution emphatically belongs to the latter class. Like such movements in the breast of the individual, those which stir an epoch have their principle in

the same craving for disentanglement of life.   This
impulse to shake off intricacies is the mark of revolutionary generations, and it was the starting-point of
all Rousseau's mental habits, and of the work in
which they expressed themselves.   His mind moved
outwards from this centre, and hence the fact that
he dealt principally with government and education,
the two great agencies which, in an old civilisation
with a thousand roots and feelers, surround external
life and internal character with complexity.   Simplification of religion by clearing away the overgrowth
of errors, simplification of social relations by equality,
of literature and art by constant return to nature, of
manners by industrious homeliness and thrift,—this
is the revolutionary process and ideal, and this is the
secret of Rousseau's hold over a generation that was
lost amid the broken maze of fallen systems.

The personality of Rousseau has most equivocal
and repulsive sides.   It has deservedly fared ill in
the esteem of the saner and more rational of those
who have judged him, and there is none in the history
of famous men and our spiritual fathers that begat
us, who make more constant demands on the patience
or pity of those who study his life.   Yet in no other
instance is the common eagerness to condense all
predication about a character into a single unqualified
proposition so fatally inadequate.   If it is indispensable that we should be for ever describing, naming,
classifying, at least it is well, in speaking of such a

nature as his, to enlarge the vocabulary beyond the pedantic formulas of unreal ethics, and to be as sure as we know how to make ourselves, that each of the sympathies and faculties which together compose our power of spiritual observation, is in a condition of free and patient energy. Any less open and liberal method, which limits our sentiments to absolute approval or disapproval, and fixes the standard either at the balance of common qualities which constitutes mediocrity, or at the balance of uncommon qualities which is divinity as in a Shakespeare, must leave in a cloud of blank incomprehensibleness those singular spirits who come from time to time to quicken the germs of strange thought and shake the quietness of the earth.

We may forget much in our story that is grievous or hateful, in reflecting that if any man now deems a day basely passed in which he has given no thought to the hard life of garret and hovel, to the forlorn children and trampled women of wide squalid wildernesses in cities, it was Rousseau who first in our modern time sounded a new trumpet note for one more of the great battles of humanity. He makes the poor very proud, it was truly said. Some of his contemporaries followed the same vein of thought, as we shall see, and he was only continuing work which others had prepared. But he alone had the gift of the golden mouth. It was in Rousseau that polite Europe first hearkened to strange voices and faint reverberation from out of the vague and cavernous shadow in which the common people move. Science has to feel the way towards light and solution, to prepare, to organise. But the race owes something to one who helped to state the problem, writing up in letters of flame at the brutal feast of kings and the rich that civilisation is as yet only a mockery, and did furthermore inspire a generation of men and women with the stern resolve that they would rather perish than live on in a world where such things can be.

CHAPTER II.

YOUTH.

JEAN JACQUES ROUSSEAU was born at Geneva, June 28, 1712. He was of old French stock. His ancestors had removed from Paris to the famous city of refuge as far back as 1529, a little while before Farel came thither to establish the principles of the Reformation, and seven years before the first visit of the more extraordinary man who made Geneva the mother city of a new interpretation of Christianity, as Rome was the mother city of the old. Three generations in a direct line separated Jean Jacques from Didier Rousseau, the son of a Paris bookseller, and the first emigrant.[1] Thus Protestant tradition in the Rousseau family dates

[1] Here is the line :—

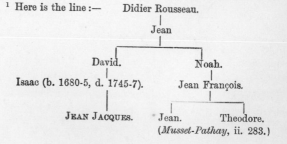

Didier Rousseau.
Jean
David.   Noah.
Isaac (b. 1680-5, d. 1745-7).   Jean François.
JEAN JACQUES.   Jean.   Theodore.
(*Musset-Pathay*, ii. 283.)

from the appearance of Protestantism in Europe, and seems to have exerted the same kind of influence upon them as it did, in conjunction with the rest of the surrounding circumstances, upon the other citizens of the ideal state of the Reformation. It is computed by the historians that out of three thousand families who composed the population of Geneva towards the end of the seventeenth century, there were hardly fifty who before the Reformation had acquired the position of burgess-ship. The curious set of conditions which thus planted a colony of foreigners in the midst of a free polity, with a new doctrine and newer discipline, introduced into Europe a fresh type of character and manners. People declared they could recognise in the men of Geneva neither French vivacity, nor Italian subtlety and clearness, nor Swiss gravity. They had a zeal for religion, a vigorous energy in government, a passion for freedom, a devotion to ingenious industries, which marked them with a stamp unlike that of any other community.[1] Towards the close of the seventeenth century some of the old austerity and rudeness was sensibly modified under the influence of the great neighbouring monarchy. One striking illustration of this tendency was the rapid decline of the Savoyard patois in popular use. The movement had not gone far enough when Rousseau was born, to take away from the manners and spirit of his country their special quality and individual note.

[1] Picot's *Hist. de Genève*, iii. 114.

The mother of Jean Jacques, who seems to have been a simple, cheerful, and tender woman, was the daughter of a Genevan minister; her maiden name, Bernard. The birth of her son was fatal to her, and the most touching and pathetic of all the many shapes of death was the fit beginning of a life preappointed to nearly unlifting cloud. "I cost my mother her life," he wrote, "and my birth was the first of my woes." [1] Destiny thus touches us with magical finger, long before consciousness awakens to the forces that have been set to work in our personality, launching us into the universe with country, forefathers, and physical predispositions, all fixed without choice of ours. Rousseau was born dying, and though he survived this first crisis by the affectionate care of one of his father's sisters, yet his constitution remained infirm and disordered.

Inborn tendencies, as we perceive on every side, are far from having unlimited irresistible mastery, if they meet early encounter from some wise and patient external will. The father of Rousseau was unfortunately cast in the same mould as his mother, and the child's own morbid sensibility was stimulated and deepened by the excessive sensibility of his first companion. Isaac Rousseau, in many of his traits, was a reversion to an old French type. In all the Genevese there was an underlying tendency of this kind. "Under a phlegmatic and cool air," wrote Rousseau, when warning his countrymen against the

[1] *Conf.*, i. 7.

inflammatory effects of the drama, "the Genevese hide an ardent and sensitive character, that is more easily moved than controlled."[1] And some of the episodes in their history during the eighteenth century might be taken for scenes from the turbulent dramas of Paris. But Isaac Rousseau's restlessness, his eager emotion, his quick and punctilious sense of personal dignity, his heedlessness of ordered affairs, were not common in Geneva, fortunately for the stability of her society and the prosperity of her citizens. This disorder of spirit descended in modified form to the son; it was inevitable that he should be indirectly affected by it. Before he was seven years old he had learnt from his father to indulge a passion for the reading of romances. The child and the man passed whole nights in a fictitious world, reading to one another in turn, absorbed by vivid interest in imaginary situations, until the morning note of the birds recalled them to a sense of the conditions of more actual life, and made the elder cry out in confusion that he was the more childish of the two.

The effect of this was to raise passion to a premature exaltation in the young brain. "I had no idea of real things," he said, "though all the sentiments were already familiar to me. Nothing had come to me by conception, everything by sensation. These confused emotions, striking me one after another, did not warp a reason that I did not yet possess, but they gradually shaped in me a reason of another cast and

[1] *Lettre à D'Alembert*, p. 187. Also *Nouv. Hél.*, VI. v. 239.

temper, and gave me bizarre and romantic ideas of
human life, of which neither reflection nor experience
has ever been able wholly to cure me."[1] Thus these
first lessons, which have such tremendous influence
over all that follow, had the direct and fatal effect in
Rousseau's case of deadening that sense of the actual
relations of things to one another in the objective world,
which is the master-key and prime law of sanity.

In time the library of romances came to an end
(1719), and Jean Jacques and his father fell back on
the more solid and moderated fiction of history and
biography. The romances had been the possession
of the mother; the more serious books were inherited
from the old minister, her father. Such books as
Nani's History of Venice, and Le Sueur's History of
the Church and the Empire, made less impression on
the young Rousseau than the admirable Plutarch;
and he used to read to his father during the hours of
work, and read over again to himself during all hours,
those stories of free and indomitable souls which are
so proper to kindle the glow of generous fire. Plutarch was dear to him to the end of his life; he read
him in the late days when he had almost ceased to
read, and he always declared Plutarch to be nearly
the only author to whom he had never gone without
profit.[2] "I think I see my father now," he wrote

---

[1] *Conf.*, i. 9. Also Second Letter to M. de Malesherbes, p. 356.
[2] *Rêveries*, iv. p. 189. "My master and counsellor, Plutarch,"
he says, when he lends a volume to Madame d'Epinay in 1756.
Corr., i. 265.

when he had begun to make his mark in Paris, "living by the work of his hands, and nourishing his soul on the sublimest truths. I see Tacitus, Plutarch, and Grotius, lying before him along with the tools of his craft. I see at his side a cherished son receiving instruction from the best of fathers, alas, with but too little fruit."[1] This did little to implant the needed impressions of the actual world. Rousseau's first training continued to be in an excessive degree the exact reverse of our common method ; this stirs the imagination too little, and shuts the young too narrowly within the strait pen of present and visible reality. The reader of Plutarch at the age of ten actually conceived himself a Greek or a Roman, and became the personage whose strokes of constancy and intrepidity transported him with sympathetic ecstasy, made his eyes sparkle, and raised his voice to heroic pitch. Listeners were even alarmed one day as he told the tale of Scaevola at table, to see him imitatively thrust forth his arm over a hot chafing-dish.[2]

Rousseau had one brother, on whom the spirit of the father came down in ample measure, just as the sensibility of the mother descended upon Jean Jacques. He passed through a boyhood of revolt, and finally ran away into Germany, where he was lost from sight and knowledge of his kinsmen for ever. Jean Jacques was thus left virtually an only child,[3] and he com-

---

[1] Dedication of the *Discours sur l'Origine de l'Inégalité*, p. 201. (June, 1754.)

[2] *Conf.*, i. 11.   [3] *Ib.* i. 12.

memorates the homely tenderness and care with which his early years were surrounded. Except in the hours which he passed in reading by the side of his father, he was always with his aunt, in the self-satisfying curiosity of childhood watching her at work with the needle and busy about affairs of the house, or else listening to her with contented interest, as she sang the simple airs of the common people. The impression of this kind and cheerful figure was stamped on his memory to the end ; her tone of voice, her dress, the quaint fashion of her hair. The constant recollection of her shows, among many other signs, how he cherished that conception of the true unity of a man's life, which places it in a closely-linked chain of active memories, and which most of us lose in wasteful dispersion of sentiment and poor fragmentariness of days. When the years came in which he might well say, I have no pleasure in them, and after a manhood of distress and suspicion and diseased sorrows had come to dim those blameless times, he could still often surprise himself unconsciously humming the tune of one of his aunt's old songs, with many tears in his eyes.[1]

This affectionate schooling came suddenly to an end. Isaac Rousseau in the course of a quarrel in which he had involved himself, believed that he saw

[1] The tenacity of this grateful recollection is shown in letters to her (Madame Gonceru)—one in 1754 (*Corr.*, i. 204), another as late as 1770 (vi. 129), and a third in 1762 (*Œuvr. et Corr. Inéd.*, 392).

unfairness in the operation of the law, for the offender
had kinsfolk in the Great Council. He resolved to
leave his country rather than give way, in circumstances which compromised his personal honour and
the free justice of the republic. So his house was
broken up, and his son was sent to school at the
neighbouring village of Bossey (1722), under the care
of a minister, " there to learn along with Latin all
the medley of sorry stuff with which, under the name
of education, they accompany Latin."[1] Rousseau
tells us nothing of the course of his intellectual
instruction here, but he marks his two years' sojourn
under the roof of M. Lambercier by two forward
steps in that fateful acquaintance with good and evil,
which is so much more important than literary knowledge. Upon one of these fruits of the tree of nascent
experience, men usually keep strict silence. Rousseau
is the only person that ever lived who proclaimed to
the whole world as a part of his own biography
the ignoble circumstances of the birth of sensuality
in boyhood. Nobody else ever asked us to listen
while he told of the playmate with which unwarned
youth takes its heedless pleasure, which waxes and
strengthens with years, until the man suddenly
awakens to find the playmate grown into a master,
grotesque and foul, whose unclean grip is not to be
shaken off, and who poisons the air with the goatish
fume of the satyr. It is on this side that the
unspoken plays so decisive a part, that most of the

[1] *Conf.*, i. 17-32.

spoken seems but as dust in the balance; it is here that the flesh spreads gross clouds over the firmament of the spirit. Thinking of it, we flee from talk about the high matters of will and conscience, of purity of heart and the diviner mind, and hurry to the physician. Manhood commonly saves itself by its own innate healthiness, though the decent apron bequeathed to us in the old legend of the fall, the thick veil of a more than legendary reserve, prevents us from really measuring the actual waste of delicacy and the finer forces. Rousseau, most unhappily for himself, lacked this innate healthiness; he never shook off the demon which would be so ridiculous, if it did not hide such terrible power. With a moral courage, that it needs hardly less moral courage in the critic firmly to refrain from calling cynical or shameless, he has told the whole story of this lifelong depravation. In the present state of knowledge, which in the region of the human character the false shamefacedness of science, aided and abetted by the mutilating hand of religious asceticism, has kept crude and imperfect, there is nothing very profitable to be said on all this. When the great art of life has been more systematically conceived in the long processes of time and endeavour, and when more bold, effective, and far-reaching advance has been made in defining those pathological manifestations which deserve to be seriously studied, as distinguished from those of a minor sort which are barely worth registering, then we should know better how to speak, or how to be silent, in the present most unwelcome instance. As it is, we perhaps do best in chronicling the fact and passing on. The harmless young are allowed to play without monition or watching among the deep open graves of temperament; and Rousseau, telling the tale of his inmost experience, unlike the physician and the moralist who love decorous surfaces of things, did not spare himself nor others a glimpse of the ignominies to which the body condemns its high tenant, the soul.[1]

The second piece of experience which he acquired at Bossey was the knowledge of injustice and wrongful suffering as things actual and existent. Circumstances brought him under suspicion of having broken the teeth of a comb which did not belong to him. He was innocent, and not even the most terrible punishment could wring from him an untrue confession of guilt. The root of his constancy was not in an abhorrence of falsehood, which is exceptional in youth, and for which he takes no credit, but in a furious and invincible resentment against the violent pressure that was unjustly put upon him. "Picture a character, timid and docile in ordinary life, but ardent, impetuous, indomitable in its passions; a child always governed by the voice of reason, always treated with equity, gentleness, and consideration, who had not even the idea of injustice, and who for the first time experiences an injustice so terrible, from the very people whom he most cherishes and respects ! What a con-

[1] See also *Conf.*, i. 43 ; iii. 185 ; vii. 73 ; xii. 188, *n.* 2.

fusion of ideas, what disorder of sentiments, what
revolution in heart, in brain, in every part of his
moral and intellectual being !" He had not learnt, any
more than other children, either to put himself in the
place of his elders, or to consider the strength of the
apparent case against him. All that he felt was the
rigour of a frightful chastisement for an offence of
which he was innocent. And the association of ideas
was permanent. " This first sentiment of violence
and injustice has remained so deeply engraved in my
soul, that all the ideas relating to it bring my first
emotion back to me ; and this sentiment, though
only relative to myself in its origin, has taken such
consistency, and become so disengaged from all personal interest, that my heart is inflamed at the sight
or story of any wrongful action, just as much as if its
effect fell on my own person. When I read of the
cruelties of some ferocious tyrant, or the subtle
atrocities of some villain of a priest, I would fain
start on the instant to poniard such wretches, though
I were to perish a hundred times for the deed. . . .
This movement may be natural to me, and I believe
it is so ; but the profound recollection of the first
injustice I suffered was too long and too fast bound
up with it, not to have strengthened it enormously." [1]

To men who belong to the silent and phlegmatic
races like our own, all this may possibly strike on the
ear like a false or strained note. Yet a tranquil
appeal to the real history of one's own strongest im-

[1] *Conf.*, i. 27-31.

pressions may disclose their roots in facts of childish
experience, which remoteness of time has gradually
emptied of the burning colour they once had.   This
childish discovery of the existence in his own world
of that injustice which he had only seen through a
glass very darkly in the imaginary world of his reading, was for Rousseau the angry dismissal from the
primitive Eden, which in one shape and at one time
or another overtakes all men.   "Here," he says, "was
the term of the serenity of my childish days.   From
this moment I ceased to enjoy a pure happiness, and
I feel even at this day that the reminiscence of the
delights of my infancy here comes to an end. . . .
Even the country lost in our eyes that charm of sweetness and simplicity which goes to the heart ; it seemed
sombre and deserted, and was as if covered by a veil,
hiding its beauties from our sight.   We no longer
tended our little gardens, our plants, our flowers.
We went no more lightly to scratch the earth, shout-
ing for joy as we discovered the germ of the seed we
had sown."

Whatever may be the degree of literal truth in the
Confessions, the whole course of Rousseau's life forbids
us to pass this passionate description by as over-
charged or exaggerated.   We are conscious in it of
a constitutional infirmity.   We perceive an absence
of healthy power of reaction against moral shock.
Such shocks are experienced in many unavoidable
forms by all save the dullest natures, when they first
come into contact with the sharp tooth of outer cir-

cumstance. Indeed, a man must be either miraculously happy in his experiences, or exceptionally obtuse in observing and feeling, or else be the creature of base and cynical ideals, if life does not to the end continue to bring many a repetition of that first day of incredulous bewilderment. But the urgent demands for material activity quickly recall the mass of men to normal relations with their fellows and the outer world. A vehement objective temperament, like Voltaire's, is instantly roused by one of these penetrative stimuli into angry and tenacious resistance. A proud and collected soul, like Goethe's, loftily follows its own inner aims, without taking any heed of the perturbations that arise from want of self-collection in a world still spelling its rudiments. A sensitive and depressed spirit, like Rousseau's or Cowper's, finds itself without any of these reacting kinds of force, and the first stroke of cruelty or oppression is the going out of a divine light.

Leaving Bossey, Rousseau returned to Geneva, and passed two or three years with his uncle, losing his time for the most part, but learning something of drawing and something of Euclid, for the former of which he showed special inclination.[1] It was a question whether he was to be made a watchmaker, a lawyer, or a minister. His own preference, as his after-life might have led us to suppose, was in favour of the last of the three; "for I thought it a fine thing," he says, "to preach." The uncle was a man

[1] *Conf.*, i. 38-47.

of pleasure, and as often happens in such circumstances, his love of pleasure had the effect of turning his wife into a pietist. Their son was Rousseau's constant comrade. " Our friendship filled our hearts so amply, that if we were only together, the simplest amusements were a delight." They made kites, cages, bows and arrows, drums, houses ; they spoiled the tools of their grandfather, in trying to make watches like him. In the same cheerful imitative spirit, which is the main feature in childhood when it is not disturbed by excess of literary teaching, after Geneva had been visited by an Italian showman with a troop of marionettes, they made puppets and composed comedies for them ; and when one day the uncle read aloud an elegant sermon, they abandoned their comedies, and turned with blithe energy to exhortation. They had glimpses of the rougher side of life in the biting mockeries of some schoolboys of the neighbourhood. These ended in appeal to the god of youthful war, who pronounced so plainly for the bigger battalions, that the release of their enemies from school was the signal for the quick retreat of our pair within doors. All this is an old story in every biography written or unwritten. It seldom fails to touch us, either in the way of sympathetic reminiscence, or if life should have gone somewhat too hardly with a man, then in the way of irony, which is not less real and poetic than the eironeia of a Greek dramatist, for being concerned with more unheroic creatures.

And this rough play of the streets always seemed

to Rousseau a manlier schooling than the effeminate tendencies which he thought he noticed in Genevese youth in after years. "In my time," he says admiringly, "children were brought up in rustic fashion and had no complexion to keep. . . . Timid and modest before the old, they were bold, haughty, combative among themselves; they had no curled locks to be careful of; they defied one another at wrestling, running, boxing. They returned home sweating, out of breath, torn; they were true blackguards, if you will, but they made men who have zeal in their heart to serve their country and blood to shed for her. May we be able to say as much one day of our fine little gentlemen, and may these men at fifteen not turn out children at thirty." [1]

Two incidents of this period remain to us, described in Rousseau's own words, and as they reveal a certain sweetness in which his life unhappily did not afterwards greatly abound, it may help our equitable balance of impressions about him to reproduce them. Every Sunday he used to spend the day at Pâquis at Mr. Fazy's, who had married one of his aunts, and who carried on the production of printed calicoes. "One day I was in the drying-room, watching the rollers of the hot press; their brightness pleased my eye; I was tempted to lay my fingers on them, and I was moving them up and down with much satisfaction along the smooth cylinder, when young Fazy placed himself in the wheel and gave it a half-quarter

[1] *Lettre à D'Alembert* (1758), 178, 179.

turn so adroitly, that I had just the ends of my two longest fingers caught, but this was enough to crush the tips and tear the nails. I raised a piercing cry; Fazy instantly turned back the wheel, and the blood gushed from my fingers. In the extremity of consternation he hastened to me, embraced me, and besought me to cease my cries, or he would be undone. In the height of my own pain, I was touched by his; I instantly fell silent, we ran to the pond, where he helped me to wash my fingers and to staunch the blood with moss. He entreated me with tears not to accuse him ; I promised him that I would not, and I kept my word so well that twenty years after no one knew the origin of the scar. I was kept in bed for more than three weeks, and for more than two months was unable to use my hand. But I persisted that a large stone had fallen and crushed my fingers."[1]

The other story is of the same tenour, though there is a new touch of sensibility in its concluding words. "I was playing at ball at Plain Palais, with one of my comrades named Plince. We began to quarrel over the game ; we fought, and in the fight he dealt me on my bare head a stroke so well directed, that with a stronger arm it would have dashed my brains out. I fell to the ground, and there never was agitation like that of this poor lad, as he saw the blood in my hair. He thought he had killed me. He threw himself upon me, and clasped me eagerly in his arms, while his tears poured down his cheeks, and he uttered

---

[1] *Rêveries*, iv. 211, 212.

shrill cries. I returned his embrace with all my force,
weeping like him, in a state of confused emotion
which was not without a kind of sweetness. Then
he tried to stop the blood which kept flowing, and
seeing that our two handkerchiefs were not enough,
he dragged me off to his mother's ; she had a small
garden hard by. The good woman nearly fell sick at
sight of me in this condition; she kept strength
enough to dress my wound, and after bathing it well,
she applied flower-de-luce macerated in brandy, an
excellent remedy much used in our country. Her
tears and those of her son, went to my very heart, so
that I looked upon them for a long while as my
mother and my brother."[1]

If it were enough that our early instincts should
be thus amiable and easy, then doubtless the dismal
sloughs in which men and women lie floundering
would occupy a very much more insignificant space
in the field of human experience. The problem, as
we know, lies in the discipline of this primitive goodness. For character in a state of society is not a
tree that grows into uprightness by the law of its
own strength, though an adorable instance here and
there of rectitude and moral loveliness that seem in-
tuitive may sometimes tempt us into a moment's belief
in a contrary doctrine. In Rousseau's case this serious
problem was never solved ; there was no deliberate
preparation of his impulses, prepossessions, notions ;
no foresight on the part of elders, and no gradual

[1] *Conf.* 212, 213.

acclimatisation of a sensitive and ardent nature in the
fixed principles which are essential to right conduct
in the frigid zone of our relations with other people.
It was one of the most elementary of Rousseau's many
perverse and mischievous contentions, that it is their
education by the older which ruins or wastes the
abundant capacity for virtue that subsists naturally
in the young. His mind seems never to have sought
much more deeply for proof of this, than the fact
that he himself was innocent and happy so long as he
was allowed to follow without disturbance the easy
simple proclivities of his own temperament. Circumstances were not indulgent enough to leave the
experiment to complete itself within these very rudimentary conditions.

Rousseau had been surrounded, as he is always
careful to protest, with a religious atmosphere. His
father, though a man of pleasure, was possessed also
not only of probity but of religion as well. His three
aunts were all in their degrees gracious and devout.
M Lambercier at Bossoy, "although Churchman and
preacher," was still a sincere believer and nearly as
good in act as in word. His inculcation of religion
was so hearty, so discreet, so reasonable, that his
pupils, far from being wearied by the sermon, never
came away without being touched inwardly and
stirred to make virtuous resolutions. With his Aunt
Bernard devotion was rather more tiresome, because
she made a business of it.[1] It would be a distinct

[1] *Conf.*, ii. 102, 103.

error to suppose that all this counted for nothing, for
let us remember that we are now engaged with the
youth of the one great religious writer of France in
the eighteenth century. When after many years
Rousseau's character hardened, the influences which
had surrounded his boyhood came out in their full
force and the historian of opinion soon notices in his
spirit and work a something which had no counterpart in the spirit and work of men who had been
trained in Jesuit colleges. At the first outset, however, every trace of religious sentiment was obliterated
from sight, and he was left unprotected against the
shocks of the world and the flesh.

At the age of eleven Jean Jacques was sent into a
notary's office, but that respectable calling struck him
in the same repulsive and insufferable way in which
it has struck many other boys of genius in all countries.
Contrary to the usual rule, he did not rebel, but was
ignominiously dismissed by his master [1] for dulness
and inaptitude; his fellow-clerks pronounced him
stupid and incompetent past hope. He was next
apprenticed to an engraver,[2] a rough and violent man,
who seems to have instantly plunged the boy into a
demoralised stupefaction. The reality of contact
with this coarse nature benumbed as by touch of
torpedo the whole being of a youth who had hitherto
lived on pure sensations and among those ideas which
are nearest to sensations. There were no longer
heroic Romans in Rousseau's universe. "The vilest

---

[1] M. Masseron.   [2] M. Ducommun.

tastes, the meanest bits of rascality, succeeded to
my simple amusements, without even leaving the
least idea behind. I must, in spite of the worthiest
education, have had a strong tendency to degenerate."
The truth was that he had never had any education
in its veritable sense, as the process, on its negative
side, of counteracting the inborn. There are two
kinds, or perhaps we should more correctly say two
degrees, of the constitution in which the reflective
part is weak. There are the men who live on sensation, but who do so lustily, with a certain fulness of
blood and active energy of muscle. There are others
who do so passively, not searching for excitement,
but acquiescing. The former by their sheer force
and plenitude of vitality may, even in a world where
reflection is a first condition, still go far. The latter
succumb, and as reflection does nothing for them,
and as their sensations in such a world bring them
few blandishments, they are tolerably early surrounded
with a self-diffusing atmosphere of misery. Rousseau
had none of this energy which makes oppression
bracing. For a time he sank.

It would be a mistake to let the story of the
Confessions carry us into exaggerations. The brutality
of his master and the harshness of his life led him to
nothing very criminal, but only to wrong acts which
are despicable by their meanness, rather than in any
sense atrocious. He told lies as readily as the truth.
He pilfered things to eat. He cunningly found a
means of opening his master's private cabinet, and of

using his master's best instruments by stealth. He
wasted his time in idle and capricious tasks. When
the man, with all the gravity of an adult moralist,
describes these misdeeds of the boy, they assume a
certain ugliness of mien, and excite a strong disgust
which, when the misdeeds themselves are before us
in actual life, we experience in a far more considerate
form. The effect of calm, retrospective avowal is to
create a kind of feeling which is essentially unlike
our feeling at what is actually avowed. Still it is
clear that his unlucky career as apprentice brought
out in Rousseau slyness, greediness, slovenliness,
untruthfulness, and the whole ragged regiment of the
squalider vices. The evil of his temperament now
and always was of the dull smouldering kind, seldom
breaking out into active flame. There is a certain
sordidness in the scene. You may complain that the
details which Rousseau gives of his youthful days are
insipid. Yet such things are the web and stuff of
life, and these days of transition from childhood to
full manhood in every case mark a crisis. These
insipidities test the education of home and family,
and they presage definitely what is to come. The
roots of character, good or bad, are shown for this
short space, and they remain unchanged, though most
people learn from their fellows the decent and useful
art of covering them over with a little dust, in the
shape of accepted phrases and routine customs and a
silence which is not oblivion.

After a time the character of Jean Jacques was

absolutely broken down.   He says little of the blows
with which his offences were punished by his master,
but he says enough to enable us to discern that they
were terrible to him.   This cowardice, if we choose
to give the name to an overmastering physical horror,
at length brought his apprentice days to an end.
He was now in his sixteenth year.   He was dragged
by his comrades into sports for which he had little
inclination, though he admits that once engaged in
them he displayed an impetuosity that carried him
beyond the others.   Such pastimes naturally led them
beyond the city walls, and on two occasions Rousseau
found the gates closed on his return.   His master
when he presented himself in the morning gave him
such greeting as we may imagine, and held out things
beyond imagining as penalty for a second sin in this
kind.   The occasion came, as, alas, it nearly always
does.   "Half a league from the town," says Rousseau,
'I hear the retreat sounded, and redouble my pace;
I hear the drum beat, and run at the top of my speed:
I arrive out of breath, bathed in sweat ; my heart
beats violently, I see from a distance the soldiers at
their post, and call out with choking voice.   It was
too late.   Twenty paces from the outpost sentinel, I
saw the first bridge rising.   I shuddered, as I watched
those terrible horns, sinister and fatal augury of the inevitable lot which that moment was opening for me."[1]

In manhood when we have the resource of our
own will to fall back upon, we underestimate the

[1] *Conf.*, i. 69.

unsurpassed horror and anguish of such moments as
this in youth, when we know only the will of others,
and that this will is inexorable against us. Rousseau
dared not expose himself to the fulfilment of his
master's menace, and he ran away (1728). But for
this, wrote the unhappy man long years after, "I
should have passed, in the bosom of my religion, of
my native land, of my family, and my friends, a mild
and peaceful life, such as my character required, in
the uniformity of work which suited my taste, and of
a society after my heart. I should have been a good
Christian, good citizen, good father of a family, good
friend, good craftsman, good man in all. I should
have been happy in my condition, perhaps I might
have honoured it; and after living a life obscure and
simple, but even and gentle, I should have died peacefully in the midst of my own people. Soon forgotten,
I should at any rate have been regretted as long as
any memory of me was left." [1]

As a man knows nothing about the secrets of his
own individual organisation, this illusory mapping out
of a supposed Possible need seldom be suspected of the
smallest insincerity. The poor madman who declares
that he is a king kept out of his rights only moves
our pity, and we perhaps owe pity no less to those
in all the various stages of aberration uncertificated
by surgeons, down to the very edge of most respectable
sanity, who accuse the injustice of men of keeping
them out of this or that kingdom, of which in truth

[1] *Conf.*, i. 72.

their own composition finally disinherited them at the
moment when they were conceived in a mother's
womb. The first of the famous Five Propositions of
Jansen, which were a stumbling-block to popes and to
the philosophy of the eighteenth-century foolishness,
put this clear and permanent truth into a mystic and
perishable formula, to the effect that there are some
commandments of God which righteous and good men
are absolutely unable to obey, though ever so disposed
to do them, and God does not give them so much
grace that they are able to observe them.

If Rousseau's sensations in the evening were those
of terror, the day and its prospect of boundless adventures soon turned them into entire delight. The
whole world was before him, and all the old conceptions
of romance were instantly revived by the supposed
nearness of their realisation. He roamed for two or
three days among the villages in the neighbourhood
of Geneva, finding such hospitality as he needed in
the cottages of friendly peasants. Before long his wanderings brought him to the end of the territory of the
little republic. Here he found himself in the domain
of Savoy, where dukes and lords had for ages been the
traditional foes of the freedom and the faith of Geneva,
Rousseau came to the village of Confignon, and the
name of the priest of Confignon recalled one of the
most embittered incidents of the old feud. This feud
had come to take new forms; instead of midnight
expeditions to scale the city walls, the descendants of
the Savoyard marauders of the sixteenth century were

now intent with equivocal good will on rescuing the souls of the descendants of their old enemies from deadly heresy. At this time a systematic struggle was going on between the priests of Savoy and the ministers of Geneva, the former using every effort to procure the conversion of any Protestant on whom they could lay hands.[1] As it happened, the priest of Confignon was one of the most active in this good work.[2] He made the young Rousseau welcome, spoke to him of the heresies of Geneva and of the authority of the holy Church, and gave him some dinner. He could hardly have had a more easy convert, for the nature with which he had to deal was now swept and garnished, ready for the entrance of all devils or gods. The dinner went for much. "I was too good a guest," writes Rousseau in one of his few passages of humour, "to be a good theologian, and his Frangi wine, which struck me as excellent, was such a triumphant argument on his side, that I should have blushed to oppose so capital a host."[3] So it was agreed that he should be put in a way to be further instructed of these matters. We may accept Rousseau's assurance that he was not exactly a hypocrite in this rapid complaisance. He admits that any one who should have seen the artifices

[1] J. Gaberel's *Histoire de l'Église de Genève* (Geneva, 1853-62), vol. iii. p. 285.

[2] There is a minute in the register of the company of ministers, to the effect that the Sieur de Pontverre "is attracting many young men from this town, and changing their religion, and that the public ought to be warned." (Gaberel, iii. 224.)

[3] *Conf.*, ii. 76.

to which he resorted, might have thought him very
false.   But, he argues, "flattery, or rather concession,
is not always a vice; it is oftener a virtue, especially
in the young.   The kindness with which a man receives
us, attaches us to him; it is not to make a fool of him
that we give way, but to avoid displeasing him, and not
to return him evil for good."   He never really meant
to change his religion; his fault was like the coquet-
ting of decent women, who sometimes, to gain their
ends, without permitting anything or promising anything, lead men to hope more than they mean to hold
good.[1]   Thereupon follow some austere reflections on
the priest, who ought to have sent him back to his
friends; and there are strictures even upon the ministers of all dogmatic religions, in which the essential
thing is not to do but to believe; their priests therefore,
provided that they can convert a man to their faith,
are wholly indifferent alike as to his worth and his
worldly interests.   All this is most just; the occasion
for such a strain of remark, though so apposite on one
side, is hardly well chosen to impress us.   We wonder,
as we watch the boy complacently hoodwinking his
entertainer, what has become of the Roman severity
of a few months back.   This nervous eagerness to
please, however, was the complementary element of a
character of vague ambition, and it was backed by a
stealthy consciousness of intellectual superiority, which
perhaps did something, though poorly enough, to make
such ignominy less deeply degrading.

[1] *Conf.*, ii. 77.

The die was cast. M. Pontverre despatched his brand plucked from the burning to a certain Madame de Warens, a lady living at Annecy, and counted zealous for the cause of the Church. In an interview whose minutest circumstances remained for ever stamped in his mind (March 21, 1728), Rousseau exchanged his first words with this singular personage, whose name and character he has covered with doubtful renown. He expected to find some gray and wrinkled woman, saving a little remnant of days in good works. Instead of this, there turned round upon him a person not more than eight-and-twenty years old, with gentle caressing air, a fascinating smile, a tender eye. Madame de Warens read the letters he brought, and entertained their bearer cheerfully. It was decided after consultation that the heretic should be sent to a monastery at Turin, where he might be brought over in form to the true Church. At the monastery not only would the spiritual question of faith and the soul be dealt with, but at the same time the material problem of shelter and subsistence for the body would be solved likewise. Elated with vanity at the thought of seeing before any of his comrades the great land of promise beyond the mountains, heedless of those whom he had left, and heedless of the future before him and the object which he was about, the young outcast made his journey over the Alps in all possible lightness of heart. "Seeing country is an allurement which hardly any Genevese can ever resist. Everything that met my eye seemed the guarantee of my approaching happiness. In the houses I imagined rustic festivals ; in the fields, joyful sports ; along the streams, bathing and fishing ; on the trees, delicious fruits ; under their shade, voluptuous interviews ; on the mountains, pails of milk and cream, a charming idleness, peace, simplicity, the delight of going forward without knowing whither."[1] He might justly choose out this interval as more perfectly free from care or anxiety than any other of his life. It was the first of the too rare occasions when his usually passive sensuousness was stung by novelty and hope into an active energy.

The seven or eight days of the journey came to an end, and the youth found himself at Turin without money or clothes, an inmate of a dreary monastery, among some of the very basest and foulest of mankind, who pass their time in going from one monastery to another through Spain and Italy, professing themselves Jews or Moors for the sake of being supported while the process of their conversion was going slowly forward. At the Hospice of the Catechumens the work of his conversion was begun in such earnest as the insincerity of at least one of the parties to it might allow. It is needless to enter into the circumstances of Rousseau's conversion to Catholicism. The mischievous zeal for theological proselytising has led to thousands of such hollow and degrading performances, but it may safely be said that none of them was ever hollower than this. Rousseau avows that he had been

[1] *Conf.*, ii. 90-97.

brought up in the heartiest abhorrence of the older
church, and that he never lost this abhorrence. He
fully explains that he accepted the arguments with
which he was not very energetically plied, simply
because he could not bear the idea of returning to
Geneva, and he saw no other way out of his present
destitute condition. "I could not dissemble from
myself that the holy deed I was about to do, was at
the bottom the action of a bandit." "The sophism
which destroyed me," he says in one of those eloquent
pieces of moralising, which bring ignoble action into
a relief that exaggerates our condemnation, "is that
of most men, who complain of lack of strength when
it is already too late for them to use it. It is only
through our own fault that virtue costs us anything;
if we could be always sage, we should rarely feel the
need of being virtuous. But inclinations that might
be easily overcome, drag us on without resistance; we
yield to light temptations of which we despise the
hazard. Insensibly we fall into perilous situations,
against which we could easily have shielded ourselves,
but from which we can afterwards only make a way
out by heroic efforts that stupefy us, and so we sink
into the abyss, crying aloud to God, Why hast thou
made me so weak? But in spite of ourselves, God
gives answer to our conscience, 'I made thee too weak
to come out from the pit, because I made thee strong
enough to avoid falling into it.'"[1] So the hopeful
convert did fall in, not as happens to the pious soul

[1] *Conf.*, ii. 107.

"too hot for certainties in this our life," to find rest
in liberty of private judgment and an open Bible, but
simply as a means of getting food, clothing, and shelter.[1]
The boy was clever enough to make some show of
resistance, and he turned to good use for this purpose
the knowledge of Church history and the great Reformation controversy which he had picked up at M.
Lambercier's.   He was careful not to carry things too
far, and exactly nine days after his admission into the
Hospice, he "abjured the errors of the sect."[2]   Two
days after that he was publicly received into the
kindly bosom of the true Church with all solemnity,
to the high edification of the devout of Turin, who
marked their interest in the regenerate soul by contributions to the extent of twenty francs in small
money.

   With that sum and formal good wishes the fathers
of the Hospice of the Catechumens thrust him out of

---

[1] See *Émile*, iv. 124, 125, where the youth who was born a
Calvinist, finding himself a stranger in a strange land, without
resource, "changed his religion to get bread."
[2] In the *Confessions* (ii. 115) he has grace enough to make the
period a month ; but the extract from the register of his baptism
(Gaberel's *Hist. de l'Église de Genève*, iii. 224), which has been
recently published, shows that this is untrue : "Jean Jacques
Rousseau, de Genève (Calviniste), entré à l'hospice à l'âge de 16
ans, le 12 avril, 1728.   Abjura les erreurs de la secte le 21 ; et
le 23 du même mois lui fut administré le saint baptême, ayant
pour parrain le sieur André Ferrero et pour marraine Françoise
Christine Rora (ou Rovea)."
   A little further on (p. 119) he speaks of having been shut up
"for two months," but this is not true even on his own showing.

their doors into the broad world. The youth who
had begun the day with dreams of palaces, found
himself at night sleeping in a den where he paid a
halfpenny for the privilege of resting in the same
room with the rude woman who kept the house, her
husband, her five or six children, and various other
lodgers.   This rough awakening produced no consciousness of hardship in a nature which, beneath all
fantastic dreams, always remained true to its first
sympathy with the homely lives of the poor.   The
woman of the house swore like a carter, and was
always dishevelled and disorderly : this did not prevent Rousseau from recognising her kindness of heart
and her staunch readiness to befriend.   He passed
his days in wandering about the streets of Turin,
seeing the wonders of a capital, and expecting some
adventure that should raise him to unknown heights.
He went regularly to mass, watched the pomp of the
court, and counted upon stirring a passion in the
breast of a princess.   A more important circumstance
was the effect of the mass in awakening in his own
breast his latent passion for music ; a passion so
strong that the poorest instrument, if it were only in
tune, never failed to give him the liveliest pleasure.
The king of Sardinia was believed to have the best
performers in Europe ; less than that was enough to
quicken the musical susceptibility which is perhaps
an invariable element in the most completely sensuous
natures.

When the end of the twenty francs began to seem

a thing possible, he tried to get work as an engraver.
A young woman in a shop took pity on him, gave
him work and food, and perhaps permitted him to
make dumb and grovelling love to her, until her
husband returned home and drove her client away
from the door with threats and the waving of a wand
not magical.[1] Rousseau's self-love sought an explanation in the natural fury of an Italian husband's
jealousy; but we need hardly ask for any other
cause than a shopkeeper's reasonable objection to
vagabonds.

The next step of this youth, who was always
dreaming of the love of princesses, was to accept with
just thankfulness the position of lackey or footboy in
the household of a widow. With Madame de Vercellis
he passed three months, and at the end of that time
she died. His stay here was marked by an incident
that has filled many pages with stormful discussion.
When Madame de Vercellis died, a piece of old rose-
coloured ribbon was missing; Rousseau had stolen it,
and it was found in his possession. They asked him
whence he had taken it. He replied that it had been
given to him by Marion, a young and comely maid
in the house. In her presence and before the whole
household he repeated his false story, and clung to it
with a bitter effrontery that we may well call diabolic,
remembering how the nervous terror of punishment
and exposure sinks the angel in man. Our phrase,
want of moral courage, really denotes in the young

[1] Madame Basile. *Conf.*, ii. 121-135.

an excruciating physical struggle, often so keen that the victim clutches after liberation with the spontaneous tenacity and cruelty of a creature wrecked in mastering waters. Undisciplined sensations constitute egoism in the most ruthless of its shapes, and at this epoch, owing either to the brutalities which surrounded his apprentice life at Geneva, or to that rapid tendency towards degeneration which he suspected in his own character, Rousseau was the slave of sensations which stained his days with baseness. "Never," he says, in his account of this hateful action, "was wickedness further from me than at this cruel moment; and when I accused the poor girl, it is contradictory and yet it is true that my affection for her was the cause of what I did. She was present to my mind, and I threw the blame from myself on to the first object that presented itself. When I saw her appear my heart was torn, but the presence of so many people was too strong for my remorse. I feared punishment very little; I only feared disgrace, but I feared that more than death, more than crime, more than anything in the world. I would fain have buried myself in the depths of the earth; invincible shame prevailed over all, shame alone caused my effrontery, and the more criminal I became, the more intrepid was I made by the fright of confessing it. I could see nothing but the horror of being recognised and declared publicly to my face a thief, liar, and traducer."[1] When he says that he

[1] *Conf.* ii. ad finem.

feared punishment little, his analysis of his mind is
most likely wrong, for nothing is clearer than that a
dread of punishment in any physical form was a
peculiarly strong feeling with him at this time.
However that may have been, the same over-excited
imagination which put every sense on the alarm and
led him into so abominable a misdemeanour, brought
its own penalties.   It led him to conceive a long
train of ruin as having befallen Marion in consequence
of his calumny against her, and this dreadful thought
haunted him to the end of his life.   In the long
sleepless nights he thought he saw the unhappy girl
coming to reproach him with a crime that seemed as
fresh to him as if it had been perpetrated the day
before.[1]   Thus the same brooding memory which
brought back to him the sweet pain of his gentle
kinswoman's household melody, preserved the darker
side of his history with equal fidelity and no less
perfect continuousness.   Rousseau expresses a hope
and belief that this burning remorse would serve as
expiation for his fault; as if expiation for the
destruction of another soul could be anything but a
fine name for self-absolution.   We may, however,
charitably and reasonably think that the possible
consequences of his fault to the unfortunate Marion
were not actual, but were as much a hallucination as
the midnight visits of her reproachful spirit.   Indeed,
we are hardly condoning evil, in suggesting that the
whole story from its beginning is marked with exag-

[1] *Conf.*, ii. 144.

geration, and that we who have our own lives to lead
shall find little help in criticising at further length
the exact heinousness of the ignoble falsehood of a
boy who happened to grow up into a man of genius.[1]

After an interval of six weeks, which were passed
in the garret or cellar of his rough patroness with
kind heart and ungentle tongue, Rousseau again
found himself a lackey in the house of a Piedmontese
person of quality. This new master, the Count of
Gouvon, treated him with a certain unusual considerateness, which may perhaps make us doubt the
narrative. His son condescended to teach the youth
Latin, and Rousseau presumed to entertain a passion
for one of the daughters of the house, to whom he
paid silent homage in the odd shape of attending to
her wants at table with special solicitude. In this
situation he had, or at least he supposed that he had,
an excellent chance of ultimate advancement. But
advancement here or elsewhere means a measure of
stability, and Rousseau's temperament in his youth
was the archtype of the mutable. An old comrade
from Geneva visited him,[2] and as almost any incident
is stimulating enough to fire the restlessness of
imaginative youth, the gratitude which he professed
to the Count of Gouvon and his family, the prudence
with which he marked his prospects, the industry

---

[1] Another version of the story mentioned by Musset-Pathay
(i. 7) makes the object of the theft a diamond, but there is
really no evidence in the matter beyond that given by Rousseau
himself.   [2] Bacle, by name.

with which he profited by opportunity, all faded
quickly into mere dead and disembodied names of
virtues. His imagination again went over the journey
across the mountains; the fields, the woods, the
streams, began to absorb his whole life. He recalled
with delicious satisfaction how charming the journey
had seemed to him, and thought how far more
charming it would be in the society of a comrade of
his own age and taste, without duty, or constraint,
or obligation to go or stay other than as it might
please them. " It would be madness to sacrifice such
a piece of good fortune to projects of ambition, which
were slow, difficult, doubtful of execution, and which,
even if they should one day be realised, were not
with all their glory worth a quarter of an hour of
true pleasure and freedom in youth."[1]

On these high principles he neglected his duties so
recklessly that he was dismissed from his situation,
and he and his comrade began their homeward wanderings with more than apostolic heedlessness as to what
they should eat or wherewithal they should be clothed.
They had a toy fountain; they hoped that in return
for the amusement to be conferred by this wonder
they should receive all that they might need. Their
hopes were not fulfilled. The exhibition of the toy
fountain did not excuse them from their reckoning.
Before long it was accidentally broken, and to their
secret satisfaction, for it had lost its novelty. Their
naked vagrancy was thus undisguised. They made

[1] *Conf.*, iii. 168.

their way by some means or other across the mountains, and their enjoyment of vagabondage was undisturbed by any thought of a future. "To understand my delirium at this moment," Rousseau says, in words which shed much light on darker parts of his history than fits of vagrancy, "it is necessary to know to what a degree my heart is subject to get aflame with the smallest things, and with what force it plunges into the imagination of the object that attracts it, vain as that object may be. The most grotesque, the most childish, the maddest schemes come to caress my favourite idea, and to show me the reasonableness of surrendering myself to it."[1] It was this deep internal vehemence which distinguished Rousseau all through his life from the commonplace type of social revolter. A vagrant sensuous temperament, strangely compounded with Genevese austerity; an ardent and fantastic imagination, incongruously shot with threads of firm reason; too little conscience and too much; a monstrous and diseased love of self, intertwined with a sincere compassion and keen interest for the great fellowship of his brothers; a wild dreaming of dreams that were made to look like sanity by the close and specious connection between conclusions and premisses, though the premisses happened to have the fault of being profoundly unreal:—this was the type of character that lay unfolded in the youth who, towards the autumn of 1729, reached Annecy, penni-

[1] *Conf.*, iii. 170. A slightly idealised account of the situation is given in *Émile*, Bk. iv. 125.

less and ragged, throwing himself once more on the charity of the patroness who had given him shelter eighteen months before. Few figures in the world at that time were less likely to conciliate the favour or excite the interest of an observer, who had not studied the hidden convolutions of human character deeply enough to know that a boy of eighteen may be sly, sensual, restless, dreamy, and yet have it in him to say things one day which may help to plunge a world into conflagration.

CHAPTER III.

SAVOY.

THE commonplace theory which the world takes for granted as to the relations of the sexes, makes the woman ever crave the power and guidance of her physically stronger mate. Even if this be a true account of the normal state, there is at any rate a kind of temperament among the many types of men, in which it seems as if the elements of character remain mere futile and dispersive particles, until compelled into unity and organisation by the creative shock of feminine influence. There are men, famous or obscure, whose lives might be divided into a number of epochs, each defined and presided over by the influence of a woman. For the inconstant such a calendar contains many divisions, for the constant it is brief and simple; for both alike it marks the great decisive phases through which character has moved.

Rousseau's temperament was deeply marked by this special sort of susceptibility in one of its least agreeable forms. His sentiment was neither robustly and courageously animal, nor was it an intellectual demand for the bright and vivacious sympathies in which women sometimes excel. It had neither bold virility, nor that sociable energy which makes close emotional companionship an essential condition of freedom of faculty and completeness of work. There is a certain close and sickly air round all his dealings with women and all his feeling for them. We seem to move not in the star-like radiance of love, nor even in the fiery flames of lust, but among the humid heats of some unknown abode of things not wholesome or manly. "I know a sentiment," he writes, "which is perhaps less impetuous than love, but a thousand times more delicious, which sometimes is joined to love, and which is very often apart from it. Nor is this sentiment friendship only; it is more voluptuous, more tender; I do not believe that any one of the same sex could be its object; at least I have been a friend, if ever man was, and I never felt this about any of my friends."[1] He admits that he can only describe this sentiment by its effects; but our lives are mostly ruled by elements that defy definition, and in Rousseau's case the sentiment which he could not describe was a paramount trait of his mental constitution. It was as a voluptuous garment; in it his imagination was cherished into activity, and protected against that outer air of reality which braces ordinary men, but benumbs and disintegrates the whole vital apparatus of such an organisation as Rousseau's. If he had been devoid of this feeling about women, his character might very possibly have remained sterile.

[1] Conf., iii. 177.

That feeling was the complementary contribution,
without which could be no fecundity.

When he returned from his squalid Italian expedition in search of bread and a new religion, his mind
was clouded with the vague desire, the sensual moodi-
ness, which in such natures stains the threshold of
manhood. This unrest, with its mysterious torments
and black delights, was banished, or at least soothed
into a happier humour, by the influence of a person
who is one of the most striking types to be found in
the gallery of fair women.

L.

A French writer in the eighteenth century, in a
story which deals with a rather repulsive theme of
action in a tone that is graceful, simple, and pathetic,
painted the portrait of a creature for whom no moralist
with a reputation to lose can say a word ; and we may,
if we choose, fool ourselves by supposing her to be
without a counterpart in the better-regulated world
of real life, but, in spite of both these objections, she
is an interesting and not untouching figure to those
who like to know all the many-webbed stuff out of
which their brothers and sisters are made. The
Manon Lescaut of the unfortunate Abbé Prevost,
kindly, bright, playful, tender, but devoid of the very
germ of the idea of that virtue which is counted the
sovereign recommendation of woman, helps us to
understand Madame de Warens. There are differ-

ences enough between them, and we need not mistake
them for one and the same type.   Manon Lescaut is
a prettier figure, because romance has fewer limita-
tions than real life; but if we think of her in reading
of Rousseau's benefactress, the vision of the imaginary
woman tends to soften our judgment of the actual
one, as well as to enlighten our conception of a character that eludes the instruments of a commonplace
analysis.[1]

She was born at Vevai in 1700; she married early,
and early disagreed with her husband, from whom
she eventually went away, abandoning family, religion,
country, and means of subsistence, with all gaiety of
heart.   The King of Sardinia happened to be keeping
his court at a small town on the southern shores of
the lake of Geneva, and the conversion of Madame
de Warens to catholicism by the preaching of the
Bishop of Annecy,[2] gave a zest to the royal visit, as
being a successful piece of sport in that great spiritual
hunt which Savoy loved to pursue at the expense of
the reformed church in Switzerland.   The king, to
mark his zeal for the faith of his house, conferred on

---

[1] Lamartine in *Raphael* defies "a reasonable man to recom-
pose with any reality the character that Rousseau gives to his
mistress, out of the contradictory elements which he associates
in her nature.   One of these elements excludes the other."   It
is worth while for any who care for this kind of study to compare Madame de Warens with the Marquise de Courcelles, whom
Sainte-Beuve has well called the Manon Lescaut of the seventeenth century.

[2] Described by Rousseau in a memorandum for the biographer
of M. de Bernex, printed in *Mélanges*, pp. 139-144.

the new convert a small pension for life; but as the
tongues of the scandalous imputed a less pure motive
for such generosity in a parsimonious prince, Madame
de Warens removed from the court and settled at
Annecy. Her conversion was hardly more serious
than Rousseau's own, because seriousness was no condition of her intelligence on any of its sides or in any
of its relations. She was extremely charitable to the
poor, full of pity for all in misfortune, easily moved
to forgiveness of wrong or ingratitude; careless, gay,
open-hearted; having, in a word, all the good qualities
which spring in certain generous soils from human
impulse, and hardly any of those which spring from
reflection, or are implanted by the ordering of society.
Her reason had been warped in her youth by an instructor of the devil's stamp;[1] finding her attached
to her husband and to her duties, always cold, argumentative, and impregnable on the side of the senses,
he attacked her by sophisms, and at last persuaded
her that the union of the sexes is in itself a matter of
the most perfect indifference, provided only that
decorum of appearance be preserved, and the peace
of mind of persons concerned be not disturbed.[2]

[1] De Tavel, by name. Disorderly ideas as to the relations
of the sexes began to appear in Switzerland along with the
reformation of religion. In the sixteenth century a woman
appeared at Geneva with the doctrine that it is as inhuman and
as unjustifiable to refuse the gratification of this appetite in a man
as to decline to give food and drink to the starving. Picot's
Hist. de Genève, vol. ii.

[2] *Conf.*, v. 341. Also ii. 83 ; and vi. 401.

This execrable lesson, which greater and more unsel-
fish men held and propagated in grave books before
the end of the century, took root in her mind. If
we accept Rousseau's explanation, it did so the more
easily as her temperament was cold, and thus cor-
roborated the idea of the indifference of what public
opinion and private passion usually concur in investing
with such enormous weightiness. " I will even dare
to say," Rousseau declares, " that she only knew one
true pleasure in the world, and that was to give
pleasure to those whom she loved."[1] He is at great
pains to protest how compatible this coolness of
temperament is with excessive sensibility of character ; and neither ethological theory nor practical
observation of men and women is at all hostile to
what he is so anxious to prove. The cardinal element
of character is the speed at which its energies move ;
its rapidity or its steadiness, concentration or vola-
tility ; whether the thought and feeling travel as
quickly as light or as slowly as sound. A rapid and
volatile constitution like that of Madame de Warens
is inconsistent with ardent and glowing warmth,
which belongs to the other sort, but it is essentially
bound up with sensibility, or readiness of sympathetic
answer to every cry from another soul. It is the
slow, brooding, smouldering nature, like Rousseau's
own, in which we may expect to find the tropics.

To bring the heavy artillery of moral reprobation
to bear upon a poor soul like Madame de Warens is

[1] *Conf.*, v. 345.

as if one should denounce flagrant want of moral purpose in the busy movements of ephemera. Her activity was incessant, but it ended in nothing better than debt, embarrassment, and confusion. She inherited from her father a taste for alchemy, and spent much time in search after secret elixirs and the like. "Quacks, taking advantage of her weakness, made themselves her master, constantly infested her, ruined her, and wasted, in the midst of furnaces and chemicals, intelligence, talents, and charms which would have made her the delight of the best societies."[1] Perhaps, however, the too notorious vagrancy of her amours had at least as much to do with her failure to delight the best societies as her indiscreet passion for alchemy. Her person was attractive enough. "She had those points of beauty," says Rousseau, "which are desirable, because they reside rather in expression than in feature. She had a tender and caressing air, a soft eye, a divine smile, light hair of uncommon beauty. You could not see a finer head or bosom, finer arms or hands."[2] She was full of tricks and whimsies. She could not endure the first smell of the soup and meats at dinner; when they were placed on the table she nearly swooned, and her disgust lasted some time, until at the end of half an hour or so she took her first morsel.[3] On the whole, if we accept the current standard of sanity, Madame de Warens must be pronounced ever so little flighty; but a monotonous

---

[1] *Conf.*, ii. 83.   [2] *Ib.* ii. 82.
[3] *Ib.* iii. 179.   See also 200.

world can afford to be lenient to people with a slight
craziness, if it only has hearty benevolence and cheerfulness in its company, and is free from egoism or
rapacious vanity.

This was the person within the sphere of whose
attraction Rousseau was decisively brought in the
autumn of 1729, and he remained, with certain breaks
of vagabondage, linked by a close attachment to her
until 1738. It was in many respects the truly forma-
tive portion of his life. He acquired during this time
much of his knowledge of books, such as it was, and
his principles of judging them. He saw much of the
lives of the poor and of the world's ways with them.
Above all his ideal was revolutionised, and the recent
dreams of Plutarchian heroism, of grandeur, of palaces,
princesses, and a glorious career full in the world's
eye, were replaced by a new conception of blessedness
of life, which never afterwards faded from his vision,
and which has held a front place in the imagination
of literary Europe ever since. The notions or aspirations which he had picked up from a few books gave
way to notions and aspirations which were shaped
and fostered by the scenes of actual life into which
he was thrown, and which found his character soft
for their impression. In one way the new pictures
of a future were as dissociated from the conditions of
reality as the old had been, and the sensuous life of the
happy valley in Savoy as little fitted a man to compose
ideals for our gnarled and knotted world as the mental
life among the heroics of sentimental fiction had done.

Rousseau's delight in the spot where Madame de Warens lived at Annecy was the mark of the new ideal which circumstances were to engender in him, and after him to spread in many hearts. His room looked over gardens and a stream, and beyond them stretched a far landscape. "It was the first time since leaving Bossey that I had green before my windows. Always shut in by walls, I had nothing under my eye but house-tops and the dull gray of the streets. How moving and delicious this novelty was to me! It brightened all the tenderness of my disposition. I counted the landscape among the kindnesses of my dear benefactress; it seemed as if she had brought it there expressly for me. I placed myself there in all peacefulness with her; she was present to me everywhere among the flowers and the verdure; her charms and those of spring were all mingled together in my eyes. My heart, which had hitherto been stifled, found itself more free in this ample space, and my sighs had more liberal vent among these orchard gardens."[1] Madame de Warens was the semi-divine figure who made the scene live, and gave it perfect and harmonious accent. He had neither transports nor desires by her side, but existed in a state of ravishing calm, enjoying without knowing what. "I could have passed my whole life and eternity itself in this way, without an instant of weariness. She is the only person with whom I never felt that dryness in conversation, which turns

[1] *Conf.*, iii. 177, 178.

the duty of keeping it up into a torment.   Our intercourse was not so much conversation as an inex-
haustible stream of chatter, which never came to an
end until it was interrupted from without.   I only
felt all the force of my attachment for her when she
was out of my sight.   So long as I could see her I
was merely happy and satisfied, but my disquiet in
her absence went so far as to be painful.   I shall
never forget how one holiday, while she was at
vespers, I went for a walk outside the town, my heart
full of her image and of an eager desire to pass all
my days by her side.   I had sense enough to see that
for the present this was impossible, and that the bliss
which I relished so keenly must be brief.   This gave
to my musing a sadness which was free from everything sombre, and which was moderated by pleasing
hope.   The sound of the bells, which has always
moved me to a singular degree, the singing of the
birds, the glory of the weather, the sweetness of the
landscape, the scattered rustic dwellings in which my
imagination placed our common home ;—all this so
struck me with a vivid, tender, sad, and touching
impression that I saw myself as in an ecstasy transported into the happy time and the happy place where
my heart, possessed of all the felicity that could bring
it delight, without even dreaming of the pleasures of
sense, should share joys inexpressible."[1]

There was still, however, a space to be bridged
between the doubtful now and this delicious future.

[1] *Conf.*, iii. 183.

The harshness of circumstance is ever interposing with a money question, and for a vagrant of eighteen the first of all problems is a problem of economics. Rousseau was submitted to the observation of a kinsman of Madame de Warens,[1] and his verdict corresponded with that of the notary of Geneva, with whom years before Rousseau had first tried the critical art of making a living. He pronounced that in spite of an animated expression, the lad was, if not thoroughly inept, at least of very slender intelligence, without ideas, almost without attainments, very narrow indeed in all respects, and that the honour of one day becoming a village priest was the highest piece of fortune to which he had any right to aspire.[2] So he was sent to the seminary, to learn Latin enough for the priestly offices. He began by conceiving a deadly antipathy to his instructor, whose appearance happened to be displeasing to him. A second was found,[2] and the patient and obliging temper, the affectionate and sympathetic manner of his new teacher made a great impression on the pupil, though the progress in intellectual acquirement was as unsatisfactory in one case as in the other. It is characteristic of that subtle impressionableness to physical comeliness, which in ordinary natures is rapidly effaced by press of more urgent considerations, but which Rousseau's strongly sensuous quality retained, that he should have remembered, and thought worth mentioning years afterwards, that the first of his two teachers at the seminary

---

[1] M. d'Aubonne.　　　　[2] *Conf.*, iii. 192.　　　　[3] M. Gatier.

of Annecy had greasy black hair, a complexion as of gingerbread, and bristles in place of beard, while the second had the most touching expression he ever saw in his life, with fair hair and large blue eyes, and a glance and a tone which made you feel that he was one of the band predestined from their birth to unhappy days.   While at Turin, Rousseau had made the acquaintance of another sage and benevolent priest,[1] and uniting the two good men thirty years after he conceived and drew the character of the Savoyard Vicar.[2]

Shortly the seminarists reported that, though not vicious, their pupil was not even good enough for a priest, so deficient was he in intellectual faculty.   It was next decided to try music, and Rousseau ascended for a brief space into the seventh heaven of the arts. This was one of the intervals of his life of which he says that he recalls not only the times, places, persons, but all the surrounding objects, the temperature of the air, its odour, its colour, a certain local impression only felt there, and the memory of which stirs the old transports anew.   He never forgot a certain tune, because one Advent Sunday he heard it from his bed being sung before daybreak on the steps of the cathedral ; nor an old lame carpenter who played the counter-bass, nor a fair little abbé who played the violin in the choir.[3]   Yet he was in so dreamy, absent, and distracted a state, that neither his goodwill nor his assiduity availed, and he could learn nothing, not

---

[1] M. Gaime.   [2] *Conf.*, iii. 204.   [3] *Ib*. iii. 209, 210.

even music. His teacher, one Le Maître, belonged
to that great class of irregular and disorderly natures
with which Rousseau's destiny, in the shape of an
irregular and disorderly temperament of his own, so
constantly brought him into contact. Le Maître could
not work without the inspiration of the wine cup, and
thus his passion for his art landed him a sot. He
took offence at a slight put upon him by the precentor
of the cathedral of which he was choir-master, and
left Annecy in a furtive manner along with Rousseau,
whom the too comprehensive solicitude of Madame
de Warens despatched to bear him company. They
went together as far as Lyons; here the unfortunate
musician happened to fall into an epileptic fit in the
street. Rousseau called for help, informed the crowd
of the poor man's hotel, and then seizing a moment
when no one was thinking about him, turned the street
corner and finally disappeared, the musician being thus
"abandoned by the only friend on whom he had a
right to count."[1] It thus appears that a man may be
exquisitely moved by the sound of bells, the song of
birds, the fairness of smiling gardens, and yet be capable all the time without a qualm of misgiving of
leaving a friend senseless in the road in a strange
place. It has ceased to be wonderful how many ugly
and cruel actions are done by people with an extraordinary sense of the beauty and beneficence of nature.
At the moment Rousseau only thought of getting back
to Annecy and Madame de Warens. "It is not," he

[1] *Conf.*, iii., 217-222.

says in words of profound warning, which many men
have verified in those two or three hours before the
tardy dawn that swell into huge purgatorial æons,—
"it is not when we have just done a bad action, that
it torments us; it is when we recall it long after, for
the memory of it can never be thrust out."[1]

II.

When he made his way homewards again, he found
to his surprise and dismay that his benefactress had
left Annecy, and had gone for an indefinite time to
Paris. He never knew the secret of this sudden departure, for no man, he says, was ever so little curious
as to the private affairs of his friends. His heart,
completely occupied with the present, filled its whole
capacity and entire space with that, and except for
past pleasures no empty corner was ever left for what
was done with.[2] He says he was too young to take
the desertion deeply to heart. Where he found subsistence we do not know. He was fascinated by a
flashy French adventurer,[3] in whose company he
wasted many hours, and the precious stuff of youthful opportunity. He passed a summer day in joyful
rustic fashion with two damsels whom he hardly ever
saw again, but the memory of whom and of the holiday that they had made with him remained stamped in

---

[1] *Conf.*, iv. 227.   [2] *Ib.* iii. 224.

[3] One Venture de Villeneuve, who visited him years afterwards (1755) in Paris, when Rousseau found that the idol of
old days was a crapulent debauchee. *Ib.* viii. 221.

his brain, to be reproduced many a year hence in some of the traits of the new Heloïsa and her friend Claire.[1] Then he accepted an invitation from a former waiting-woman of Madame de Warens to attend her home to Freiburg. On this expedition he paid an hour's visit to his father, who had settled and remarried at Nyon. Returning from Freiburg, he came to Lausanne, where, with an audacity that might be taken for the first presage of mental disturbance, he undertook to teach music. "I have already," he says, "noted some moments of inconceivable delirium, in which I ceased to be myself. Behold me now a teacher of singing, without knowing how to decipher an air. Without the least knowledge of composition, I boasted of my skill in it before all the world; and without ability to score the slenderest vaudeville, I gave myself out for a composer. Having been presented to M. de Treytorens, a professor of law, who loved music and gave concerts at his house, I insisted on giving him a specimen of my talent, and I set to work to compose a piece for his concert with as much effrontery as if I knew all about it." The performance came off duly, and the strange impostor conducted it with as much gravity as the profoundest master. Never since the beginning of opera has the like charivari greeted the ears of men.[2] Such an opening was fatal to all chance of scholars, but the friendly tavern-keeper who had first taken him in did not lack either hope or charity.

[1] Mdlles. de Graffenried and Galley. *Conf.*, iv. 231.
[2] *Ib.* iv. 254-256.

"How is it," Rousseau cried, many years after this, "that having found so many good people in my youth, I find so few in my advanced life? Is their stock exhausted? No; but the class in which I have to seek them now is not the same as that in which I found them then. Among the common people, where great passions only speak at intervals, the sentiments of nature make themselves heard oftener. In the higher ranks they are absolutely stifled, and under the mask of sentiment it is only interest or vanity that speaks."[1]

From Lausanne he went to Neuchâtel, where he had more success, for, teaching others, he began himself to learn. But no success was marked enough to make him resist a vagrant chance. One day in his rambles falling in with an archimandrite of the Greek church, who was traversing Europe in search of subscriptions for the restoration of the Holy Sepulchre, he at once attached himself to him in the capacity of interpreter. In this position he remained for a few weeks, until the French minister at Soleure took him away from the Greek monk, and despatched him to Paris to be the attendant of a young officer.[2] A few days in the famous city, which he now saw for the first time, and which disappointed his expecta-

---

[1] *Conf.*, iv. 253.

[2] While in the ambassador's house at Soleure, he was lodged in a room which had once belonged to his namesake, Jean Baptiste Rousseau (*b.* 1670—*d.* 1741), whom the older critics astonishingly insist on counting the first of French lyric poets. There was a third Rousseau, Pierre (*b.* 1725—*d.* 1785), who

tions just as the sea and all other wonders disappointed them,[1] convinced him that here was not what he sought, and he again turned his face southwards in search of Madame de Warens and more familiar lands.

The interval thus passed in roaming over the eastern face of France, and which we may date in the summer of 1732,[2] was always counted by Rousseau

wrote plays and did other work now well forgotten.   There are some lines imperfectly commemorative of the trio—

> Trois auteurs que Rousseau l'on nomme,
> Connus de Paris jusqu'à Rome,
> Sont différens ; voici par où ;
> Rousseau de Paris fut grand homme ;
> Rousseau de Genève est un fou ;
> Rousseau de Toulouse un atome.

Jean Jacques refers to both his namesakes in his letter to Voltaire, Jan. 30, 1750. *Corr.*, i. 145.

[1] The only object which ever surpassed his expectation was the great Roman structure near Nismes, the Pont du Gard. *Conf.*, vi. 446.

[2] Rousseau gives 1732 as the probable date of his return to Chambéri, after his first visit to Paris (*Conf.*, v. 305), and the only objection to this is his mention of the incident of the march of the French troops, which could not have happened until the winter of 1733, as having taken place "some months" after his arrival.   Musset-Pathay accepts this as decisive, and fixes the return in the spring of 1733 (i. 12).   My own conjectural chronology is this : Returns from Turin towards the autumn of 1729 ; stays at Annecy until the spring of 1731 ; passes the winter of 1731-2 at Neuchâtel ; first visits Paris in spring of 1732 ; returns to Savoy in the early summer of 1732. But a precise harmonising of the dates in the Confessions is impossible ; Rousseau wrote them three and thirty years after our present point (in 1766 at Wootton), and never claimed to be exact in minuteness of date.   Fortunately such matters in the present case are absolutely devoid of importance.

among the happy epochs of his life, though the weeks
may seem grievously wasted to a generation which
is apt to limit its ideas of redeeming the time to the
two pursuits of reading books or making money.
He travelled alone and on foot from Soleure to Paris
and from Paris back again to Lyons, and this was part
of the training which served him in the stead of books.
Scarcely any great writer since the revival of letters
has been so little literary as Rousseau, so little
indebted to literature for the most characteristic part
of his work.   He was formed by life; not by life in
the sense of contact with a great number of active
and important persons, or with a great number of
persons of any kind, but in the rarer sense of free
surrender to the plenitude of his own impressions.
A world composed of such people, all dispensing with
the inherited portion of human experience, and living
independently on their own stock, would rapidly fall
backwards into dissolution.   But there is no more rash
idea of the right composition of a society than one
which leads us to denounce a type of character for
no better reason than that, if it were universal, society
would go to pieces.   There is very little danger of
Rousseau's type becoming common, unless lunar or
other great physical influences arise to work a vast
change in the cerebral constitution of the species.
We may safely trust the prodigious *vis inertiæ* of
human nature to ward off the peril of an eccentricity
beyond bounds spreading too far.   At present, however, it is enough, without going into the general

question, to notice the particular fact that while the
other great exponents of the eighteenth century movement, Hume, Voltaire, Diderot, were nourishing their
natural strength of understanding by the study and
practice of literature, Rousseau, the leader of the
reaction against that movement, was wandering a
beggar and an outcast, craving the rude fare of the
peasant's hut, knocking at roadside inns, and passing
nights in caves and holes in the fields, or in the great
desolate streets of towns.

If such a life had been disagreeable to him, it
would have lost all the significance that it now has
for us.　But where others would have found affliction,
he had consolation, and where they would have lain
desperate and squalid, he marched elate and ready to
strike the stars.　"Never," he says, "did I think so
much, exist so much, be myself so much, as in the
journeys that I have made alone and on foot.　Walking has something about it which animates and
enlivens my ideas.　I can hardly think while I am
still ; my body must be in motion, to move my mind.
The sight of the country, the succession of agreeable
views, open air, good appetite, the freedom of the
alehouse, the absence of everything that could make
me feel dependence, or recall me to my situation—all
this sets my soul free, gives me a greater boldness of
thought.　I dispose of all nature as its sovereign
lord ; my heart, wandering from object to object,
mingles and is one with the things that soothe it,
wraps itself up in charming images, and is intoxi-

cated by delicious sentiment. Ideas come as they
please, not as I please : they do not come at all, or
they come in a crowd, overwhelming me with their
number and their force. When I came to a place I
only thought of eating, and when I left it I only
thought of walking. I felt that a new paradise
awaited me at the door, and I thought of nothing
but of hastening in search of it."[1]

Here again is a picture of one whom vagrancy
assuredly did not degrade :—"I had not the least
care for the future, and I awaited the answer [as to
the return of Madame de Warens to Savoy], lying out
in the open air, sleeping stretched out on the ground
or on some wooden bench, as tranquilly as on a bed
of roses. I remember passing one delicious night
outside the town [Lyons], in a road which ran by the
side of either the Rhone or the Saône, I forget which
of the two. Gardens raised on a terrace bordered the
other side of the road. It had been very hot all day,
and the evening was delightful ; the dew moistened
the parched grass, the night was profoundly still, the
air fresh without being cold ; the sun in going down
had left red vapours in the heaven, and they turned
the water to rose colour ; the trees on the terrace
sheltered nightingales, answering song for song. I
went on in a sort of ecstasy, surrendering my heart
and every sense to the enjoyment of it all, and only
sighing for regret that I was enjoying it alone.
Absorbed in the sweetness of my musing, I prolonged

[1] *Conf.*, iv. 279, 280.

my ramble far into the night, without ever perceiving
that I was tired.   At last I found it out.   I lay down
luxuriously on the shelf of a niche or false doorway
made in the wall of the terrace ; the canopy of my
bed was formed by overarching tree-tops ; a nightingale was perched exactly over my head, and I fell
asleep to his singing.   My slumber was delicious, my
awaking more delicious still.   It was broad day, and
my opening eyes looked on sun and water and green
things, and an adorable landscape.   I rose up and
gave myself a shake ; I felt hungry and started gaily
for the town, resolved to spend on a good breakfast
the two pieces of money which I still had left.   I
was in such joyful spirits that I went along the road
singing lustily."[1]

There is in this the free expansion of inner sympathy ; the natural sentiment spontaneously respond-
ing to all the delicious movement of the external
world on its peaceful and harmonious side, just as if
the world of many-hued social circumstance which
man has made for himself had no existence.   We are
conscious of a full nervous elation which is not the
product of literature, such as we have seen so many
a time since, and which only found its expression in
literature in Rousseau's case by accident.   He did
not feel in order to write, but felt without any thought
of writing.   He dreamed at this time of many lofty
destinies, among them that of marshal of France, but
the fame of authorship never entered into his dreams.

[1] *Conf.*, iv. 290, 291.

When the time for authorship actually came, his work had all the benefit of the absence of self-consciousness, it had all the disinterestedness, so to say, with which the first fresh impressions were suffered to rise in his mind.

One other picture of this time is worth remembering, as showing that Rousseau was not wholly blind to social circumstances, and as illustrating, too, how it was that his way of dealing with them was so much more real and passionate, though so much less sagacious in some of its aspects, than the way of the other revolutionists of the century. One day, when he had lost himself in wandering in search of some site which he expected to find beautiful, he entered the house of a peasant, half dead with hunger and thirst. His entertainer offered him nothing more restoring than coarse barley bread and skimmed milk. Presently, after seeing what manner of guest he had, the worthy man descended by a small trap into his cellar, and brought up some good brown bread, some meat, and a bottle of wine, and an omelette was added afterwards. Then he explained to the wondering Rousseau, who was a Swiss, and knew none of the mysteries of the French fisc, that he hid away his wine on account of the duties, and his bread on account of the *taille*, and declared that he would be a ruined man if they suspected that he was not dying of hunger. All this made an impression on Rousseau which he never forgot. "Here," he says, "was the germ of the inextinguishable hatred which afterwards

grew up in my heart against the vexations that harass
the common people, and against all their oppressors.
This man actually did not dare to eat the bread
which he had won by the sweat of his brow, and
only avoided ruin by showing the same misery as
reigned around him."[1]

It was because he had thus seen the wrongs of the
poor, not from without but from within, not as a
pitying spectator but as of their own company, that
Rousseau by and by brought such fire to the attack
upon the old order, and changed the blank practice
of the elder philosophers into a deadly affair of ball
and shell. The man who had been a servant, who
had wanted bread, who knew the horrors of the
midnight street, who had slept in dens, who had
been befriended by rough men and rougher women,
who saw the goodness of humanity under its coarsest
outside, and who above all never tried to shut these
things out from his memory, but accepted them as
the most interesting, the most touching, the most
real of all his experiences, might well be expected to
penetrate to the root of the matter, and to protest to
the few who usurp literature and policy with their
ideas, aspirations, interests, that it is not they but
the many, whose existence stirs the heart and fills
the eye with the great prime elements of the human
lot.

[1] *Conf.*, iv. 281-283.

III.

It was, then, some time towards the middle of 1732
that Rousseau arrived at Chambéri, and finally took
up his residence with Madame de Warens, in the
dullest and most sombre room of a dull and sombre
house. She had procured him employment in connection with a land survey which the government of
Charles Emmanuel III. was then executing. It was
only temporary, and Rousseau's function was no
loftier than that of clerk, who had to copy and reduce
arithmetical calculations. We may imagine how
little a youth fresh from nights under the summer
sky would relish eight hours a day of surly toil in a
gloomy office, with a crowd of dirty and ill-smelling
fellow-workers.[1] If Rousseau was ever oppressed by
any set of circumstances, his method was invariable :
he ran away from them. So now he threw up his
post, and again tried to earn a little money by
that musical instruction in which he had made so
many singular and grotesque endeavours. Even
here the virtues which make ordinary life a possible
thing were not his. He was pleased at his lessons
while there, but he could not bear the idea of being
bound to be there, nor the fixing of an hour. In
time this experiment for a subsistence came to the
same end as all the others. He next rushed to
Besançon in search of the musical instruction which
he wished to give to others, but his baggage was

[1] *Conf.*, v. 325.

confiscated at the frontier, and he had to return.[1]
Finally he abandoned the attempt, and threw himself
loyally upon the narrow resources of Madame de
Warens, whom he assisted in some singularly indefinite way in the transaction of her very indefinite
and miscellaneous affairs,—if we are here, as so often,
to give the name of affairs to a very rapid and heedless passage along a shabby road to ruin.

The household at this time was on a very remarkable footing. Madame de Warens was at its head,
and Claude Anet, gardener, butler, steward, was her
factotum. He was a discreet person, of severe probity
and few words, firm, thrifty, and sage. The too
comprehensive principles of his mistress admitted
him to the closest intimacy, and in due time, when
Madame de Warens thought of the seductions which
ensnare the feet of youth, Rousseau was delivered
from them in an equivocal way by solicitous application of the same maxims of comprehension. "Although Claude Anet was as young as she was, he
was so mature and so grave, that he looked upon us
as two children worthy of indulgence, and we both
looked upon him as a respectable man, whose esteem
it was our business to conciliate. Thus there grew
up between us three a companionship, perhaps without another example like it upon earth. All our
wishes, our cares, our hearts were in common;
nothing seemed to pass outside our little circle.
The habit of living together, and of living together

[1] *Conf.* v. 360-364. *Corr.*, i. 21-24.

exclusively, became so strong that if at our meals
one of the three was absent, or there came a fourth,
all was thrown out; and in spite of our peculiar
relations, a *tête-à-tête* was less sweet than a meeting
of all three."[1]   Fate interfered to spoil this striking
attempt after a new type of the family, developed on
a duandric base.   Claude Anet was seized with
illness, a consequence of excessive fatigue in an
Alpine expedition in search of plants, and he came
to his end.[2]   In him Rousseau always believed that
he lost the most solid friend he ever possessed, " a
rare and estimable man, in whom nature served
instead of education, and who nourished in obscure
servitude all the virtues of great men."[3]   The day
after his death, Rousseau was speaking of their lost
friend to Madame de Warens with the liveliest and
most sincere affliction, when suddenly in the midst of
the conversation he remembered that he should
inherit the poor man's clothes, and particularly a
handsome black coat.   A reproachful tear from his
Maman, as he always somewhat nauseously called
Madame de Warens, extinguished the vile thought
and washed away its last traces.[4]   After all, those
men and women are exceptionally happy, who have
no such involuntary meanness of thought standing
against themselves in that unwritten chapter of their

[1] *Conf.*, v. 349, 350.

[2] Apparently in the summer of 1736, though the reference
to the return of the French troops at the peace (*Ib.* v. 365)
would place it in 1735.

[3] *Ib.* v. 356.   [4] *Ib.*

lives which even the most candid persons keep
privately locked up in shamefast recollection.

Shortly after his return to Chambéri, a wave from
the great tide of European affairs surged into the
quiet valleys of Savoy. In the February of 1733,
Augustus the Strong died, and the usual disorder
followed in the choice of a successor to him in the
kingship of Poland. France was for Stanislaus, the
father-in-law of Lewis xv., while the Emperor Charles
vi. and Anne of Russia were for August iii., elector
of Saxony. Stanislaus was compelled to flee, and
the French Government, taking up his quarrel,
declared war against the Emperor (October 14, 1733).
The first act of this war, which was to end in the
acquisition of Naples and the two Sicilies by Spanish
Bourbons, and of Lorraine by France, was the
despatch of a French expedition to the Milanese
under Marshall Villars, the husband of one of Voltaire's first idols. This took place in the autumn of
1733, and a French column passed through Chambéri,
exciting lively interest in all minds, including Rousseau's. He now read the newspapers for the first
time, with the most eager sympathy for the country
with whose history his own name was destined to be
so permanently associated. "If this mad passion,"
he says, "had only been momentary, I should not
speak of it; but for no visible reason it took such
root in my heart, that when I afterwards at Paris
played the stern republican, I could not help feeling
in spite of myself a secret predilection for the very

nation that I found so servile, and the government I
made bold to assail."[1]   This fondness for France was
strong, constant, and invincible, and found what was
in the eighteenth century a natural complement in a
corresponding dislike of England.[2]

Rousseau's health began to show signs of weakness.
His breath became asthmatic, he had palpitations, he
spat blood, and suffered from a slow feverishness from
which he never afterwards became entirely free.[3]
His mind was as feverish as his body, and the morbid
broodings which active life reduces to their lowest
degree in most young men, were left to make full
havoc along with the seven devils of idleness and
vacuity.   An instinct which may flow from the unrecognised animal lying deep down in us all, suggested
the way of return to wholesomeness.   Rousseau prevailed upon Madame de Warens to leave the stifling
streets for the fresh fields, and to deliver herself by
retreat to rural solitude from the adventurers who
made her their prey.   Les Charmettes, the modest
farm-house to which they retired, still stands.   The
modern traveller, with a taste for relieving an imagination strained by great historic monuments and secular
landmarks, with the sight of spots associated with the
passion and meditation of some far-shining teacher of
men, may walk a short league from where the gray

---

[1] Conf., v. 315, 316.

[2] Ib. iv. 276.   Nouv. Hél., II. xiv. 381, etc.

[3] He refers to the ill-health of his youth, Conf., vii. 32, and
describes an ominous head seizure while at Chambéri, Ib. vi. 396.

slate roofs of dull Chambéri bake in the sun, and
ascending a gently mounting road, with high leafy
bank on the right throwing cool shadows over his
head, and a stream on the left making music at his
feet, he sees an old red housetop lifted lonely above
the trees. The homes in which men have lived now
and again lend themselves to the beholder's subjective
impression; they seemed to be brooding in forlorn
isolation like some life-wearied gray-beard over ancient
and sorrow-stricken memories. At Les Charmettes
a pitiful melancholy penetrates you. The supreme
loveliness of the scene, the sweet-smelling meadows,
the orchard, the water-ways, the little vineyard with
here and there a rose glowing crimson among the
yellow stunted vines, the rust-red crag of the Nivolet
rising against the sky far across the broad valley; the
contrast between all this peace, beauty, silence, and
the diseased miserable life of the famous man who
found a scanty span of paradise in the midst of it,
touches the soul with a pathetic spell. We are for
the moment lifted out of squalor, vagrancy, and disorder, and seem to hear some of the harmonies which
sounded to this perturbed spirit, soothing it, exalting
it, and stirring those inmost vibrations which in
truth make up all the short divine part of a man's
life.[1]

[1] Rousseau's description of Les Charmettes is at the end of
the fifth book. The present proprietor keeps the house arranged
as it used to be, and has gathered one or two memorials of its
famous tenant, including his poor *clavecin* and his watch. In an
outside wall, Hérault de Sechelles, when Commissioner from

"No day passes," he wrote in the very year in which he died, "in which I do not recall with joy and tender effusion this single and brief time in my life, when I was fully myself, without mixture or hindrance, and when I may say in a true sense that I lived. I may almost say, like the prefect when disgraced and proceeding to end his days tranquilly in the country, 'I have passed seventy years on the earth, and I have lived but seven of them.' But for this brief and precious space, I should perhaps have remained uncertain about myself; for during all the rest of my life I have been so agitated, tossed, plucked hither and thither by the passions of others, that, being nearly passive in a life so stormy, I should find it hard to distinguish what belonged to me in my own conduct,—to such a degree has harsh necessity weighed upon me. But during these few years I did what I wished to do, I was what I wished to be."[1] The secret of such rare felicity is hardly to be described in words. It was the ease of a profoundly sensuous nature with every sense gratified and fascinated. Caressing and undivided affection within doors, all the sweetness and movement of nature without, solitude, freedom, and the busy idleness of life in gardens, —these were the conditions of Rousseau's ideal state. "If my happiness," he says, in language of strange

the Convention in the department of Mont Blanc, inserted a little white stone with two most lapidary stanzas inscribed upon it, about *génie, solitude, fierté, gloire, vérité, envie,* and the like.

[2] *Rêveries,* x. 336 (1778).

felicity, " consisted in facts, actions, or words, I might
then describe and represent it in some way ; but how
say what was neither said nor done nor even thought,
but only enjoyed and felt without my being able to
point to any other object of my happiness than the
very feeling itself ?   I arose with the sun and I was
happy ; I went out of doors and I was happy ; I saw
Maman and I was happy ; I left her and I was happy ;
I went among the woods and hills, I wandered about
in the dells, I read, I was idle, I dug in the garden,
I gathered fruit, I helped them indoors, and everywhere happiness followed me.   It was not in any
given thing, it was all in myself, and could never
leave me for a single instant."[1]   This was a true
garden of Eden, with the serpent in temporary quiescence, and we may count the man rare since the fall
who has found such happiness in such conditions, and
not less blessed than he is rare.   The fact that he
was one of this chosen company was among the foremost of the circumstances which made Rousseau seem
to so many men in the eighteenth century as a spring
of water in a thirsty land.

All innocent and amiable things moved him.   He
used to spend hours together in taming pigeons ; he
inspired them with such confidence that they would
follow him about, and allow him to take them wherever
he would, and the moment that he appeared in the
garden two or three of them would instantly settle on
his arms or his head.   The bees, too, gradually came to

[1] *Conf.*, vi. 393.

put the same trust in him, and his whole life was surrounded with gentle companionship. He always began the day with the sun, walking on the high ridge above the slope on which the house lay, and going through his form of worship. "It did not consist in a vain moving of the lips, but in a sincere elevation of heart to the author of the tender nature whose beauties lay spread out before my eyes. This act passed rather in wonder and contemplation than in requests; and I always knew that with the dispenser of true blessings, the best means of obtaining those which are needful for us, is less to ask than to deserve them."[1] These effusions may be taken for the beginning of the deistical reaction in the eighteenth century. While the truly scientific and progressive spirits were occupied in laborious preparation for adding to human knowledge and systematising it, Rousseau walked with his head in the clouds among gods, beneficent authors of nature, wise dispensers of blessings, and the like. "Ah, madam," he once said, "sometimes in the privacy of my study, with my hands pressed tight over my eyes or in the darkness of the night, I am of his opinion [that there is no God]. But look yonder (pointing with his hand to the sky, with head erect, and an inspired glance): the rising of the sun, as it scatters the mists that cover the earth and lays bare the wondrous glittering scene of nature, disperses at the same moment all cloud from my soul. I find my faith again, and my God, and

[1] *Conf.*, vi. 412.

my belief in him. I admire and adore him, and I
prostrate myself in his presence."[1] As if that settled
the question affirmatively, any more than the absence
of such theistic emotion in many noble spirits settles
it negatively. God became the highest known formula
for sensuous expansion, the synthesis of all complacent
emotions, and Rousseau filled up the measure of his
delight by creating and invoking a Supreme Being to
match with fine scenery and sunny gardens. We
shall have a better occasion to mark the attributes of
this important conception when we come to *Emilius*,
where it was launched in a panoply of resounding
phrases upon a Europe which was grown too strong
for Christian dogma, and was not yet grown strong
enough to rest in a provisional ordering of the results
of its own positive knowledge. Walking on the
terrace at Les Charmettes, you are at the very birth-
place of that particular Être Suprême to whom Robespierre offered the incense of an official festival.

Sometimes the reading of a Jansenist book would
make him unhappy by the prominence into which it
brought the displeasing idea of hell, and he used now
and then to pass a miserable day in wondering whether
this cruel destiny should be his. Madame de Warens,
whose softness of heart inspired her with a theology
that ought to have satisfied a seraphic doctor, had
abolished hell, but she could not dispense with purga-
tory because she did not know what to do with the

---

[1] *Mém. de Mdme. d'Epinay*, i. 394. (M. Boiteau's edition :
Charpentier. 1865.)

souls of the wicked, being unable either to damn them,
or to instal them among the good until they had been
purified into goodness. In truth it must be confessed,
says Rousseau, that alike in this world and the other
the wicked are extremely embarrassing.[1] His own
search after knowledge of his fate is well known.
One day, amusing himself in a characteristic manner
by throwing stones at trees, he began to be tormented
by fear of the eternal pit. He resolved to test his
doom by throwing a stone at a particular tree; if
he hit, then salvation; if he missed, then perdition.
With a trembling hand and beating heart he threw;
as he had chosen a large tree and was careful not to
place himself too far away, all was well.[2] As a rule,
however, in spite of the ugly phantoms of theology,
he passed his days in a state of calm. Even when
illness brought it into his head that he should soon
know the future lot by more assured experiment, he
still preserved a tranquillity which he justly qualifies
as sensual.

In thinking of Rousseau's peculiar feeling for nature,
which acquired such a decisive place in his character
during his life at Les Charmettes, it is to be remembered that it was entirely devoid of that stormy and
boisterous quality which has grown up in more modern
literature, out of the violent attempt to press nature
in her most awful moods into the service of the great

[1] *Conf.*, vi. 399.
[2] *Ib.* vi. 424. Goethe made a similar experiment; see
Mr. Lewes's *Life*, p. 126.

revolt against a social and religious tradition that can
no longer be endured.   Of this revolt Rousseau was
a chief, and his passion for natural aspects was connected with this attitude, but he did not seize those
of them which the poet of *Manfred*, for example,
forced into an imputed sympathy with his own rebel-
lion.   Rousseau always loved nature best in her moods
of quiescence and serenity, and in proportion as she
lent herself to such moods in men.   He liked rivulets
better than rivers.   He could not bear the sight of the
sea ; its infertile bosom and blind restless tumblings
filled him with melancholy.   The ruins of a park
affected him more than the ruins of castles.[1]   It is
true that no plain, however beautiful, ever seemed so
in his eyes ; he required torrents, rocks, dark forests,
mountains, and precipices.[2]   This does not affect the
fact that he never moralised appalling landscape, as
post-revolutionary writers have done, and that the
Alpine wastes which throw your puniest modern into
a rapture, had no attraction for him.   He could steep
himself in nature without climbing fifteen thousand
feet to find her.   In landscape, as has been said by
one with a right to speak, Rousseau was truly a great
artist, and you can, if you are artistic too, follow him
with confidence in his wanderings ; he understood that
beauty does not require a great stage, and that the

[1] Bernardin de Saint Pierre tells us this.   *Œuvres* (Ed. 1818),
xii. 70, etc.
[2] *Conf.*, iv. 297.   See also the description of the scenery of
the Valais, in the *Nouv. Hél.*, Pt. I. Let. xxiii.

effect of things lies in harmony.[1] The humble heights of the Jura, and the lovely points of the valley of Chambéri, sufficed to give him all the pleasure of which he was capable. In truth a man cannot escape from his time, and Rousseau at least belonged to the eighteenth century in being devoid of the capacity for feeling awe, and the taste for objects inspiring it. Nature was a tender friend with softest bosom, and no sphinx with cruel enigma. He felt neither terror, nor any sense of the littleness of man, nor of the mysteriousness of life, nor of the unseen forces which make us their sport, as he peered over the precipice and heard the water roaring at the bottom of it; he only remained for hours enjoying the physical sensation of dizziness with which it turned his brain, with a break now and again for hurling large stones, and watching them roll and leap down into the torrent, with as little reflection and as little articulate emotion as if he had been a child.[2]

Just as it is convenient for purposes of classification to divide a man into body and soul, even when we believe the soul to be only a function of the body, so people talk of his intellectual side and his emotional side, his thinking quality and his feeling quality, though in fact and at the roots these qualities are not two but one, with temperament for the common substratum. During this period of his life the whole of

[1] George Sand in *Mademoiselle la Quintinie* (p. 27), a book containing some peculiarly subtle appreciations of the Savoy landscape. [2] *Conf.*, iv. 298.

Rousseau's true force went into his feelings, and at all times feeling predominated over reflection, with many drawbacks and some advantages of a very critical kind for subsequent generations of men. Nearly every one who came into contact with him in the way of testing his capacity for being instructed pronounced him hopeless. He had several excellent opportunities of learning Latin, especially at Turin in the house of Count Gouvon, and in the seminary at Annecy, and at Les Charmettes he did his best to teach himself, but without any better result than a very limited power of reading. In learning one rule he forgot the last; he could never master the most elementary laws of versification; he learnt and re-learnt twenty times the Eclogues of Virgil, but not a single word remained with him.[1] He was absolutely without verbal memory, and he pronounces himself wholly incapable of learning anything from masters. Madame de Warens tried to have him taught both dancing and fencing; he could never achieve a minuet, and after three months of instruction he was as clumsy and helpless with his foil as he had been on the first day. He resolved to become a master at the chessboard; he shut himself up in his room, and worked night and day over the books with indescribable efforts which covered many weeks. On proceeding to the café to manifest his powers, he found that all the moves and combinations had got mixed up in his head, he saw nothing but

---

[1] *Conf.*, vi. 416, 422, etc.; iii. 164; iii. 203; v. 347; v. 383, 384. Also vii. 53.

clouds on the board, and as often as he repeated the
experiment he only found himself weaker than before.
Even in music, for which he had a genuine passion
and at which he worked hard, he never could acquire
any facility at sight, and he was an inaccurate scorer,
even when only copying the score of others.[1]

Two things nearly incompatible, he writes in an
important passage, are united in me without my being
able to think how ; an extremely ardent temperament,
lively and impetuous passions, along with ideas that
are very slow in coming to birth, very embarrassed,
and which never arise until after the event.   " One
would say that my heart and my intelligence do not
belong to the same individual. . . . I feel all, and see
nothing ; I am carried away, but I am stupid. . . .
This slowness of thinking, united with such vivacity
of feeling, possesses me not only in conversation, but
when I am alone and working.   My ideas arrange
themselves in my head with incredible difficulty ; they
circulate there in a dull way and ferment until they
agitate me, fill me with heat, and give me palpitations ;
in the midst of this stir I see nothing clearly, I could
not write a single word.   Insensibly the violent
emotion grows still, the chaos is disentangled, everything falls into its place, but very slowly and after
long and confused agitation."[2]

So far from saying that his heart and intelligence
belonged to two persons, we might have been quite

[1] *Conf.*, v. 313, 367 ; iv. 293 ; ix. 353.   Also *Mém. de Mdme.
d'Epinay*, ii. 151.   [2] *Ib.* iii. 192, 193.

sure, knowing his heart, that his intelligence must be exactly what he describes its process to have been. The slow-burning ecstasy in which he knew himself at his height and was most conscious of fulness of life, was incompatible with the rapid and deliberate generation of ideas. The same soft passivity, the same receptiveness, which made his emotions like the surface of a lake under sky and breeze, entered also into the working of his intellectual faculties. But it happens that in this region, in the attainment of knowledge, truth, and definite thoughts, even receptiveness implies a distinct and active energy, and hence the very quality of temperament which left him free and eager for sensuous impressions, seemed to muffle his intelligence in a certain opaque and resisting medium, of the indefinable kind that interposes between will and action in a dream. His rational part was fatally protected by a non-conducting envelope of sentiment; this intercepted clear ideas on their passage, and even cut off the direct and true impress of those objects and their relations, which are the material of clear ideas. He was no doubt right in his avowal that objects generally made less impression on him than the recollection of them; that he could see nothing of what was before his eyes, and had only his intelligence in cases where memories were concerned; and that of what was said or done in his presence, he felt and penetrated nothing.[1] In other words, this is to say that his material of thought was not fact but image.

[1] *Conf.*, iv. 301 ; iii. 195.

When he plunged into reflection, he did not deal with
the objects of reflection at first hand and in themselves,
but only with the reminiscences of objects, which he
had never approached in a spirit of deliberate and
systematic observation, and with those reminiscences,
moreover, suffused and saturated by the impalpable
but most potent essences of a fermenting imagination.
Instead of urgently seeking truth with the patient
energy, the wariness, and the conscience, with the
sharpened instruments, the systematic apparatus, and
the minute feelers and tentacles of the genuine thinker
and solid reasoner, he only floated languidly on a
summer tide of sensation, and captured premiss and
conclusion in a succession of swoons.   It would be a
mistake to contend that no work can be done for the
world by this method, or that truth only comes to
those who chase her with logical forceps.   But one
should always try to discover how a teacher of men
came by his ideas, whether by careful toil, or by the
easy bequest of generous phantasy.

To give a zest to rural delight, and partly perhaps
to satisfy the intellectual interest which must have
been an instinct in one who became so consummate
a master in the great and noble art of composition,
Rousseau, during the time when he lived with Madame
de Warens, tried as well as he knew how to acquire a
little knowledge of what fruit the cultivation of the
mind of man had hitherto brought forth.   According
to his own account, it was Voltaire's Letters on the
English which first drew him seriously to study, and

nothing which that illustrious man wrote at this time
escaped him. His taste for Voltaire inspired him with
the desire of writing with elegance, and of imitating
"the fine and enchanting colour of Voltaire's style"[1]
—an object in which he cannot be held to have in
the least succeeded, though he achieved a superb style
of his own. On his return from Turin Madame de
Warens had begun in some small way to cultivate a
taste for letters in him, though he had lost the enthusiasm of his childhood for reading. Saint Evremond,
Puffendorff, the Henriade, and the Spectator happened
to be in his room, and he turned over their pages. The
Spectator, he says, pleased him greatly and did him
much good.[2] Madame de Warens was what he calls
protestant in literary taste, and would talk for ever of
the great Bayle, while she thought more of Saint Evremond than she could ever persuade Rousseau to think.
Two or three years later than this he began to use his
own mind more freely, and opened his eyes for the first
time to the greatest question that ever dawns upon any
human intelligence that has the privilege of discerning
it, the problem of a philosophy and a body of doctrine.

His way of answering it did not promise the best
results. He read an introduction to the Sciences,

---

[1] Conf., v. 372, 373. The mistaken date assigned to the
correspondence between Voltaire and Frederick is one of many
instances how little we can trust the Confessions for minute
accuracy, though their substantial veracity is confirmed by all
the collateral evidence that we have.

[2] Ib. iii. 188. For his debt in the way of education to
Madame de Warens, see also Ib. vii. 46.

then he took an Encyclopædia and tried to learn all
things together, until he repented and resolved to
study subjects apart. This he found a better plan for
one to whom long application was so fatiguing, that
he could not with any effect occupy himself for half
an hour on any one matter, especially if following the
ideas of another person.[1] He began his morning's
work, after an hour or two of dispersive chat, with
the Port-Royal Logic, Locke's Essay on the Human
Understanding, Malebranche, Leibnitz, Descartes.[2]
He found these authors in a condition of such perpetual contradiction among themselves, that he formed
the chimerical design of reconciling them with one
another. This was tedious, so he took up another
method, on which he congratulated himself to the
end of his life. It consisted in simply adopting and
following the ideas of each author, without comparing
them either with one another or with those of other
writers, and above all without any criticism of his
own. Let me begin, he said, by collecting a store of
ideas, true or false, but at any rate clear, until my
head is well enough stocked to enable me to compare
and choose. At the end of some years passed "in
never thinking exactly, except after other people,
without reflecting so to speak, and almost without
reasoning," he found himself in a state to think for
himself. "In spite of beginning late to exercise my
judicial faculty, I never found that it had lost its

[1] *Conf.*, vi. 409.
[2] *Ib.* vi. 413.   He adds a suspicious-looking "*et cetera.*"

vigour, and when I came to publish my own ideas, I
was hardly accused of being a servile disciple."[1]

To that fairly credible account of the matter, one
can only say that this mutually exclusive way of learning the thoughts of others, and developing thoughts
of your own, is for an adult probably the most mischievous, where it is not the most impotent, fashion
in which intellectual exercise can well be taken. It is
exactly the use of the judicial faculty, criticising, comparing, and defining, which is indispensable in order
that a student should not only effectually assimilate
the ideas of a writer, but even know what those ideas
come to and how much they are worth. And so
when he works at ideas of his own, a judicial faculty
which has been kept studiously slumbering for some
years, is not likely to revive in full strength without
any preliminary training. Rousseau was a man of
singular genius, and he set an extraordinary mark on
Europe, but this mark would have been very different
if he had ever mastered any one system of thought, or
if he had ever fully grasped what systematic thinking
means. Instead of this, his debt to the men whom
he read was a debt of piecemeal, and his obligation
an obligation for fragments; and this is perhaps the
worst way of acquiring an intellectual lineage, for it
leaves out the vital continuity of temper and method.
It is a small thing to accept this or that of Locke's
notions upon education or the origin of ideas, if you
do not see the merit of his way of coming by his

[1] *Conf.*, vi. 414

notions. In short, Rousseau has distinctions in abundance, but the distinction of knowing how to think, in
the exact sense of that term, was hardly among them,
and neither now nor at any other time did he go
through any of that toilsome and vigorous intellectual
preparation to which the ablest of his contemporaries,
Diderot, Voltaire, D'Alembert, Turgot, Condorcet,
Hume, all submitted themselves. His comfortable view
was that " the sensible and interesting conversations
of a woman of merit are more proper to form a young
man than all the pedantical philosophy of books."[1]

Style, however, in which he ultimately became
such a proficient, and which wrought such marvels
as only style backed by passion can work, already
engaged his serious attention. We have already seen
how Voltaire implanted in him the first root idea,
which so many of us never perceive at all, that there
is such a quality of writing as style. He evidently
took pains with the form of expression and thought
about it, in obedience to some inborn harmonious
predisposition which is the source of all veritable
eloquence, though there is no strong trace now nor
for many years to come of any irresistible inclination
for literary composition. We find him, indeed, in
1736 showing consciousness of a slight skill in writing,[2] but he only thought of it as a possible recommendation for a secretaryship to some great person.
He also appears to have practised verses, not for their

[1] *Conf.*, iv. 295. See also v. 346.
[2] *Corr.*, 1736, pp. 26, 27.

own sake, for he always most justly thought his own
verses mediocre, and they are even worse; but on the
ground that verse-making is a rather good exercise
for breaking one's self to elegant inversions, and
learning a greater ease in prose.[1] At the age of one
and twenty he composed a comedy, long afterwards
damned as *Narcisse*. Such prelusions, however, were
of small importance compared with the fact of his
being surrounded by a moral atmosphere in which
his whole mind was steeped. It is not in the study
of Voltaire or another, but in the deep soft soil of
constant mood and old habit that such a style as
Rousseau's has its growth.

It was the custom to return to Chambéri for the
winter, and the day of their departure from Les
Charmettes was always a day blurred and tearful for
Rousseau; he never left it without kissing the ground,
the trees, the flowers; he had to be torn away from it
as from a loved companion. At the first melting of
the winter snows they left their dungeon in Chambéri,
and they never missed the earliest song of the nightingale. Many a joyful day of summer peace remained
vivid in Rousseau's memory, and made a mixed heaven
and hell for him long years after in the stifling dingy
Paris street, and the raw and cheerless air of a Derbyshire winter.[1] "We started early in the morning,"

[1] *Conf.*, iv. 271, where he says further that he never found
enough attraction in French poetry to make him think of pursu-
ing it.

[2] The first part of the Confessions was written in Wootton in
Derbyshire, in the winter of 1766-1767.

he says, describing one of these simple excursions on the day of St. Lewis, who was the very unconscious patron saint of Madame de Warens, "together and alone; I proposed that we should go and ramble about the side of the valley opposite to our own, which we had not yet visited. We sent our provisions on before us, for we were to be out all day. We went from hill to hill and wood to wood, sometimes in the sun and often in the shade, resting from time to time and forgetting ourselves for whole hours; chatting about ourselves, our union, our dear lot, and offering unheard prayers that it might last. All seemed to conspire for the bliss of this day. Rain had fallen a short time before; there was no dust, and the little streams were full; a light fresh breeze stirred the leaves, the air was pure, the horizon without a cloud, and the same serenity reigned in our own hearts. Our dinner was cooked in a peasant's cottage, and we shared it with his family. These Savoyards are such good souls! After dinner we sought shade under some tall trees, where, while I collected dry sticks for making our coffee, Maman amused herself by botanising among the bushes, and the expedition ended in transports of tenderness and effusion."[1] This is one of such days as the soul turns back to when the misery that stalks after us all has seized it, and a man is left to the sting and smart of the memory of irrecoverable things.

He was resolved to bind himself to Madame de

[1] *Conf.*, vi. 422.

Warens with an inalterable fidelity for all the rest of
his days; he would watch over her with all the dutiful
and tender vigilance of a son, and she should be to
him something dearer than mother or wife or sister.
What actually befell was this. He was attacked by
vapours, which he characterises as the disorder of the
happy. One symptom of his disease was the conviction derived from the rash perusal of surgeon's
treatises, that he was suffering from a polypus in the
heart. On the not very chivalrous principle that if
he did not spend Madame de Warens' money, he was
only leaving it for adventurers and knaves, he proceeded to Montpellier to consult the physicians, and
took the money for his expenses out of his benefactress's store, which was always slender because it was
always open to any hand. While on the road, he fell
into an intrigue with a travelling companion, whom
critics have compared to the fair Philina of Wilhelm
Meister. In due time, the Montpellier doctor being
unable to discover a disease, declared that the patient
had none. The scenery was dull and unattractive,
and this would have counterbalanced the weightiest
prudential reasons with him at any time. Rousseau
debated whether he should keep tryst with his gay
fellow-traveller, or return to Chambéri. Remorse
and that intractable emptiness of pocket which is the
iron key to many a deed of ingenuous-looking self-
denial and Spartan virtue, directed him homewards.
Here he had a surprise, and perhaps learnt a lesson.
He found installed in the house a personage whom

he describes as tall, fair, noisy, coxcombical, flat-faced, flat-souled. Another triple alliance seemed a thing odious in the eyes of a man whom his travelling diversions had made a Pharisee for the hour. He protested, but Madame de Warens was a woman of principle, and declined to let Rousseau, who had profited by the doctrine of indifference, now set up in his own favour the contrary doctrine of a narrow and churlish partiality. So a short, delicious, and never-forgotten episode came to an end : this pair who had known so much happiness together were happy together no more, and the air became peopled for Rousseau with wan spectres of dead joys and fast gathering cares.

The dates of the various events described in the fifth and sixth books of the Confessions are inextricable, and the order is evidently inverted more than once. The inversion of order is less serious than the contradictions between the dates of the Confessions and the more authentic and unmistakable dates of his letters. For instance, he describes a visit to Geneva as having been made shortly before Lautrec's temporary pacification of the civic troubles of that town ; and that event took place in the spring of 1738. This would throw the Montpellier journey, which he says came after the visit to Geneva, into 1738, but the letters to Madame de Warens from Grenoble and Montpellier are dated in the autumn and winter of 1737.[1] Minor verifications attest the

[1] *Corr.*, i. 43, 46, 62, etc.

exactitude of the dates of the letters,[1] and we may therefore conclude that he returned from Montpellier, found his place taken and lost his old delight in Les Charmettes, in the early part of 1738. In the tenth of the Rêveries he speaks of having passed "a space of four or five years" in the bliss of Les Charmettes, and it is true that his connection with it in one way and another lasted from the middle of 1736 until about the middle of 1741. But as he left for Montpellier in the autumn of 1737, and found the obnoxious Vinzenried installed in 1738, the pure and characteristic felicity of Les Charmettes perhaps only lasted about a year or a year and a half. But a year may set a deep mark on a man, and give him imperishable taste of many things bitter and sweet.

[1] Musset-Pathay, i. 23, *n*.

CHAPTER IV.

THERESA LE VASSEUR.

MEN like Rousseau, who are most heedless in letting their delight perish, are as often as not most loth to bury what they have slain, or even to perceive that life has gone out of it. The sight of simple hearts trying to coax back a little warm breath of former days into a present that is stiff and cold with indifference, is touching enough. But there is a certain grossness around the circumstances in which Rousseau now and too often found himself, that makes us watch his embarrassment with some composure. One cannot easily think of him as a simple heart, and we feel perhaps as much relief as he, when he resolves after making all due efforts to thrust out the intruder and bring Madame de Warens over from theories which had become too practical to be interesting, to leave Les Charmettes and accept a tutorship at Lyons. His new patron was a De Mably, elder brother of the philosophic abbé of the same name (1709-85), and of the still more notable Condillac (1714-80).

The future author of the most influential treatise on education that has ever been written, was not

successful in the practical and far more arduous side
of that master art.[1]   We have seen how little training
he had ever given himself in the cardinal virtues of
collectedness and self-control, and we know this to
be the indispensable quality in all who have to shape
young minds for a humane life.   So long as all went
well, he was an angel, but when things went wrong,
he is willing to confess that he was a devil.   When
his two pupils could not understand him, he became
frantic ; when they showed wilfulness or any other
part of the disagreeable materials out of which, along
with the rest, human excellence has to be ingeniously
and painfully manufactured, he was ready to kill
them.   This, as he justly admits, was not the way to
render them either well learned or sage.   The moral
education of the teacher himself was hardly complete,
for he describes how he used to steal his employer's
wine, and the exquisite draughts which he enjoyed
in the secrecy of his own room, with a piece of cake
in one hand and some dear romance in the other.
We should forgive greedy pilferings of this kind
more easily if Rousseau had forgotten them more
speedily.   These are surely offences for which the
best expiation is oblivion in a throng of worthier
memories.

[1] In theory he was even now curiously prudent and almost
sagacious ; witness the Projet pour l'Education, etc., submitted
to M. de Mably, and printed in the volume of his Works entitled *Mélanges*, pp. 106-136.   In the matter of Latin, it may
be worth noting that Rousseau rashly or otherwise condemns
the practice of writing it, as a vexatious superfluity (p. 132).

It is easy to understand how often Rousseau's mind turned from the deadly drudgery of his present employment to the beatitude of former days. "What rendered my present condition insupportable was the recollection of my beloved Charmettes, of my garden, my trees, my fountain, my orchard, and above all of her for whom I felt myself born and who gave life to it all. As I thought of her, of our pleasures, our guileless days, I was seized by a tightness in my heart, a stopping of my breath, which robbed me of all spirit."[1] For years to come this was a kind of far-off accompaniment, thrumming melodiously in his ears under all the discords of a miserable life. He made another effort to quicken the dead. Throwing up his office with his usual promptitude in escaping from the irksome, after a residence of something like a year at Lyons (April, 1740—spring of 1741), he made his way back to his old haunts. The first half-hour with Madame de Warens persuaded him that happiness here was really at an end. After a stay of a few months, his desolation again overcame him. It was agreed that he should go to Paris to make his fortune by a new method of musical notation which he had invented, and after a short stay at Lyons, he found himself for the second time in the famous city which in the eighteenth century had become for the moment the centre of the universe.[2]

It was not yet, however, destined to be a centre

[1] *Conf.*, vi. 471.   [2] *Ib.*, vi. 472-475 ; vii. 8.

for him.   His plan of musical notation was examined
by a learned committee of the Academy, no member
of whom was instructed in the musical art.   Rousseau,
dumb, inarticulate, and unready as usual, was amazed
at the ease with which his critics by the free use of
sounding phrases demolished arguments and objections which he perceived that they did not at all understand.   His experience on this occasion suggested to
him the most just reflection, how even without
breadth of intelligence, the profound knowledge of
any one thing is preferable in forming a judgment
about it, to all possible enlightenment conferred by
the cultivation of the sciences, without study of the
special matter in question.   It astonished him that
all these learned men, who knew so many things,
could yet be so ignorant that a man should only pre-
tend to be a judge in his own craft. [1]

His musical path to glory and riches thus blocked
up, he surrendered himself not to despair but to
complete idleness and peace of mind.   He had a few
coins left, and these prevented him from thinking of
a future.   He was presented to one or two great
ladies, and with the blundering gallantry habitual to
him he wrote a letter to one of the greatest of them,
declaring his passion for her.   Madame Dupin was
the daughter of one, and the wife of another, of the
richest men in France, and the attentions of a man
whose acquaintance Madame Beuzenval had begun
by inviting him to dine in the servants' hall, were

[1] *Conf.*, vii. 18, 19.

not pleasing to her.[1]   She forgave the impertinence
eventually, and her stepson, M. Francueil, was Rousseau's patron for some years.[2]   On the whole, however,
in spite of his own account of his social ineptitude,
there cannot have been anything so repulsive in his
manners as this account would lead us to think.
There is no grave anachronism in introducing here
the impression which he made on two fine ladies
not many years after this.   " He pays compliments,
yet he is not polite, or at least he is without the air
of politeness.   He seems to be ignorant of the usages
of society, but it is easily seen that he is infinitely
intelligent.   He has a brown complexion, while eyes
that overflow with fire give animation to his expression.   When he has spoken and you look at him, he
appears comely ; but when you try to recall him,
his image is always extremely plain.   They say that
he has bad health, and endures agony which from

[1] Musset-Pathay (ii. 72) quotes the passage from Lord Chester-
field's Letters, where the writer suggests Madame Dupin as a
proper person with whom his son might in a regular and business-
like manner open the elevating game of gallant intrigue.

[2] M. Dupin deserves honourable mention as having helped the
editors of the Encyclopædia by procuring information for them
as to salt-works (D'Alembert's *Discours Préliminaire*).   His
son M. Dupin de Francueil, it may be worth noting, is a link
in the genealogical chain between two famous personages.   In
1777, the year before Rousseau's death, he married (in the
chapel of the French embassy in London) Aurora de Saxe, a
natural daughter of the marshal, himself the natural son of
August the Strong, King of Poland.   From this union was
born Maurice Dupin, and Maurice Dupin was the father of
Madame George Sand.   M. Francueil died in 1787.

some motive of vanity he most carefully conceals. It is this, I fancy, which gives him from time to time an air of sullenness."[1] The other lady, who saw him at the same time, speaks of "the poor devil of an author, who's as poor as Job for you, but with wit and vanity enough for four. . . . They say his history is as queer as his person, and that is saying a good deal. . . . Madame Maupeou and I tried to guess what it was. 'In spite of his face,' said she (for it is certain he is uncommonly plain), 'his eyes tell that love plays a great part in his romance.' 'No,' said I, 'his nose tells me that it is vanity.' 'Well then, 'tis both one and the other.'"[2]

One of his patronesses took some trouble to procure him the post of secretary to the French ambassador at Venice, and in the spring of 1743 our much-wandering man started once more in quest of meat and raiment in the famous city of the Adriatic. This was one of those steps of which there are not a few in a man's life, that seem at the moment to rank foremost in the short line of decisive acts, and then are presently seen not to have been decisive at all, but mere interruptions conducting nowhither. In truth the critical moments with us are mostly as points in slumber. Even if the ancient oracles of the gods were to regain their speech once more on the earth, men would usually go to consult them on days when the answer would have least significance,

---

[1] *Mém. de Mdme. d'Epinay*, vol. i. ch. iv. p. 176.
[2] *Ib.* vol. i. ch. iv. pp. 178, 179.

and could guide them least far. That one of the
most heedless vagrants in Europe, and as it happened
one of the men of most extraordinary genius also,
should have got a footing in the train of the ambassador of a great government, would naturally seem to
him and others as chance's one critical stroke in his
life. In reality it was nothing. The Count of
Montaigu, his master, was one of the worst characters
with whom Rousseau could for his own profit have
been brought into contact. In his professional quality
he was not far from imbecile. The folly and weakness of the government at Versailles during the reign
of Lewis xv., and its indifference to competence in
every department except perhaps partially in the
fisc, was fairly illustrated in its absurd representative
at Venice. The secretary, whose renown has preserved his master's name, has recorded more amply
than enough the grounds of quarrel between them.
Rousseau is for once eager to assert his own efficiency,
and declares that he rendered many important services
for which he was repaid with ingratitude and persecution.[1] One would be glad to know what the
Count of Montaigu's version of matters was, for in
truth Rousseau's conduct in previous posts makes us
wonder how it was that he who had hitherto always

---

[1] *Conf.*, vii. 46, 51, 52, etc. A diplomatic piece in Rousseau's
handwriting has been found in the archives of the French
consulate at Constantinople, as M. Girardin informs us. Voltaire unworthily spread the report that Rousseau had been the
ambassador's private attendant. For Rousseau's reply to the
calumny, see *Corr.*, v. 75 (Jan. 5, 1767) ; also iv. 150.

been unfaithful over few things, suddenly touched perfection when he became lord over many.

There is other testimony, however, to the ambassador's morbid quality, of which, after that general imbecility which was too common a thing among men in office to be remarkable, avarice was the most striking trait. For instance, careful observation had persuaded him that three shoes are equivalent to two pairs, because there is always one of a pair which is more worn than its fellow; and hence he habitually ordered his shoes in threes.[1] It was natural enough that such a master and such a secretary should quarrel over perquisites. That slightly cringing quality which we have noticed on one or two occasions in Rousseau's hungry youthful time, had been hardened out of him by circumstance or the strengthening of inborn fibre. He would now neither dine in a servants' hall because a fine lady forgot what was due to a musician, nor share his fees with a great ambassador who forgot what was due to himself. These sordid disputes are of no interest now to anybody, and we need only say that after a period of eighteen months passed in uncongenial company, Rousseau parted from his count in extreme dudgeon, and the diplomatic career which he had promised to himself came to the same close as various other careers had already done.

He returned to Paris towards the end of 1744, burning with indignation at the unjust treatment which he believed himself to have suffered, and laying

[1] Bernardin de St. Pierre, *Œuv.*, xii. 55 *seq.*

memorial after memorial before the minister at home.
He assures us that it was the justice and the futility
of his complaints, that left in his soul the germ of
exasperation against preposterous civil institutions,
"in which the true common weal and real justice are
always sacrificed to some seeming order or other, which
is in fact destructive of all order, and only adds the
sanction of public authority to the oppression of the
weak and the iniquity of the strong."[1]

One or two pictures connected with the Venetian
episode remain in the memory of the reader of the
Confessions, and among them perhaps with most
people is that of the quarantine at Genoa in Rousseau's voyage to his new post. The travellers had
the choice of remaining on board the felucca, or passing the time in an unfurnished lazaretto. This, we
may notice in passing, was his first view of the sea;
he makes no mention of the fact, nor does the sight
or thought of the sea appear to have left the least
mark in any line of his writings. He always disliked
it, and thought of it with melancholy. Rousseau, as
we may suppose, found the want of space and air in
the boat the most intolerable of evils, and preferred
to go alone to the lazaretto, though it had neither
window-sashes nor tables nor chairs nor bed, nor even
a truss of straw to lie down upon. He was locked up
and had the whole barrack to himself. "I manufactured," he says, "a good bed out of my coats and
shirts, sheets out of towels which I stitched together,

[1] *Conf.*, vii. 92.

a pillow out of my old cloak rolled up. I made myself a seat of one trunk placed flat, and a table of the other. I got out some paper and my writing-desk, and arranged some dozen books that I had by way of library. In short I made myself so comfortable, that, with the exception of curtains and windows, I was nearly as well off in this absolutely naked lazaretto as in my lodgings in Paris. My meals were served with much pomp; two grenadiers, with bayonets at their musket-ends, escorted them; the staircase was my dining-room, the landing did for table and the lower step for a seat, and when my dinner was served, they rang a little bell as they withdrew, to warn me to seat myself at table. Between my meals, when I was neither writing nor reading, nor busy with my furnishing, I went for a walk in the Protestant graveyard, or mounted into a lantern which looked out on to the port, and whence I could see the ships sailing in and out. I passed a fortnight in this way, and I could have spent the whole three weeks of the quarantine without feeling an instant's weariness."[1]

These are the occasions when we catch glimpses of the true Rousseau; but his residence in Venice was on the whole one of his few really sociable periods. He made friends and kept them, and there was even a certain gaiety in his life. He used to tell people their fortunes in a way that an earlier century would have counted unholy.[2] He rarely sought pleasure in those of her haunts for which the Queen of the Adri-

---

[1] *Conf.*, vii. 38, 39.   [2] *Lettres de la Montagne*, iii. 266.

atic had a guilty renown, but he has left one singular
anecdote, showing the degree to which profound
sensibility is capable of doing the moralist's work in
a man, and how a stroke of sympathetic imagination
may keep one from sin more effectually than an ethical
precept.[1]   It is pleasanter to think of him as working
at the formation of that musical taste which ten years
afterwards led him to amaze the Parisians by proving
that French melody was a hollow idea born of national
self-delusion.   A Venetian experiment, whose evidence
in the special controversy is less weighty perhaps than
Rousseau supposed, was among the facts which persuaded him that Italian is the language of music.   An
Armenian who had never heard any music was invited
to listen first of all to a French monologue, and then
to an air of Galuppi's.   Rousseau observed in the
Armenian more surprise than pleasure during the
performance of the French piece.   The first notes of
the Italian were no sooner struck, than his eyes and
whole expression softened; he was enchanted, surrendered his whole soul to the ravishing impressions of
the music, and could never again be induced to listen
to the performance of any French air.[2]

More important than this was the circumstance that
the sight of the defects of the government of the
Venetian Republic first drew his mind to political

[1] *Conf.*, vii. 75-84. Also a second example, 84-86. For
Byron's opinion of one of these stories, see Lockhart's *Life of
Scott*, vi. 132. (Ed. 1837.)

[2] *Lettre sur la Musique Française* (1753), p. 186.

speculation, and suggested to him the composition of a book that was to be called Institutions Politiques.[1] The work, as thus designed and named, was never written, but the idea of it, after many years of medi-tation, ripened first in the Discourse on Inequality, and then in the Social Contract.

If Rousseau's departure for Venice was a wholly insignificant element in his life, his return from it was almost immediately followed by an event which counted for nothing at the moment, which his friends by and by came to regard as the fatal and irretrievable disaster of his life, but which he persistently described as the only real consolation that heaven permitted him to taste in his misery, and the only one that enabled him to bear his many sore burdens.[2]

He took up his quarters at a small and dirty hotel not far from the Sorbonne, where he had alighted on the occasion of his second arrival in Paris.[3] Here was a kitchen-maid, some two-and-twenty years old, who used to sit at table with her mistress and the guests

---

[1] Conf., ix. 232.   [2] Ib. vii. 97.

[3] Hôtel St. Quentin, rue des Cordiers, a narrow street run-ning between the rue St. Jacques and the rue Victor Cousin. The still squalid hostelry is now visible as Hôtel J. J. Rousseau. There is some doubt whether he first saw Theresa in 1743 or 1745. The account in Bk. vii. of the Confessions is for the latter date (see also Corr., ii. 207), but in the well-known letter to her in 1769 (Ib. vi. 79), he speaks of the twenty-six years of their union. Their so-called marriage took place in 1768, and writing in that year he speaks of the five-and-twenty years of their attachment (Ib. v. 323), and in the Confessions (ix. 249) he

of the house.   The company was rough, being mainly
composed of Irish and Gascon abbés, and other people
to whom graces of mien and refinement of speech had
come neither by nature nor cultivation.   The hostess
herself pitched the conversation in merry Rabelaisian
key, and the apparent modesty of her serving-woman
gave a zest to her own licence.   Rousseau was moved
with pity for a maid defenceless against a ribald storm,
and from pity he advanced to some warmer sentiment,
and he and Theresa Le Vasseur took each other for
better for worse, in a way informal but sufficiently
effective.   This was the beginning of a union which
lasted for the length of a generation and more, down
to the day of Rousseau's most tragical ending.[1]   She
thought she saw in him a worthy soul ; and he was
convinced that he saw in her a woman of sensibility,
simple and free from trick, and neither of the two, he
says, was deceived in respect of the other.   Her intellectual quality was unique. She could never be taught
to read with any approach to success.   She could
never follow the order of the twelve months of the
year, nor master a single arithmetical figure, nor count
a sum of money, nor reckon the price of a thing.   A
month's instruction was not enough to give knowledge
of the hours of the day on the dial-plate.   The words

fixes their marriage at the same date ; also in the letter to
Saint-Germain (vi. 152).   Musset-Pathay, though giving
1745 in one place (i. 45), and 1743 in another (ii. 198), has
with less than his usual care paid no attention to the discrepancy.

[1] *Conf.*, vii. 97-100.

she used were often the direct opposites of the words
that she meant to use.[1]

The marriage choice of others is the inscrutable
puzzle of those who have no eye for the fact that such
choice is the great match of cajolery between purpose
and invisible hazard; the blessedness of many lives is
the stake, as intention happens to cheat accident or
to be cheated by it. When the match is once over,
deep criticism of a game of pure chance is time wasted.
The crude talk in which the unwise deliver their judgments upon the conditions of success in the relations
between men and women, has flowed with unpro-
fitable copiousness as to this not very inviting case.
People construct an imaginary Rousseau out of his
writings, and then fetter their elevated, susceptible,

---

[1] *Conf.*, vii. 101. A short specimen of her composition may
be interesting, at any rate to hieroglyphic students: "Mesi-
ceuras ancor mieu re mies quan geu ceures o pres deu vous, e deu
vous temoes tous la goies e latandres deu mon querque vous cones
ces que getou gour e rus pour vous, e qui neu finiraes quotobocs
ces mon quere qui vous paleu ces paes mes le vre. . . . ge sui
avestous lamities e la reu conec caceu posible e la tacheman mon
cher bonnamies votreau enble e bon amiess theress le vasseur.'
Of which dark words this is the interpretation :—"Mais il sera
encore mieux remis quand je sera auprès de vous, et de vous
témoigner toute la joie et la tendresse de mon cœur que vous
connaissez que j'ai toujours eue pour vous, et qui ne finira qu'au
tombeau ; c'est mon cœur qui vous parle, c'est pas mes lèvres.
. . . Je suis avec toute l'amitié et la reconnaissance possibles.
et l'attachement, mon cher bon ami, votre humble et bonne
amie, Thérèse Le Vasseur." (*Rousseau, ses Amis et ses Ennemis,*
ii. 450.) Certainly it was not learning and arts which hindered
Theresa's manners from being pure.

sensitive, and humane creation, to the unfortunate
woman who could never be taught that April is the
month after March, or that twice four and a half are
nine. Now we have already seen enough of Rousseau
to know for how infinitely little he counted the gift
of a quick wit, and what small store he set either on
literary varnish or on capacity for receiving it. He
was touched in people with whom he had to do, not
by attainment, but by moral fibre or his imaginary
impression of their moral fibre. Instead of analysing
a character, bringing its several elements into the
balance, computing the more or less of this faculty or
that, he loved to feel its influence as a whole, indivisible, impalpable, playing without sound or agitation
around him like soft light and warmth and the foster-
ing air. The deepest ignorance, the dullest incapacity,
the cloudiest faculties of apprehension, were nothing
to him in man or woman, provided he could only be
sensible of that indescribable emanation from voice
and eye and movement, that silent effusion of serenity
around spoken words, which nature has given to some
tranquillising spirits, and which would have left him
free in an even life of indolent meditation and un-
fretted sense. A woman of high, eager, stimulating
kind would have been a more fatal mate for him
than the most stupid woman that ever rivalled the
stupidity of man. Stimulation in any form always
meant distress to Rousseau. The moist warmth of
the Savoy valleys was not dearer to him than the
subtle inhalations of softened and close enveloping

companionship, in which the one needful thing is
not intellectual equality, but easy, smooth, constant
contact of feeling about the thousand small matters
that make up the existence of a day. This is not the
highest ideal of union that one's mind can conceive
from the point of view of intense productive energy,
but Rousseau was not concerned with the conditions
of productive energy. He only sought to live, to be
himself, and he knew better than any critics can know
for him, what kind of nature was the best supplement
for his own. As he said in an apophthegm with a
deep melancholy lying at the bottom of it,—you never
can cite the example of a thoroughly happy man, for
no one but the man himself knows anything about it.[1]
"By the side of people we love," he says very truly,
"sentiment nourishes the intelligence as well as the
heart, and we have little occasion to seek ideas elsewhere. I lived with my Theresa as pleasantly as
with the finest genius in the universe."[2]

Theresa Le Vasseur would probably have been
happier if she had married a stout stable-boy, as
indeed she did some thirty years hence by way of
gathering up the fragments that were left; but there
is little reason to think that Rousseau would have
been much happier with any other mate than he was
with Theresa. There was no social disparity between
the two. She was a person accustomed to hardship

---

[1] Œuv. et Corr. Inéd., 365.

[2] Conf., vii. 102. See also Corr., v. 373 (Oct. 10, 1768).
On the other hand, Conf., ix. 249.

and coarseness, and so was he. And he always
systematically preferred the honest coarseness of the
plain people from whom he was sprung and among
whom he had lived, to the more hateful coarseness of
heart which so often lurks under fine manners and a
complete knowledge of the order of the months in
the year and the arithmetical table. Rousseau had
been a serving-man, and there was no deterioration
in going with a serving-woman.[1] However this may
be, it is certain that for the first dozen years or so of
his partnership—and many others as well as he are
said to have found in this term a limit to the conditions of the original contract,—Rousseau had perfect
and entire contentment in the Theresa whom all his
friends pronounced as mean, greedy, jealous, degrading, as she was avowedly brutish in understanding.
Granting that she was all these things, how much of
the responsibility for his acts has been thus shifted
from the shoulders of Rousseau himself, whose connection with her was from beginning to end entirely
voluntary? If he attached himself deliberately to an
unworthy object by a bond which he was indisputably
free to break on any day that he chose, were not the

[1] M. St. Marc Girardin, in one of his admirable papers on
Rousseau, speaks of him as "a bourgeois unclassed by an alliance
with a tavern servant" (*Rev. des Deux Mondes*, Nov. 1852, p.
759) ; but surely Rousseau had unclassed himself long before,
in the houses of Madame Vercellis, Count Gouvon, and even
Madame de Warens, and by his repudiation, from the time
when he ran away from Geneva, of nearly every bourgeois virtue
and bourgeois prejudice.

effects of such a union as much due to his own character which sought, formed, and perpetuated it, as to
the character of Theresa Le Vasseur? Nothing, as
he himself said in a passage to which he appends a
vindication of Theresa, shows the true leanings and
inclinations of a man better than the sort of attach-
ments which he forms.[1]

It is a natural blunder in a literate and well-
mannered society to charge a mistake against a man
who infringes its conventions in this particular way.
Rousseau knew what he was about, as well as politer
persons. He was at least as happy with his kitchen
wench as Addison was with his countess, or Voltaire
with his marchioness, and he would not have been
what he was, nor have played the part that he did
play in the eighteenth century, if he had felt anything derogatory or unseemly in a kitchen wench.
The selection was probably not very deliberate; as it
happened, Theresa served as a standing illustration
of two of his most marked traits, a contempt for mere
literary culture, and a yet deeper contempt for social
accomplishments and social position. In time he
found out the grievous disadvantages of living in
solitude with a companion who did not know how to
think, and whose stock of ideas was so slight that
the only common ground of talk between them was
gossip and quodlibets. But her lack of sprightliness,
beauty, grace, refinement, and that gentle initiative by
which women may make even a sombre life so various,

[1] *Conf.*, vii. 11. Also footnote.

went for nothing with him.   What his friends missed
in her, he did not seek and would not have valued;
and what he found in her, they were naturally unable
to appreciate, for they never were in the mood for
detecting it.   "I have not seen much of happy men,"
he wrote when near his end, "perhaps nothing; but
I have many a time seen contented hearts, and of all
the objects that have struck me, I believe it is this
which has always given most contentment to myself."[1]
This moderate conception of felicity, which was always
so characteristic with him, as an even, durable, and
rather low-toned state of the feelings, accounts for his
prolonged acquiescence in a companion whom men
with more elation in their ideal would assuredly
have found hostile even to the most modest contentment.

"The heart of my Theresa," he wrote long after
the first tenderness had changed into riper emotion
on his side, and, alas, into indifference on hers, "was
that of an angel; our attachment waxed stronger with
our intimacy, and we felt more and more each day
that we were made for one another.   If our pleasures
could be described, their simplicity would make you
laugh; our excursions together out of town, in which
I would munificently expend eight or ten halfpence in
some rural tavern; our modest suppers at my window,
seated in front of one another on two small chairs
placed on a trunk that filled up the breadth of the
embrasure.   Here the window did duty for a table,

---

[1] *Rêveries*, ix. 309.

we breathed the fresh air, we could see the neighbourhood and the people passing by, and though on the
fourth story, could look down into the street as we
ate.   Who shall describe, who shall feel the charms
of those meals, consisting of a coarse quartern loaf,
some cherries, a tiny morsel of cheese, and a pint of
wine which we drank between us ?   Ah, what delicious
seasoning there is in friendship, confidence, intimacy,
gentleness of soul !   We used sometimes to remain
thus until midnight, without once thinking of the
time." [1]

Men and women are often more fairly judged by
the way in which they bear the burden of what they
have done, than by the prime act which laid the burden
on their lives. [2]   The deeper part of us shows in the
manner of accepting consequences.   On the whole,
Rousseau's relations with this woman present him in
a better light than those with any other person whatever.   If he became with all the rest of the world
suspicious, angry, jealous, profoundly diseased in a
word, with her he was habitually trustful, affectionate,
careful, most long-suffering.   It sometimes even occurs
to us that his constancy to Theresa was only another
side of the morbid perversity of his relations with the
rest of the world.   People of a certain kind not seldom
make the most serious and vital sacrifices for bare love

[1] *Conf.*, viii. 142, 143.
[2] The other day I came for the first time upon the following
in the sayings of Madame de Lambert :—" Ce ne sont pas toujours les fautes qui nous perdent ; c'est la manière de se conduire
aprés les avoir faites."   [1877.]

of singularity, and a man like Rousseau was not un-
likely to feel an eccentric pleasure in proving that he
could find merit in a woman who to everybody else
was desperate.   One who is on bad terms with the
bulk of his fellows may contrive to save his self-respect
and confirm his conviction that they are all in the
wrong, by preserving attachment to some one to whom
general opinion is hostile ; the private argument being
that if he is capable of this degree of virtue and
friendship in an unfavourable case, how much more
could he have practised it with others, if they would
only have allowed him.   Whether this kind of
apology was present to his mind or not, Rousseau
could always refer those who charged him with
black caprice, to his steady kindness towards Theresa
Le Vasseur.   Her family were among the most
odious of human beings, greedy, idle, and ill-hum
oured, while her mother had every fault that a
woman could have in Rousseau's eyes, including that
worst fault of setting herself up for a fine wit. Yet
he bore with them all for years, and did not break
with Madame Le Vasseur until she had poisoned the
mind of her daughter, and done her best by rapa-
city and lying to render him contemptible to all
his friends.

In the course of years Theresa herself gave him
unmistakable signs of a change in her affections.   "I
began to feel," he says, at a date of sixteen or seven-
teen years from our present point, "that she was no
longer for me what she had been in our happy years,

and I felt it all the more clearly as I was still the same towards her."[1]   This was in 1762, and her estrangement grew deeper and her indifference more open, until at length, seven years afterwards, we find that she had proposed a separation from him.   What the exact reasons for this gradual change may have been we do not know, nor have we any right in ignorance of the whole facts to say that they were not adequate and just.   There are two good traits recorded of the woman's character.   She could never console herself for having let her father be taken away to end his days miserably in a house of charity.[2]   And the repudiation of her children, against which the glowing egoism of maternity always rebelled, remained a cruel dart in her bosom as long as she lived.   We may suppose that there was that about household life with Rousseau which might have bred disgusts even in one as little fastidious as Theresa was.   Among other things which must have been hard to endure, we know that in composing his works he was often weeks together without speaking a word to her.[3]   Perhaps again it would not be difficult to produce some passages in Rousseau's letters and in the Confessions, which show traces of that subtle contempt for women that lurks undetected in many who would blush to avow it.   Whatever the causes may have been, from indifference she passed to something like aversion, and

---

[1] *Conf.*, xii. 187, 188.   [2] *Ib.*, viii. 221.
[3] Bernardin de St. Pierre, *Œuv.*, xii. 103.   See *Conf.*, xii. 188, and *Corr.*, v. 324.

in the one place where a word of complaint is wrung
from him, he describes her as rending and piercing his
heart at a moment when his other miseries were at
their height. His patience at any rate was inexhaust-
ible; now old, worn by painful bodily infirmities,
racked by diseased suspicion and the most dreadful
and tormenting of the minor forms of madness, nearly
friendless, and altogether hopeless, he yet kept unabated
the old tenderness of a quarter of a century before,
and expressed it in words of such gentleness, gravity,
and self-respecting strength, as may touch even those
whom his books leave unmoved, and who view his
character with deepest distrust. "For the six-and-
twenty years, dearest, that our union has lasted, I
have never sought my happiness except in yours,
and have never ceased to try to make you happy;
and you saw by what I did lately,[1] that your honour
and happiness were one as dear to me as the other. I
see with pain that success does not answer my solicitude, and that my kindness is not as sweet to you to
receive, as it is sweet to me to show. I know that
the sentiments of honour and uprightness with which
you were born will never change in you; but as for
those of tenderness and attachment which were once
reciprocal between us, I feel that they now only exist
on my side. Not only, dearest of all friends, have you
ceased to find pleasure in my company, but you have
to tax yourself severely even to remain a few minutes

---

[1] Referring, no doubt, to the ceremony which he called their
marriage, and which had taken place in 1768.

with me out of complaisance. You are at your ease
with all the world but me. I do not speak to you of
many other things. We must take our friends with
their faults, and I ought to pass over yours, as you
pass over mine. If you were happy with me I could
be content, but I see clearly that you are not, and this
is what makes my heart sore. If I could do better for
your happiness, I would do it and hold my peace; but
that is not possible. I have left nothing undone that
I thought would contribute to your felicity. At this
moment, while I am writing to you, overwhelmed with
distress and misery, I have no more true or lively
desire than to finish my days in closest union with
you. You know my lot,—it is such as one could not
even dare to describe, for no one could believe it. I
never had, my dearest, other than one single solace,
but that the sweetest; it was to pour out all my heart
in yours; when I talked of my miseries to you, they
were soothed; and when you had pitied me, I needed
pity no more. My every resource, my whole confidence, is in you and in you only; my soul cannot exist
without sympathy, and cannot find sympathy except
with you. It is certain that if you fail me and I am
forced to live alone, I am as a dead man. But I
should die a thousand times more cruelly still, if we
continued to live together in misunderstanding, and
if confidence and friendship were to go out between
us. It would be a hundred times better to cease to
see each other; still to live, and sometimes to regret
one another. Whatever sacrifice may be necessary on

my part to make you happy, be so at any cost, and I shall be content.   We have faults to weep over and to expiate, but no crimes; let us not blot out by the imprudence of our closing days the sweetness and purity of those we have passed together."[1]   Think ill as we may of Rousseau's theories, and meanly as we may of some parts of his conduct, yet to those who can feel the pulsing of a human life apart from a man's formulæ, and can be content to leave to sure circumstance the tragic retaliation for evil behaviour, this letter is like one of the great master's symphonies, whose theme falls in soft strokes of melting pity on the heart.   In truth, alas, the union of this now diverse pair had been stained by crimes shortly after its beginning.   In the estrangement of father and mother in their late years we may perhaps hear the rustle and spy the pale forms of the avenging spectres of their lost children.

At the time when the connection with Theresa Le Vasseur was formed, Rousseau did not know how to gain bread.   He composed the musical diversion of the Muses Galantes, which Rameau rightly or wrongly pronounced a plagiarism, and at the request of Richelieu he made some minor re-adaptations in Voltaire's Princesse de Navarre, which Rameau had set to music —that "farce of the fair" to which the author of Zaïre owed his seat in the Academy.[2]   But neither

[1] Corr., vi. 79-86.   August 12, 1769.
[2] Composed in 1745.   The Fêtes de Ramire was represented at Versailles at the very end of this year.

task brought him money, and he fell back on a sort
of secretaryship, with perhaps a little of the valet in
it, to Madame Dupin and her son-in-law, M. de
Francueil, for which he received the too moderate
income of nine hundred francs. On one occasion he
returned to his room expecting with eager impatience
the arrival of a remittance, the proceeds of some small
property which came to him by the death of his
father.[1] He found the letter, and was opening it
with trembling hands, when he was suddenly smitten
with shame at his want of self-control; he placed it
unopened on the chimney-piece, undressed, slept better
than usual, and when he awoke the next morning, he
had forgotten all about the letter until it caught his
eye. He was delighted to find that it contained his
money, but "I can swear," he adds, "that my liveliest
delight was in having conquered myself." An occasion
for self-conquest on a more considerable scale was at
hand. In these tight straits, he received grievous
news from the unfortunate Theresa. He made up his
mind cheerfully what to do; the mother acquiesced
after sore persuasion and with bitter tears; and the
new-born child was dropped into oblivion in the box
of the asylum for foundlings. Next year the same
easy expedient was again resorted to, with the same
heedlessness on the part of the father, the same
pain and reluctance on the part of the mother. Five
children in all were thus put away, and with such
entire absence of any precaution with a view to their

[1] Some time in 1746-7. *Conf.*, vii. 113, 114.

identification in happier times, that not even a note was kept of the day of their birth.[1]

People have made a great variety of remarks upon this transaction, from the economist who turns it into an illustration of the evil results of hospitals for foundlings in encouraging improvident unions, down to the theologian who sees in it new proof of the inborn depravity of the human heart and the fall of man. Others have vindicated it in various ways, one of them courageously taking up the ground that Rousseau had good reason to believe that the children were not his own, and therefore was fully warranted in sending the poor creatures kinless into the universe.[2] Perhaps it is not too transcendental a thing to hope that civilisation may one day reach a point when a plea like this shall count for an aggravation rather than a palliative; when a higher conception of the duties of humanity, familiarised by the practice of adoption as well as by the spread of both rational and compassionate considerations as to the blameless little ones, shall have expelled what is surely as some red and naked beast's emotion of fatherhood. What may be an excellent reason for repudiating a woman, can

[1] Probably in the winter of 1746-7. *Corr.*, ii. 207. *Conf.*, vii. 120-124. *Ib.*, viii. 148. *Corr.*, ii. 208. June 12, 1761, to the Maréchale de Luxembourg.

[2] George Sand,—in an eloquent piece entitled *À Propos des Charmettes* (*Revue des Deux Mondes*, November 15, 1863), in which she expresses her own obligations to Jean Jacques. In 1761 Rousseau declares that he had never hitherto had the least reason to suspect Theresa's fidelity. *Corr.*, ii. 209.

never be a reason for abandoning a child, except with
those whom reckless egoism has made willing to
think it a light thing to fling away from us the
moulding of new lives and the ensuring of salutary
nurture for growing souls.

We are, however, dispensed from entering into
these questions of the greater morals by the very
plain account which the chief actor has given us,
almost in spite of himself. His crime like most others
was the result of heedlessness, of the overriding of
duty by the short dim-eyed selfishness of the moment.
He had been accustomed to frequent a tavern, where
the talk turned mostly upon topics which men with
much self-respect put as far from them, as men with
little self-respect will allow them to do.   "I formed
my fashion of thinking from what I perceived to
reign among people who were at bottom extremely
worthy folk, and I said to myself, Since it is the usage
of the country, as one lives here, one may as well
follow it.   So I made up my mind to it cheerfully,
and without the least scruple."[1]   By and by he proceeded to cover this nude and intelligible explanation
with finer phrases, about preferring that his children
should be trained up as workmen and peasants rather
than as adventurers and fortune-hunters, and about his
supposing that in sending them to the hospital for
foundlings he was enrolling himself a citizen in Plato's
Republic.[2]   This is hardly more than the talk of one
become famous, who is defending the acts of his

[1] *Conf.*, vii. 123.   [2] *Ib.*, viii. 145-151.

obscurity on the high principles which fame requires. People do not turn citizens of Plato's Republic "cheerfully and without the least scruple," and if a man frequents company where the despatch of inconvenient children to the hospital was an accepted point of common practice, it is superfluous to drag Plato and his Republic into the matter. Another turn again was given to his motives when his mind had become clouded by suspicious mania. Writing a year or two before his death he had assured himself that his determining reason was the fear of a destiny for his children a thousand times worse than the hard life of foundlings, namely, being spoiled by their mother, being turned into monsters by her family, and finally being taught to hate and betray their father by his plotting enemies.[1] This is obviously a mixture in his mind of the motives which led to the abandonment of the children and justified the act to himself at the time, with the circumstances that afterwards reconciled him to what he had done ; for now he neither had any enemies plotting against him, nor did he suppose that he had. As for his wife's family, he showed himself quite capable, when the time came, of dealing resolutely and shortly with their importunities in his own case, and he might therefore well have trusted his power to deal with them in the case of his children. He was more right when in 1770, in his important letter to M. de St. Germain, he admitted that example,

---

[1] *Rêveries*, ix. 313. The same reason is given, *Conf.*, ix. 252; also in Letter to Madame B., January 17, 1770 (*Corr.*, vi. 117).

necessity, the honour of her who was dear to him, all united to make him entrust his children to the establishment provided for that purpose, and kept him from fulfilling the first and holiest of natural duties. "In this, far from excusing, I accuse myself; and when my reason tells me that I did what I ought to have done in my situation, I believe that less than my heart, which bitterly belies it."[1] This coincides with the first undisguised account given in the Confessions, which has been already quoted, and it has not that flawed ring of cant and fine words which sounds through nearly all his other references to this great stain upon his life, excepting one, and this is the only further document with which we need concern ourselves. In that,[2] which was written while the unholy work was actually being done, he states very distinctly that the motives were those which are more or less closely connected with most unholy works, motives of money—the great instrument and measure of our personal convenience, the quantitative test of our self-control in placing personal convenience behind duty to other people. "If my misery and my misfortunes rob me of the power of fulfilling a duty so dear, that is a calamity to pity me for, rather than a crime to reproach me with. I owe them subsistence, and I procured a better or at least a surer subsistence for them than I could myself have provided; this condi-

[1] *Corr.*, vi. 152, 153. Feb. 27, 1770.
[2] Letter to Madame de Francueil, April 20, 1751. *Corr.*, i. 151.

tion is above all others." Next comes the consideration
of their mother, whose honour must be kept. "You
know my situation; I gained my bread from day to
day painfully enough; how then should I feed a
family as well? And if I were compelled to fall back
on the profession of author, how would domestic cares
and the confusion of children leave me peace of mind
enough in my garret to earn a living? Writings which
hunger dictates are hardly of any use, and such a
resource is speedily exhausted. Then I should have
to resort to patronage, to intrigue, to tricks . . . in
short to surrender myself to all those infamies, for
which I am penetrated with such just horror. Support
myself, my children, and their mother on the blood of
wretches? No, madame, it were better for them to
be orphans than to have a scoundrel for their father.
. . . Why have I not married, you will ask? Madame,
ask it of your unjust laws. It was not fitting for me
to contract an eternal engagement; and it will never
be proved to me that my duty binds me to it. What
is certain is that I have never done it, and that I never
meant to do it. But we ought not to have children
when we cannot support them. Pardon me, madame;
nature means us to have offspring, since the earth
produces sustenance enough for all; but it is the rich,
it is your class, which robs mine of the bread of my
children. . . . I know that foundlings are not delicately nurtured; so much the better for them, they
become more robust. They have nothing superfluous
given to them, but they have everything that is

necessary. They do not make gentlemen of them,
but peasants or artisans. . . They would not know
how to dance, or ride on horseback, but they would
have strong unwearied legs. I would neither make
authors of them, nor clerks; I would not practise
them in handling the pen, but the plough, the file,
and the plane, instruments for leading a healthy,
laborious, innocent life. . . . I deprived myself of the
delight of seeing them, and I have never tasted the
sweetness of a father's embrace. Alas, as I have
already told you, I see in this only a claim on your
pity, and I deliver them from misery at my own
expense."[1] We may see here that Rousseau's sophistical eloquence, if it misled others, was at least as
powerful in misleading himself, and it may be noted
that this letter, with its talk of the children of the
rich taking bread out of the mouths of the children of
the poor, contains the first of those socialistic sentences
by which the writer in after times gained so famous a
name. It is at any rate clear from this that the real
motive of the abandonment of the children was wholly
material. He could not afford to maintain them, and
he did not wish to have his comfort disturbed by their
presence.

There is assuredly no word to be said by any one
with firm reason and unsophisticated conscience in extenuation of this crime. We have only to remember
that a great many other persons in that lax time, when
the structure of the family was undermined alike in

[1] *Corr.*, i. 151-155

practice and speculation, were guilty of the same crime; that Rousseau, better than they, did not erect his own criminality into a social theory, but was tolerably soon overtaken by a remorse which drove him both to confess his misdeed, and to admit that it was inexpiable; and that the atrocity of the offence owes half the blackness with which it has always been invested by wholesome opinion, to the fact that the offender was by and by the author of the most powerful book by which parental duty has been commended in its full loveliness and nobility.   And at any rate, let Rousseau be a little free from excessive reproach from all clergymen, sentimentalists, and others, who do their worst to uphold the common and rather bestial opinion in favour of reckless propagation, and who, if they do not advocate the despatch of children to public institutions, still encourage a selfish incontinence which ultimately falls in burdens on others than the offenders, and which turns the family into a scene of squalor and brutishness, producing a kind of parental influence that is far more disastrous and demoralising than the absence of it in public institutions can possibly be.   If the propagation of children without regard to their maintenance be either a virtue or a necessity, and if afterwards the only alternatives are their maintenance in an asylum on the one hand, and their maintenance in the degradation of a poverty-stricken home on the other, we should not hesitate to give people who act as Rousseau acted, all that credit for self-denial and high moral courage which he so

audaciously claimed for himself. It really seems to
be no more criminal to produce children with the
deliberate intention of abandoning them to public
charity, as Rousseau did, than it is to produce them
in deliberate reliance on the besotted maxim that he
who sends mouths will send meat, or any other of the
spurious saws which make Providence do duty for
self-control, and add to the gratification of physical
appetite the grotesque luxury of religious unction.

In 1761 the Maréchale de Luxembourg made efforts
to discover Rousseau's children, but without success.
They were gone beyond hope of identification, and
the author of *Emitius* and his sons and daughters
lived together in this world, not knowing one another.
Rousseau with singular honesty did not conceal his
satisfaction at the fruitlessness of the charitable
endeavours to restore them to him.   "The success of
your search," he wrote, "could not give me pure and
undisturbed pleasure; it is too late, too late. . . . In my
present condition this search interested me more for
another person [Theresa] than myself; and considering the too easily yielding character of the person in
question, it is possible that what she had found already
formed for good or for evil, might turn out a sorry
boon to her."[1]   We may doubt, in spite of one or two
charming and graceful passages, whether Rousseau

---

[1] August 10, 1761. *Corr.*, ii. 220. The Maréchale de
Luxembourg's note on the subject, to which this is a reply, is
given in *Rousseau, ses Amis et ses Ennemis*, i. 444.

was of a nature to have any feeling for the pathos of
infancy, the bright blank eye, the eager unpurposed
straining of the hand, the many turns and changes
in murmurings that yet can tell us nothing.   He was
both too self-centred and too passionate for warm
ease and fulness of life in all things, to be truly
sympathetic with a condition whose feebleness and
immaturity touch us with half-painful hope.

Rousseau speaks in the Confessions of having
married Theresa five-and-twenty years after the beginning of their acquaintance,[1] but we hardly have to
understand that any ceremony took place which anybody but himself would recognise as constituting a
marriage.   What happened appears to have been this.
Seated at table with Theresa and two guests, one of
them the mayor of the place, he declared that she was
his wife. "This good and seemly engagement was
contracted," he says, "in all the simplicity but also in
all the truth of nature, in the presence of two men of
worth and honour. . . . During the short and simple
act, I saw the honest pair melted in tears."[2]   He had
at this time whimsically assumed the name of Renou,
and he wrote to a friend that of course he had married
in this name, for he adds, with the characteristic in-
sertion of an irrelevant bit of magniloquence, "it is
not names that are married ; no, it is persons." "Even

[1] Conf., x. 249. See above, p. 106, n.
[2] To Lalliaud, Aug 31, 1768. Corr., v. 324.   See also
D'Escherny, quoted in Musset-Pathay, i. 169, 170.

if in this simple and holy ceremony names entered as a constituent part, the one I bear would have sufficed, since I recognise no other. If it were a question of property to be assured, then it would be another thing, but you know very well that is not our case."[1] Of course, this may have been a marriage according to the truth of nature, and Rousseau was as free to choose his own rites as more sacramental performers, but it is clear from his own words about property that there was no pretence of a marriage in law. He and Theresa were on profoundly uncomfortable terms about this time,[2] and Rousseau is not the only person by many thousands who has deceived himself into thinking that some form of words between man and woman must magically transform the substance of their characters and lives, and conjure up new relations of peace and steadfastness.

We have, however, been outstripping slow-footed destiny, and have now to return to the time when Theresa did not drink brandy, nor run after stable-boys, nor fill Rousseau's soul with bitterness and suspicion, but sat contentedly with him in an evening taking a stoic's meal in the window of their garret on the fourth floor, seasoning it with "confidence, intimacy, gentleness of soul," and that general comfort of sensation which, as we know to our cost, is by no means an invariable condition either of duty done externally

[1] To Du Peyrou, Sept. 26, 1768. *Corr.*, v. 360.
[2] To Mdlle. Le Vasseur, July 25, 1768. *Corr.*, v. 116-119.

or of spiritual growth within. It is perhaps hard for
us to feel that we are in the presence of a great religious
reactionist; there is so little sign of the higher graces
of the soul, there are so many signs of the lowering
clogs of the flesh. But the spirit of a man moves in
mysterious ways, and expands like the plants of the
field with strange and silent stirrings. It is one of
the chief tests of worthiness and freedom from vulgarity of soul in us, to be able to have faith that this
expansion is a reality, and the most important of all
realities. We do not rightly seize the type of Socrates
if we can never forget that he was the husband of
Xanthippe, nor David's if we can only think of him
as the murderer of Uriah, nor Peter's if we can simply
remember that he denied his master. Our vision is
only blindness, if we can never bring ourselves to see
the possibilities of deep mystic aspiration behind the
vile outer life of a man, or to believe that this coarse
Rousseau, scantily supping with his coarse mate,
might yet have many glimpses of the great wide
horizons that are haunted by figures rather divine
than human.

CHAPTER V.

THE DISCOURSES.

THE busy establishment of local academies in the provincial centres of France only preceded the outbreak of the revolution by ten or a dozen years; but one or two of the provincial cities, such as Bordeaux, Rouen, Dijon, had possessed academies in imitation of the greater body of Paris for a much longer time. Their activity covered a very varied ground, from the mere commonplaces of literature to the most practical details of material production. If they now and then relapsed into inquiries about the laws of Crete, they more often discussed positive and scientific theses, and rather resembled our chambers of agriculture than bodies of more learned pretension. The academy of Dijon was one of the earliest of these excellent institutions, and on the whole the list of its theses shows it to have been among the most sensible in respect of the subjects which it found worth thinking about. Its members, however, could not entirely resist the intellectual atmosphere of the time. In 1742 they invited discussion of the point, whether the natural law can conduct society to perfection without the aid of political laws.[1]   In 1749 they proposed this question as a theme for their prize essay : *Has the restoration of the sciences contributed to purify or to corrupt manners ?*   Rousseau was one of fourteen competitors, and in 1750 his discussion of the academic theme received the prize.[2]   This was his first entry on the field of literature and speculation.   Three years afterwards the same academy propounded another question : *What is the origin of inequality among men, and is it authorised by the natural law ?*   Rousseau again competed, and though his essay neither gained the prize, nor created as lively an agitation as its predecessor had done, yet we may justly regard the second as a more powerful supplement to the first.

It is always interesting to know the circumstances under which pieces that have moved a world were originally composed, and Rousseau's account of the generation of his thoughts as to the influence of enlightenment on morality, is remarkable enough to be worth transcribing.   He was walking along the road from Paris to Vincennes one hot summer afternoon on a visit to Diderot, then in prison for his Letter on the Blind (1749), when he came across in a newspaper the announcement of the theme propounded by the Dijon academy.   "If ever anything resembled

[1] Delandine's *Couronnes Académiques, ou Recueil de prix proposés par les Sociétés Savantes.*   (Paris, 2 vols., 1787.)

[2] Musset-Pathay has collected the details connected with the award of the prize, ii. 365-367.

a sudden inspiration, it was the movement which began
in me as I read this.   All at once I felt myself dazzled
by a thousand sparkling lights; crowds of vivid ideas
thronged into my mind with a force and confusion
that threw me into unspeakable agitation; I felt my
head whirling in a giddiness like that of intoxication.
A violent palpitation oppressed me ; unable to walk for
difficulty of breathing, I sank under one of the trees
of the avenue, and passed half an hour there in such
a condition of excitement, that when I arose I saw
that the front of my waistcoat was all wet with my
tears, though I was wholly unconscious of shedding
them.   Ah, if I could ever have written the quarter
of what I saw and felt under that tree, with what
clearness should I have brought out all the contradictions of our social system ; with what simplicity I
should have demonstrated that man is good naturally,
and that by institutions only is he made bad." [1]
Diderot encouraged him to compete for the prize,
and to give full flight to the ideas which had come to
him in this singular way. [2]

[1] Second Letter to M. de Malesherbes, p.358. Also *Conf.*,viii.135.
[2] Diderot's account (*Vie de Sénèque*, sect. 66, *Œuv.*, iii. 98 ;
also ii. 285) is not inconsistent with Rousseau's own, so that
we may dismiss as apocryphal Marmontel's version of the story
(*Mém.* VIII.), to the effect that Rousseau was about to answer
the question with a commonplace affirmative, until Diderot persuaded him that a paradox would attract more attention.   It has
been said also that M. de Francueil, and various others, first
urged the writer to take a negative line of argument.   To suppose this possible is to prove one's incapacity for understanding
what manner of man Rousseau was.

People have held up their hands at the amazing originality of the idea that perhaps sciences and arts have not purified manners. This sentiment is surely exaggerated, if we reflect first that it occurred to the academicians of Dijon as a question for discussion, and second that, if you are asked whether a given result has or has not followed from certain circumstances, the mere form of the question suggests No quite as readily as Yes. The originality lay not in the central contention, but in the fervour, sincerity, and conviction of a most unacademic sort with which it was presented and enforced. There is less originality in denouncing your generation as wicked and adulterous than there is in believing it to be so, and in persuading the generation itself both that you believe it and that you have good reasons to give. We have not to suppose that there was any miracle wrought by agency celestial or infernal in the sudden disclosure of his idea to Rousseau. Rousseau had been thinking of politics ever since the working of the government of Venice had first drawn his mind to the subject. What is the government, he had kept asking himself, which is most proper to form a sage and virtuous nation? What government by its nature keeps closest to the law? What is this law? And whence?[1] This chain of problems had led him to what he calls the historic study of morality, though we may doubt whether history was so much his teacher as the rather meagrely nourished handmaid of his

[1] *Conf.*, ix. 232, 233.

imagination. Here was the irregular preparation,
the hidden process, which suddenly burst into light
and manifested itself with an exuberance of energy,
that passed to the man himself for an inward revolution with no precursive sign.

Rousseau's ecstatic vision on the road to Vincennes
was the opening of a life of thought and production
which only lasted a dozen years, but which in that
brief space gave to Europe a new gospel. Emilius
and the Social Contract were completed in 1761, and
they crowned a work which if you consider its origin,
influence, and meaning with due and proper breadth,
is marked by signal unity of purpose and conception.
The key to it is given to us in the astonishing transport at the foot of the wide-spreading oak. Such a
transport does not come to us of cool and rational
western temperament, but more often to the oriental
after lonely sojourning in the wilderness, or in violent
reactions on the road to Damascus and elsewhere.
Jean Jacques detected oriental quality in his own
nature,[1] and so far as the union of ardour with
mysticism, of intense passion with vague dream, is to
be defined as oriental, he assuredly deserves the name.
The ideas stirred in his mind by the Dijon problem
suddenly "opened his eyes, brought order into the
chaos in his head, revealed to him another universe.
From the active effervescence which thus began in
his soul, came sparks of genius which people saw
glittering in his writings through ten years of fever

[1] *Rousseau Juge de Jean Jacques, Dialogues,* i. 252.

and delirium, but of which no trace had been seen
in him previously, and which would probably have
ceased to shine henceforth, if he should have chanced
to wish to continue writing after the access was over.
Inflamed by the contemplation of these lofty objects,
he had them incessantly present to his mind. His
heart, made hot within him by the idea of the future
happiness of the human race, and by the honour of
contributing to it, dictated to him a language worthy
of so high an enterprise. . . . and for a moment, he
astonished Europe by productions in which vulgar
souls saw only eloquence and brightness of understanding, but in which those who dwell in the ethereal
regions recognised with joy one of their own." [1]

This was his own account of the matter quite at
the end of his life, and this is the only point of view
from which we are secure against the vulgarity of
counting him a deliberate hypocrite and conscious
charlatan. He was possessed, as holier natures than
his have been, by an enthusiastic vision, an intoxicated
confidence, a mixture of sacred rage and prodigious
love, an insensate but absolutely disinterested revolt
against the stone and iron of a reality which he was
bent on melting in a heavenly blaze of splendid
aspiration and irresistibly persuasive expression. The
last word of this great expansion was Emilius, its first
and more imperfectly articulated was the earlier of
the two Discourses.

Rousseau's often-repeated assertion that here was

[1] *Dialogues*, i. 275, 276.

the instant of the ruin of his life, and that all his
misfortunes flowed from that unhappy moment, has
been constantly treated as the word of affectation and
disguised pride. Yet, vain as he was, it may well
have represented his sincere feeling in those better
moods when mental suffering was strong enough to
silence vanity. His visions mastered him for these
thirteen years, *grande mortalis ævi spatium.* They
threw him on to that turbid sea of literature for
which he had so keen an aversion, and from which,
let it be remarked, he fled finally away, when his
confidence in the ease of making men good and happy
by words of monition had left him. It was the
torment of his own enthusiasm which rent that veil
of placid living, that in his normal moments he
would fain have interposed between his existence and
the tumult of a generation with which he was profoundly out of sympathy. In this way the first
Discourse was the letting in of much evil upon him,
as that and the next and the Social Contract were the
letting in of much evil upon all Europe.

Of this essay the writer has recorded his own
impression that, though full of heat and force, it is
absolutely wanting in logic and order, and that of all
the products of his pen, it is the feeblest in reasoning
and the poorest in numbers and harmony. "For,"
as he justly adds, "the art of writing is not learnt all
at once." [1] The modern critic must be content to
accept the same verdict ; only a generation so in love

[1] *Conf.*, viii. 138.

as this was with anything that could tickle its intellectual curiousness, would have found in the first of the two Discourses that combination of speculative and literary merit which was imputed to Rousseau on the strength of it, and which at once brought him into a place among the notables of an age that was full of them.[1] We ought to take in connection with it two at any rate of the vindications of the Discourse, which the course of controversy provoked from its author, and which serve to complete its significance. It is difficult to analyse, because in truth it is neither closely argumentative, nor is it vertebrate, even as a piece of rhetoric. The gist of the piece, however, runs somewhat in this wise :—

Before art had fashioned our manners, and taught our passions to use a too elaborate speech, men were rude but natural, and difference of conduct announced at a glance difference of character. To-day a vile and most deceptive uniformity reigns over our manners, and all minds seem as if they had been cast in a single mould. Hence we never know with what sort of person we are dealing, hence the hateful troop of suspicions, fears, reserves, and treacheries, and the concealment of impiety, arrogance, calumny, and scepticism, under a dangerous varnish of refinement. So terrible a set of effects must have a cause. History shows that the cause here is to be found in the progress of sciences and arts. Egypt, once so mighty,

[1] "It made a kind of revolution in Paris," says Grimm. *Corr. Lit.*, i. 108.

becomes the mother of philosophy and the fine arts;
straightway behold its conquest by Cambyses, by
Greeks, by Romans, by Arabs, finally by Turks.
Greece twice conquered Asia, once before Troy, once
in its own homes; then came in fatal sequence the progress of the arts, the dissolution of manners, and the
yoke of the Macedonian. Rome, founded by a shepherd and raised to glory by husbandmen, began to
degenerate with Ennius, and the eve of her ruin was
the day when she gave a citizen the deadly title of
arbiter of good taste. China, where letters carry men
to the highest dignities of the state, could not be preserved by all her literature from the conquering power
of the ruder Tartar. On the other hand, the Persians,
Scythians, Germans, remain in history as types of
simplicity, innocence, and virtue. Was not he
admittedly the wisest of the Greeks, who made of
his own apology a plea for ignorance, and a denunciation of poets, orators, and artists? The chosen people
of God never cultivated the sciences, and when the
new law was established, it was not the learned, but
the simple and lowly, fishers and workmen, to whom
Christ entrusted his teaching and its ministry.[1]

This, then, is the way in which chastisement has
always overtaken our presumptuous efforts to emerge
from that happy ignorance in which eternal wisdom
placed us; though the thick veil with which that
wisdom has covered all its operations seemed to warn
us that we were not destined to fatuous research.

[1] *Rép. au Roi de Pologne*, p. 111 and p. 113.

All the secrets that Nature hides from us are so many evils against which she would fain shelter us.

Is probity the child of ignorance, and can science and virtue be really inconsistent with one another? These sounding contrasts are mere deceits, because if you look nearly into the results of this science of which we talk so proudly, you will perceive that they confirm the results of induction from history. Astronomy, for instance, is born of superstition; geometry from the desire of gain; physics from a futile curiosity; all of them, even morals, from human pride. Are we for ever to be the dupes of words, and to believe that these pompous names of science, philosophy, and the rest, stand for worthy and profitable realities?[1] Be sure that they do not.

How many errors do we pass through on our road to truth, errors a thousandfold more dangerous than truth is useful? And by what marks are we to know truth, when we think that we have found it? And above all, if we do find it, who of us can be sure that he will make good use of it? If celestial intelligences cultivated science, only good could result; and we may say as much of great men of the stamp of Socrates, who are born to be the guides of others.[2] But the intelligences of common men are neither celestial nor Socratic.

Again, every useless citizen may be fairly regarded as a pernicious man; and let us ask those illustrious philosophers who have taught us what insects repro-

[1] *Rép. à M. Bordes*, 138.   [2] *Ib.* 137.

duce themselves curiously, in what ratio bodies attract one another in space, what curves have conjugate points, points of inflection or reflection, what in the planetary revolutions are the relations of areas traversed in equal times—let us ask those who have attained all this sublime knowledge, by how much the worse governed, less flourishing, or less perverse we should have been if they had attained none of it? Now if the works of our most scientific men and best citizens lead to such small utility, tell us what we are to think of the crowd of obscure writers and idle men of letters who devour the public substance in pure loss.

Then it is in the nature of things that devotion to art leads to luxury, and luxury, as we all know from our own experience, no less than from the teaching of history, saps not only the military virtues by which nations preserve their independence, but also those moral virtues which make the independence of a nation worth preserving. Your children go to costly establishments where they learn everything except their duties. They remain ignorant of their own tongue, though they will speak others not in use anywhere in the world; they gain the faculty of composing verses which they can barely understand; without capacity to distinguish truth from error, they possess the art of rendering them indistinguishable to others by specious arguments. Magnanimity. equity, temperance, courage, humanity, have no real meaning to them; and if they hear speak of God, it breeds more terror than awful fear.

Whence spring all these abuses, if not from the disastrous inequality introduced among men by the distinction of talents and the cheapening of virtue ?[1] People no longer ask of a man whether he has probity, but whether he is clever ; nor of a book whether it is useful, but whether it is well written. And after all, what is this philosophy, what are these lessons of wisdom, to which we give the prize of enduring fame? To listen to these sages, would you not take them for a troop of charlatans, all bawling out in the market-place, Come to me, it is only I who never cheat you, and always give good measure ? One maintains that there is no body, and that everything is mere representation ; the other that there is no entity but matter, and no God but the universe : one that moral good and evil are chimeras ; the other that men are wolves and may devour one another with the easiest conscience in the world. These are the marvellous personages on whom the esteem of contemporaries is lavished so long as they live, and to whom immortality is reserved after their death. And we have now invented the art of making their extravagances eternal, and thanks to the use of typographic characters the dangerous speculations of Hobbes and Spinoza will endure for ever. Surely when they perceive the terrible disorders which printing has

[1] "The first source of the evil is inequality ; from inequality come riches . . . from riches are born luxury and idleness ; from luxury come the fine arts, and from idleness the sciences." *Rép. au Roi de Pologne*, 120, 121.

already caused in Europe, sovereigns will take as
much trouble to banish this deadly art from their
states as they once took to introduce it.

If there is perhaps no harm in allowing one or two
men to give themselves up to the study of sciences
and arts, it is only those who feel conscious of the
strength required for advancing their subjects, who
have any right to attempt to raise monuments to the
glory of the human mind. We ought to have no
tolerance for those compilers who rashly break open
the gate of the sciences, and introduce into their
sanctuary a populace that is unworthy even to draw
near to it. It may be well that there should be
philosophers, provided only and always that the
people do not meddle with philosophising.[1]

In short, there are two kinds of ignorance: one
brutal and ferocious,. springing from a bad heart,
multiplying vices, degrading the reason, and debasing
the soul: the other "a reasonable ignorance, which
consists in limiting our curiosity to the extent of the
faculties we have received; a modest ignorance, born
of a lively love for virtue, and inspiring indifference
only for what is not worthy of filling a man's heart,
or fails to contribute to its improvement; a sweet and
precious ignorance, the treasure of a pure soul at peace
with itself, which finds all its blessedness in inward
retreat, in testifying to itself its own innocence, and

---

[1] *Rép. à M. Bordes*, 147. In the same spirit he once wrote
the more wholesome maxim, "We should argue with the wise,
and never with the public." *Corr.*, i. 191.

which feels no need of seeking a warped and hollow
happiness in the opinion of other people as to its
enlightenment."[1]

Some of the most pointed assaults in this Discourse,
such for instance as that on the pedantic parade of
wit, or that on the excessive preponderance of literary
instruction in the art of education, are due to Montaigne; and in one way, the Discourse might be
described as binding together a number of that shrewd
man's detached hints by means of a paradoxical
generalisation. But the Rousseau is more important
than the Montaigne in it. Another remark to be
made is that its vigorous disparagement of science, of
the emptiness of much that is called science, of the
deadly pride of intellect, is an anticipation in a very
precise way of the attitude taken by the various
Christian churches and their representatives now and
for long, beginning with De Maistre, the greatest of
the religious reactionaries after Rousseau. The vilifi-
cation of the Greeks is strikingly like some vehement
passages in De Maistre's estimate of their share in
sophisticating European intellect. At last Rousseau
even began to doubt whether "so chattering a people
could ever have had any solid virtues, even in primitive times."[2] Yet Rousseau's own thinking about
society is deeply marked with opinions borrowed
exactly from these very chatterers. His imagination

[1] *Rép. au Roi de Pologne*, 128, 129.
[2] *Rép. à M. Bordes*, 150-161.

was fascinated from the first by the freedom and
boldness of Plato's social speculations, to which his
debt in a hundred details of his political and educa-
tional schemes is well known.   What was more
important than any obligation of detail was the fatal
conception, borrowed partly from the Greeks and
partly from Geneva, of the omnipotence of the Lawgiver in moulding a social state after his own purpose
and ideal.   We shall presently quote the passage in
which he holds up for our envy and imitation the
policy of Lycurgus at Sparta, who swept away all
that he found existing and constructed the social
edifice afresh from foundation to roof.[1]   It is true
that there was an unmistakable decay of Greek literary
studies in France from the beginning of the eighteenth
century, and Rousseau seems to have read Plato only
through Ficinus's translation.   But his example and
its influence, along with that of Mably and others,
warrant the historian in saying that at no time did
Greek ideas more keenly preoccupy opinion than
during this century.[2]   Perhaps we may say that
Rousseau would never have proved how little learning and art do for the good of manners, if Plato had
not insisted on poets being driven out of the Republic.
The article on Political Economy, written by him for
the Encyclopædia (1755), rings with the names of
ancient rulers and lawgivers; the project of public
education is recommended by the example of Cretans,

---

[1] P. 174.
[2] Egger's *Hellénisme en France*, 28ième leçon, p. 265.

Lacedæmonians, and Persians, while the propriety of
the reservation of a state domain is suggested by
Romulus.

It may be added that one of the not too many
merits of the essay is the way in which the writer,
more or less in the Socratic manner, insists on drag-
ging people out of the refuge of sonorous general
terms, with a great public reputation of much too
well-established a kind to be subjected to the affront
of analysis. It is true that Rousseau himself contributed nothing directly to that analytic operation
which Socrates likened to midwifery, and he set up
graven images of his own in place of the idols which
he destroyed. This, however, did not wholly efface
the distinction, which he shares with all who have
ever tried to lead the minds of men into new tracks,
of refusing to accept the current coins of philosophical
speech without test or measurement. Such a treatment of the great trite words which come so easily
to the tongue and seem to weigh for so much, must
always be the first step towards bringing thought
back into the region of real matter, and confronting
phrases, terms, and all the common form of the discussion of an age, with the actualities which it is the
object of sincere discussion to penetrate.

The refutation of many parts of Rousseau's main
contention on the principles which are universally
accepted among enlightened men in modern society
is so extremely obvious that to undertake it would
merely be to draw up a list of the gratulatory common-

places of which we hear quite enough in the literature and talk of our day. In this direction, perhaps it suffices to say that the Discourse is wholly one-sided, admitting none of the conveniences, none of the alleviations of suffering of all kinds, nothing of the increase of mental stature, which the pursuit of knowledge has brought to the race. They may or may not counterbalance the evils that it has brought, but they are certainly to be put in the balance in any attempt at philosophic examination of the subject. It contains no serious attempt to tell us what those alleged evils really are, or definitely to trace them one by one, to abuse of the thirst for knowledge and defects in the method of satisfying it. It omits to take into account the various other circumstances, such as climate, government, race, and the disposition of neighbours, which must enter equally with intellectual progress into whatever demoralisation has marked the destinies of a nation. Finally it has for the base of its argument the entirely unsupported assumption of there having once been in the early history of each society a stage of mild, credulous, and innocent virtue, from which appetite for the fruit of the forbidden tree caused an inevitable degeneration. All evidence and all scientific analogy are now well known to lead to the contrary doctrine, that the history of civilisation is a history of progress and not of decline from a primary state. After all, as Voltaire said to Rousseau in a letter which only showed a superficial appreciation of the real drift of the argument, we must confess that these thorns attached to literature are only as flowers in comparison with the other evils that have deluged the earth. "It was not Cicero nor Lucretius nor Virgil nor Horace, who contrived the proscriptions of Marius, of Sulla, of the debauched Antony, of the imbecile Lepidus, of that craven tyrant basely sur-named Augustus. It was not Marot who produced the St. Bartholomew massacre, nor the tragedy of the Cid that led to the wars of the Fronde. What really makes, and always will make, this world into a valley of tears, is the insatiable cupidity and indomitable insolence of men, from Kouli Khan, who did not know how to read, down to the custom-house clerk, who knows nothing but how to cast up figures. Letters nourish the soul, they strengthen its integrity, they furnish a solace to it,"—and so on in the sense, though without the eloquence, of the famous passage in Cicero's defence of Archias the poet.[1] All this, however, in our time is in no danger of being for-gotten, and will be present to the mind of every reader. The only danger is that pointed out by Rousseau himself : "People always think they have described what the sciences do, when they have in reality only described what the sciences ought to do."[2]

What we are more likely to forget is that Rous-seau's piece has a positive as well as a negative side, and presents, in however vehement and overstated a way, a truth which the literary and speculative enthu-

[1] Voltaire to J. J. R. Aug. 30, 1755.
[2] *Rép. au Roi de Pologne*, 105.

siasm of France in the eighteenth century, as is always
the case with such enthusiasm whenever it penetrates
either a generation or an individual, was sure to make
men dangerously ready to forget.[1] This truth may
be put in different terms. We may describe it as the
possibility of eminent civic virtue existing in people,
without either literary taste or science or speculative
curiosity.   Or we may express it as the compatibility
of a great amount of contentment and order in a given
social state, with a very low degree of knowledge.
Or finally, we may give the truth its most general
expression, as the subordination of all activity to the
promotion of social aims. Rousseau's is an elaborate
and roundabout manner of saying that virtue without
science is better than science without virtue; or that
the well-being of a country depends more on the
standard of social duty and the willingness of citizens
to conform to it, than on the standard of intellectual
culture and the extent of its diffusion. In other
words, we ought to be less concerned about the speculative or scientific curiousness of our people than
about the height of their notion of civic virtue and
their firmness and persistency in realising it. It is a
moralist's way of putting the ancient preacher's monition, that they are but empty in whom is not the
wisdom of God.   The importance of stating this is in

[1] In 1753 the French Academy, by way no doubt of summon-
ing a counter-blast to Rousseau, boldly offered as the subject of
their essay the thesis that "The love of letters inspires the love
of virtue," and the prize was won fitly enough by a Jesuit professor of rhetoric.   See Delandine, i. 42.

our modern era always pressing, because there is a constant tendency on the part of energetic intellectual workers, first, to concentrate their energies on a minute specialty, leaving public affairs and interests to their own course. Second, they are apt to overestimate their contributions to the stock of means by which men are made happier, and what is more serious, to underestimate in comparison those orderly, modest, self-denying, moral qualities, by which only men are made worthier, and the continuity of society is made surer. Third, in consequence of their greater command of specious expression and their control of the organs of public opinion, they both assume a kind of supreme place in the social hierarchy, and persuade the majority of plain men unsuspectingly to take so very egregious an assumption for granted. So far as Rousseau's Discourse recalled the truth as against this sort of error it was full of wholesomeness.

Unfortunately his indignation against the overweening pretensions of the verse-writer, the gazetteer, and the great band of sciolists at large, led him into a general position with reference to scientific and speculative energy, which seems to involve a perilous misconception of the conditions of this energy producing its proper results. It is easy now, as it was easy for Rousseau in the last century, to ask in an epigrammatical manner by how much men are better or happier for having found out this or that novelty in transcendental mathematics, biology, or astronomy; and this is very well as against the discoverer of small marvels who shall give himself out for the benefactor of the human race. But both historical experience and observation of the terms on which the human intelligence works, show us that we can only make sure of intellectual activity on condition of leaving it free to work all round, in every department and in every remotest nook of each department, and that its most fruitful epochs are exactly those when this freedom is greatest, this curiosity most keen and minute, and this waste, if you choose to call the indispensable superfluity of force in a natural process waste, most copious and unsparing. You will not find your highest capacity in statesmanship, nor in practical science, nor in art, nor in any other field where that capacity is most urgently needed for the right service of life, unless there is a general and vehement spirit of search in the air. If it incidentally leads to many industrious futilities and much learned refuse, this is still the sign and the generative element of industry which is not futile, and of learning which is something more than mere water spilled upon the ground.

We may say in fine that this first Discourse and its vindications were a dim, shallow, and ineffective feeling after the great truth, that the only normal state of society is that in which neither the love of virtue has been thrust far back into a secondary place by the love of knowledge, nor the active curiosity of the understanding dulled, blunted, and made ashamed by soft, lazy ideals of life as a life only of the affections.

Rousseau now and always fell into the opposite extreme
from that against which his whole work was a protest.
We need not complain very loudly that while re-
monstrating against the restless intrepidity of the
rationalists of his generation, he passed over the
central truth, namely that the full and ever festal life
is found in active freedom of curiosity and search
taking significance, motive, force, from a warm inner
pulse of human love and sympathy. It was not given
to Rousseau to see all this, but it was given to him to
see the side of it for which the most powerful of the
men living with him had no eyes, and the first Discourse was only a moderately successful attempt to
bring his vision before Europe. It was said at the
time that he did not believe a word of what he had
written.[1] It is a natural characteristic of an age
passionately occupied with its own set of ideas, to
question either the sincerity or the sanity of anybody
who declares its sovereign conceptions to be no better
than foolishness. We cannot entertain such a suspicion. Perhaps the vehemence of controversy carries
him rather further than he quite meant to go, when
he declares that if he were a chief of an African tribe,
he would erect on his frontier a gallows, on which he
would hang without mercy the first European who
should venture to pass into his territory, and the first
native who should dare to pass out of it.[2] And there
are many other extravagances of illustration, but the
main position is serious enough, as represented in the

---

[1] Preface to *Narcisse*, 251.		[2] *Rép. à M. Bordes*, 167.

emblematic vignette with which the essay was printed
—the torch of science brought to men by Prometheus,
who warns a satyr that it burns; the satyr, seeing
fire for the first time and being fain to embrace it, is
the symbol of the vulgar men who, seduced by the
glitter of literature, insist on delivering themselves up
to its study.[1] Rousseau's whole doctrine hangs
compactly together, and we may see the signs of its
growth after leaving his hands in the crude formula
of the first Discourse, if we proceed to the more
audacious paradox of the second.

II.

The Discourse on the Origin of Inequality among
men opens with a description of the natural state
of man, which occupies considerably more than half
of the entire performance. It is composed in a vein
which is only too familiar to the student of the
literature of the time, picturing each habit and
thought, and each step to new habits and thoughts,
with the minuteness, the fulness, the precision, of one
who narrates circumstances of which he has all his
life been the close eye-witness. The natural man
reveals to us every motive, every process internal and
external, every slightest circumstance of his daily life,
and each element that gradually transformed him into
the non-natural man. One who had watched bees or
beetles for years could not give us a more full or

[1] P. 187.

confident account of their doings, their hourly goings
in and out, than it was the fashion in the eighteenth
century to give of the walk and conversation of the
primeval ancestor.   The conditions of primitive man
were discussed by very incompetent ladies and gentlemen at convivial supper parties, and settled with
complete assurance.[1]

Rousseau thought and talked about the state of
nature because all his world was thinking and talking
about it.   He used phrases and formulas with reference to it which other people used.   He required no
more evidence than they did, as to the reality of the
existence of the supposed set of conditions to which
they gave the almost sacramental name of state of
nature.   He never thought of asking, any more than
anybody else did in the middle of the eighteenth
century, what sort of proof, how strong, how direct,
was to be had, that primeval man had such and such
habits, and changed them in such a way and direction,
and for such reasons.   Physical science had reached
a stage by this time when its followers were careful
to ask questions about evidence, correct description,
verification.   But the idea of accurate method had to
be made very familiar to men by the successes of
physical science in the search after truths of one kind,
before the indispensableness of applying it in the
search after truths of all kinds had extended to the
science of the constitution and succession of social

[1] See for instance a strange discussion about *morale univer-
selle* and the like in *Mém. de Mdme. d'Epinay*, i. 217-226.

states. In this respect Rousseau was not guiltier than the bulk of his contemporaries. Voltaire's piercing common sense, Hume's deep-set sagacity, Montesquieu's caution, prevented them from launching very far on to this metaphysical sea of nature and natural laws and states, but none of them asked those critical questions in relation to such matters which occur so promptly in the present day to persons far inferior to them in intellectual strength. Rousseau took the notion of the state of nature because he found it to his hand; he fitted to it his own characteristic aspirations, expanding and vivifying a philosophic conception with all the heat of humane passion; and thus, although, at the end of the process when he had done with it, the state of nature came out blooming as the rose, it was fundamentally only the dry, current abstraction of his time, artificially decorated to seduce men into embracing a strange ideal under a familiar name.

Before analysing the Discourse on Inequality, we ought to make some mention of a remarkable man whose influence probably reached Rousseau in an indirect manner through Diderot; I mean Morelly.[1] In 1753 Morelly published a prose poem called the Basiliade, describing the corruption of manners introduced by the errors of the lawgiver, and pointing out how this corruption is to be amended by return to

[1] Often described as Morelly the Younger, to distinguish him from his father, who wrote an essay on the human heart, and another on the human intelligence.

the empire of nature and truth. He was no doubt
stimulated by what was supposed to be the central
doctrine of Montesquieu, then freshly given to the
world, that it is government and institutions which
make men what they are. But he was stimulated
into a reaction, and in 1754 he propounded his whole
theory, in a piece which in closeness, consistency, and
thoroughness is admirably different from Rousseau's
rhetoric.[1] It lacked the sovereign quality of per-
suasiveness, and so fell on deaf ears. Morelly accepts
the doctrine that men are formed by the laws, but
insists that moralists and statesmen have always led
us wrong by legislating and prescribing conduct on
the false theory that man is bad, whereas he is in
truth a creature endowed with natural probity. Then
he strikes to the root of society with a directness that
Rousseau could not imitate, by the position that
"these laws by establishing a monstrous division of
the products of nature, and even of their very elements—by dividing what ought to have remained
entire, or ought to have been restored to entireness if
any accident had divided them, aided and favoured
the break-up of all sociability." All political and all
moral evils are the effects of this pernicious cause—
private property. He says of Rousseau's first Discourse that the writer ought to have seen that the
corruption of manners which he set down to literature
and art really came from this venomous principle of

[1] *Code de la Nature, ou le véritable esprit de ses loix, de tout
tems négligé ou méconnu.*

property, which infects all that it touches.[1]   Christianity, it is true, assailed this principle and restored
equality or community of possessions, but Christianity
had the radical fault of involving such a detachment
from earthly affections, in order to deliver ourselves
to heavenly meditation, as brought about a necessary
degeneration in social activity.   The form of government is a matter of indifference, provided you can
only assure community of goods.   Political revolutions
are at bottom the clash of material interests, and until
you have equalised the one you will never prevent
the other.[2]

   Let us turn from this very definite position to one

   [1] P. 169.   Rousseau did not see it then, but he showed himself on the track.
   [2] At the end of the *Code de la Nature* Morelly places a complete set of rules for the organisation of a model community.
The base of it was the absence of private property—a condition
that was to be preserved by vigilant education of the young in
ways of thinking, that should make the possession of private property odious or inconceivable.   There are to be sumptuary laws
of a moderate kind.   The government is to be in the hands of
the elders.   The children are to be taken away from their
parents at the age of five ; reared and educated in public establishments ; and returned to their parents at the age of sixteen
or so when they will marry.   Marriage is to be dissoluble at the
end of ten years, but after divorce the woman is not to marry a
man younger than herself, nor is the man to marry a woman
younger than the wife from whom he has parted.   The children
of a divorced couple are to remain with the father, and if he
marries again, they are to be held the children of the second
wife.   Mothers are to suckle their own children (p. 220).   The
whole scheme is fuller of good ideas than such schemes usually
are.

of the least definite productions to be found in all
literature.

It will seem a little odd that more than half of a
discussion on the origin of inequality among men
should be devoted to a glowing imaginary description,
from which no reader could conjecture what thesis it
was designed to support. But we have only to remember that Rousseau's object was to persuade people
that the happier state is that in which inequality does
not subsist, that there had once been such a state,
and that this was first the state of nature, and then
the state only one degree removed from it, in which
we now find the majority of savage tribes. At the
outset he defines inequality as a word meaning two
different things ; one, natural or physical inequality,
such as difference of age, of health, of physical
strength, of attributes of intelligence and character ;
the other, moral or political inequality, consisting in
difference of privileges which some enjoy to the
detriment of the rest, such as being richer, more
honoured, more powerful. The former differences
are established by nature, the latter are authorised, if
they were not established, by the consent of men.[1]
In the state of nature no inequalities flow from the
differences among men in point of physical advantage
and disadvantage, and which remain without derivative differences so long as the state of nature endures
undisturbed. Nature deals with men as the law of

[1] P. 218.

Sparta dealt with the children of its citizens; she makes those who are well constituted strong and robust, and she destroys all the rest.

The surface of the earth is originally covered by dense forest, and inhabited by animals of every species. Men, scattered among them, imitate their industry, and so rise to the instinct of the brutes, with this advantage that while each species has only its own, man, without anything special, appropriates the instincts of all. This admirable creature, with foes on every side, is forced to be constantly on the alert, and hence to be always in full possession of all his faculties. unlike civilised man, whose native force is enfeebled by the mechanical protections with which he has surrounded himself. He is not afraid of the wild beasts around him, for experience has taught him that he is their master. His health is better than ours, for we live in a time when excess of idleness in some, excess of toil in others, the heating and over-abundant diet of the rich, the bad food of the poor, the orgies and excesses of every kind, the immoderate transport of every passion, the fatigue and strain of spirit,— when all these things have inflicted more disorders upon us than the vaunted art of medicine has been able to keep pace with. Even if the sick savage has only nature to hope from, on the other hand he has only his own malady to be afraid of. He has no fear of death, for no animal can know what death is, and the knowledge of death and its terrors is one of the first of man's terrible acquisitions after abandoning his animal condition.[1] In other respects, such as protection against weather, such as habitation, such as food, the savage's natural power of adaptation, and the fact that his demands are moderate in proportion to his means of satisfying them, forbid us to consider him physically unhappy. Let us turn to the intellectual and moral side.

If you contend that men were miserable, degraded, and outcast during these primitive centuries because the intelligence was dormant, then do not forget, first, that you are drawing an indictment against nature,— no trifling blasphemy in those days—and second, that you are attributing misery to a free creature with tranquil spirit and healthy body, and that must surely be a singular abuse of the term. We see around us scarcely any but people who complain of the burden of their lives ; but who ever heard of a savage in full enjoyment of his liberty ever dreaming of complaint about his life or of self-destruction ?

With reference to virtues and vices in a state of nature, Hobbes is wrong in declaring that man in this state is vicious, as not knowing virtue. He is not vicious, for the reason that he does not know what being good is. It is not development of en-lightenment nor the restrictions of law, but the calm of the passions and ignorance of vice, which keep

[1] This is obviously untrue. Animals do not know death in the sense of scientific definition, and probably have no abstract idea of it as a general state ; but they know and are afraid of its concrete phenomena, and so are most savages.

them from doing ill. *Tanto plus in illis proficit vitiorum ignoratio, quam in his cognitio virtutis.*

Besides man has one great natural virtue, that of pity, which precedes in him the use of reflection, and which indeed he shares with some of the brutes. Mandeville, who was forced to admit the existence of this admirable quality in man, was absurd in not perceiving that from it flow all the social virtues which he would fain deny. Pity is more energetic in the primitive condition than it is among ourselves. It is reflection which isolates one. It is philosophy which teaches the philosopher to say secretly at sight of a suffering wretch, Perish if it please thee; I am safe and sound. They may be butchering a fellow-creature under your window; all you have to do is to clap your hands to your ears, and argue a little with yourself to hinder nature in revolt from making you feel as if you were in the case of the victim.[1] The savage man has not got this odious gift. In the state of nature it is pity that takes the place of laws, manners, and virtue. It is in this natural sentiment rather than in subtle arguments that we have to seek the reluctance that every man would feel to do ill, even without the precepts of education.[2]

Finally, the passion of love, which produces such disasters in a state of society, where the jealousy of lovers and the vengeance of husbands lead each day

---

[1] This is one of the passages in the Discourse, the harshness of which was afterwards attributed by Rousseau to the influence of Diderot. *Conf.*, viii. 205, *n.*   [2] P. 261.

to duels and murders, where the duty of eternal
fidelity only serves to occasion adulteries, and where
the law of continence necessarily extends the debauch-
ing of women and the practice of procuring abortion [1]
—this passion in a state of nature, where it is purely
physical, momentary, and without any association of
durable sentiment with the object of it, simply leads
to the necessary reproduction of the species and
nothing more.

"Let us conclude, then, that wandering in the
forests, without industry, without speech, without
habitation, without war, without connection of any
kind, without any need of his fellows or without any
desire to harm them, perhaps even without ever
recognising one of them individually, savage man,
subject to few passions and sufficing to himself, had
only the sentiments and the enlightenment proper to
his condition. He was only sensible of his real wants,
and only looked because he thought he had an interest
in seeing; and his intelligence made no more progress
than his vanity. If by chance he hit on some discovery, he was all the less able to communicate it;
as he did not know even his own children. An art
perished with its inventor. There was neither education nor progress; generations multiplied uselessly;
and as each generation always started from the same

[1] As if sin really came by the law in this sense ; as if a law
defining and prohibiting a malpractice were the cause of the commission of the act which it constituted a malpractice. As if
giving a name and juristic classification to any kind of conduct
were adding to men's motives for indulging in it.

point, centuries glided away in all the rudeness of
the first ages, the race was already old, the individual
remained always a child."

This brings us to the point of the matter. For if
you compare the prodigious diversities in education
and manner of life which reign in the different orders
of the civil condition, with the simplicity and uniformity of the savage and animal life, where all find
nourishment in the same articles of food, live in the
same way, and do exactly the same things, you will
easily understand to what degree the difference
between man and man must be less in the state of
nature than in that of society.[1] Physical inequality
is hardly perceived in the state of nature, and its
indirect influences there are almost non-existent.

Now as all the social virtues and other faculties
possessed by man potentially were not bound by anything inherent in him to develop into actuality, he
might have remained to all eternity in his admirable
and most fitting primitive condition, but for the
fortuitous concurrence of a variety of external changes.
What are these different changes, which may perhaps
have perfected human reason, while they certainly
have deteriorated the race, and made men bad in
making them sociable ?

What, then, are the intermediary facts between
the state of nature and the state of civil society,
the nursery of inequality ?   What broke up the happy
uniformity of the first times ?   First, difference in soil,

[1] P. 269.

in climate, in seasons, led to corresponding differences in men's manner of living. Along the banks of rivers and on the shores of the sea, they invented hooks and lines, and were eaters of fish. In the forests they invented bows and arrows, and became hunters. In cold countries they covered themselves with the skins of beasts. Lightning, volcanoes, or some happy chance acquainted them with fire, a new protection against the rigours of winter. In company with these natural acquisitions, grew up a sort of reflection or mechanical prudence, which showed them the kind of precautions most necessary to their security. From this rudimentary and wholly egoistic reflection there came a sense of the existence of a similar nature and similar interests in their fellow-creatures. Instructed by experience that the love of well-being and comfort is the only motive of human actions, the savage united with his neighbours when union was for their joint convenience, and did his best to blind and outwit his neighbours when their interests were adverse to his own, and he felt himself the weaker. Hence the origin of certain rude ideas of mutual obligation.[1]

Soon, ceasing to fall asleep under the first tree, or to withdraw into caves, they found axes of hard stone, which served them to cut wood, to dig the ground, and to construct hovels of branches and clay. This was the epoch of a first revolution, which formed the establishment and division of families, and which introduced a rough and partial sort of property.

[1] P. 278.

Along with rudimentary ideas of property, though not connected with them, came the rudimentary forms of inequality. When men were thrown more together, then he who sang or danced the best, the strongest, the most adroit, or the most eloquent, acquired the most consideration—that is, men ceased to take uniform and equal place. And with the coming of this end of equality there passed away the happy primitive immunity from jealousy, envy, malice, hate.

On the whole, though men had lost some of their original endurance, and their natural pity had already undergone a certain deterioration, this period of the development of the human faculties, occupying a just medium between the indolence of the primitive state and the petulant activity of our modern self-love, must have been at once the happiest and the most durable epoch. The more we reflect, the more evident we find it that this state was the least subject to revolutions and the best for man. "So long as men were content with their rustic hovels, so long as they confined themselves to stitching their garments of skin with spines or fish bones, to decking their bodies with feathers and shells and painting them in different colours, to perfecting and beautifying their bows and arrows—in a word, so long as they only applied themselves to works that one person could do, and to arts that needed no more than a single hand, then they lived free, healthy, good, and happy, so far as was compatible with their natural constitution, and continued to enjoy among themselves the sweetness of independent intercourse. But from the moment that one man had need of the help of another, as soon as they perceived it to be useful for one person to have provisions for two, then equality disappeared, property was introduced, labour became necessary, and the vast forests changed into smiling fields, which had to be watered by the sweat of men, and in which they ever saw bondage and misery springing up and growing ripe with the harvests."[1]

The working of metals and agriculture have been the two great agents in this revolution. For the poet it is gold and silver, but for the philosopher it is iron and corn, that have civilised men and undone the human race. It is easy to see how the latter of the two arts was suggested to men by watching the reproducing processes of vegetation. It is less easy to be sure how they discovered metal, saw its uses, and invented means of smelting it, for nature had taken extreme precautions to hide the fatal secret. It was probably the operation of some volcano which first suggested the idea of fusing ore. From the fact of land being cultivated its division followed, and therefore the institution of property in its full shape. From property arose civil society. "The first man who, having enclosed a piece of ground, could think of saying, *This is mine*, and found people simple enough to believe him, was the real founder of civil society. How many crimes, wars, murders, miseries, and horrors would not have been spared to the human

[1] Pp. 285-287.

race by one who, plucking up the stakes, or filling in
the trench, should have called out to his fellows :
Beware of listening to this impostor ; you are undone
if you forget that the earth belongs to no one, and
that its fruits are for all." [1]

Things might have remained equal even in this
state, if talents had only been equal, and if for
example the employment of iron and the consumption
of agricultural produce had always exactly balanced
one another. But the stronger did more work ; the
cleverer got more advantage from his work ; the
more ingenious found means of shortening his labour ;
the husbandman had more need of metal, or the
smith more need of grain ; and while working equally,
one got much gain, and the other could scarcely live
This distinction between Have and Have-not led to
confusion and revolt, to brigandage on the one side
and constant insecurity on the other.

Hence disorders of a violent and interminable kind,
which gave rise to the most deeply designed project
that ever entered the human mind. This was to
employ in favour of property the strength of the very
persons who attacked it, to inspire them with other
maxims, and to give them other institutions which
should be as favourable to property as natural law
had been contrary to it. The man who conceived
this project, after showing his neighbours the mon
strous confusion which made their lives most burden-
some, spoke in this wise : "Let us unite to shield the

[1] P. 273.

weak from oppression, to restrain the proud, and to assure to each the possession of what belongs to him; let us set up rules of justice and peace, to which all shall be obliged to conform, without respect of persons, and which may repair to some extent the caprices of fortune, by subjecting the weak and the mighty alike to mutual duties. In a word, instead of turning our forces against one another, let us collect them into one supreme power to govern us by sage laws, to protect and defend all the members of the association, repel their common foes, and preserve us in never-ending concord." This, and not the right of conquest, must have been the origin of society and laws, which threw new chains round the poor and gave new might to the rich; and for the profit of a few grasping and ambitious men, subjected the whole human race henceforth and for ever to toil and bondage and wretchedness without hope.

The social constitution thus propounded and accepted was radically imperfect from the outset, and in spite of the efforts of the sagest lawgivers, it has always remained imperfect, because it was the work of chance, and because, inasmuch as it was ill begun, time, while revealing defects and suggesting remedies, could never repair its vices; *people went on incessantly repairing and patching, instead of which it was indispensable to begin by making a clean surface and by throwing aside all the old materials, just as Lycurgus did in Sparta.*

Put shortly, the main positions are these. In the state of nature each man lived in entire isolation, and therefore physical inequality was as if it did not exist. After many centuries, accident, in the shape of difference of climate and external natural conditions, enforcing for the sake of subsistence some degree of joint labour, led to an increase of communication among men, to a slight development of the reasoning and reflective faculties, and to a rude and simple sense of mutual obligation, as a means of greater comfort in the long run. The first state was good and pure, but the second state was truly perfect. It was destroyed by a fresh succession of chances, such as the discovery of the arts of metal-working and tillage, which led first to the institution of property, and second to the prominence of the natural or physical inequalities, which now began to tell with deadly effectiveness. These inequalities gradually became summed up in the great distinction between rich and poor ; and this distinction was finally embodied in the constitution of a civil society, expressly adapted to consecrate the usurpation of the rich, and to make the inequality of condition between them and the poor eternal.

We thus see that the Discourse, unlike Morelly's terse exposition, contains no clear account of the kind of inequality with which it deals. Is it inequality of material possession or inequality of political right ? Morelly tells you decisively that the latter is only an accident, flowing from the first; that the key to renovation lies in the abolition of the first. Rousseau mixes the two confusedly together under a single name, bemoans each, but shrinks from a conclusion or a recommendation as to either.   He declares property to be the key to civil society, but falls back from any ideas leading to the modification of the institution lying at the root of all that he deplores.

The first general criticism, which in itself contains and covers nearly all others, turns on Method. "Conjectures become reasons when they are the most likely that you can draw from the nature of things," and "it is for philosophy in lack of history to determine the most likely facts." In an inductive age this royal road is rigorously closed. Guesses drawn from the general nature of things can no longer give us light as to the particular nature of the things pertaining to primitive men, any more than such guesses can teach us the law of the movement of the heavenly bodies, or the foundations of jurisprudence. Nor can deduction from anything but propositions which have themselves been won by laborious induction, ever lead us to the only kind of philosophy which has fair pretension to determine the most probable of the missing facts in the chain of human history. That quantitative and differentiating knowledge which is science, was not yet thought of in connection with the movements of our own race upon the earth. It is to be said, further, that of the two possible ways of guessing about the early state, the conditions of advance from it, and the rest, Rousseau's guess that all movement away from it has been towards corruption, is less supported by subsequent knowledge than the guess

of his adversaries, that it has been a movement progressive and upwards.

This much being said as to incurable vice of method,
and there are fervent disciples of Rousseau now living
who will regard one's craving for method in talking
about men as a foible of pedantry, we may briefly
remark on one or two detached objections to Rousseau's story. To begin with, there is no certainty as
to there having ever been a state of nature of a normal
and organic kind, any more than there is any one
normal and typical state of society now. There are
infinitely diverse states of society, and there were
probably as many diverse states of nature. Rousseau
was sufficiently acquainted with the most recent meta-
physics of his time to know that you cannot think of
a tree in general, nor of a triangle in general, but only
of some particular tree or triangle.[1] In a similar way
he might have known that there never was any such
thing as a state of nature in the general and abstract,
fixed, typical, and single. He speaks of the savage
state also, which comes next, as one, identical, normal.
It is, of course, nothing of the kind. The varieties
of belief and habit and custom among the different
tribes of savages, in reference to every object that can
engage their attention, from death and the gods and
immortality down to the uses of marriage and the
art of counting and the ways of procuring subsistence,
are infinitely numerous; and the more we know about
this vast diversity, the less easy is it to think of the

[1] P. 250.

savage state in general. When Rousseau extols the savage state as the veritable youth of the world, we wonder whether we are to think of the negroes of the Gold Coast, or the Dyaks of Borneo, Papuans or Maoris, Cheyennes or Tierra-del-Fuegians or the fabled Troglodytes ; whether in the veritable youth of the world they counted up to five or only to two ; whether they used a fire-drill, and if so what kind of drill ; whether they had the notion of personal identity in so weak a shape as to practise the couvade ; and a hundred other points, which we should now require any writer to settle, who should speak of the savage state as sovereign, one, and indivisible, in the way in which Rousseau speaks of it, and holds it up to our vain admiration.

Again, if the savage state supervened upon the state of nature in consequence of certain climatic accidents of a permanent kind, such as living on the banks of a river or in a dense forest, how was it that the force of these accidents did not begin to operate at once ? How could the isolated state of nature endure for a year in face of them ? Or what was the precipitating incident which suddenly set them to work, and drew the primitive men from an isolation so profound that they barely recognised one another, into that semi-social state in which the family was founded ?

We cannot tell how the state of nature continued to subsist, or, if it ever subsisted, how and why it ever came to an end, because the agencies which are

alleged to have brought it to an end must have been
coeval with the appearance of man himself.   If gods
had brought to men seed, fire, and the mechanical
arts, as in one of the Platonic myths,[1] we could understand that there was a long stage preliminary to these
heavenly gifts.   But if the gods had no part nor lot
in it, and if the accidents that slowly led the human
creature into union were as old as that nature, of
which indeed they were actually the component elements, then man must have quitted the state of nature
the very day on which he was born into it.   And
what can be a more monstrous anachronism than to
turn a flat-headed savage into a clever, self-conscious,
argumentative utilitarian of the eighteenth century ;
working the social problem out in his flat head with
a keenness, a consistency, a grasp of first principles,
that would have entitled him to a chair in the institute
of moral sciences, and entering the social union with
the calm and reasonable deliberation of a great states-
man taking a critical step in policy ?   Aristotle was
wiser when he fixed upon sociability as an ultimate
quality of human nature, instead of making it, as
Rousseau and so many others have done, the conclusion of an unimpeachable train of syllogistic reasoning.[2]

[1] *Politicus,* 268 D-274 E.

[2] Here for instance is D'Alembert's story :—"The necessity
of shielding our own body from pain and destruction leads us to
examine among external objects those which are useful and those
which are hurtful, so that we may seek the one and flee the
others.   But we hardly begin our search into such objects before
we discover among them a great number of beings which strike

Morelly even, his own contemporary, and much less of a sage than Aristotle, was still sage enough to perceive that this primitive human machine, "though composed of intelligent parts, generally operates independently of its reason; its deliberations are forestalled, and only leave it to look on, while sentiment does its work."[1] It is the more remarkable that Rousseau should have fallen into this kind of error, as it was one of his distinctions to have perceived and partially worked out the principle, that men guide their conduct rather from passion and instinct than from reasoned enlightenment.[2] The ultimate quality which he named pity is, after all, the germ of sociability, which is only extended sympathy. But he did not firmly adhere to this ultimate quality, nor make any effort consistently to trace out its various products.

us as exactly like ourselves; that is, whose form is just like our own, and who, so far as we can judge at the first glance, appear to have the same perceptions. Everything therefore leads us to suppose that they have also the same wants, and consequently the same interest in satisfying them, whence it results that we must find great advantage in joining with them for the purpose of distinguishing in nature what has the power of preserving us from what has the power of hurting us. The communication of ideas is the principle and the stay of this union, and necessarily demands the invention of signs; such is the origin of the formation of societies." *Discours Préliminaire de l'Encyclopédie.* Contrast this with Aristotle's sensible statement (*Polit.* 1, ii. 15) that "there is in men by nature a strong impulse to enter into such union."

[1] *Code de la Nature.*

[2] See, for example, his criticism on the Abbé de St. Pierre. *Conf.*, viii. 264. And also in the analysis of this very Discourse, above, vol. i. p. 163.

We do not find, however, in Rousseau any serious attempt to analyse the composition of human nature in its primitive stages. Though constantly warning his readers very impressively against confounding domesticated with primitive men, he practically assumes that the main elements of character must always have been substantially identical with such elements and conceptions as are found after the addition of many ages of increasingly complex experience. There is something worth considering in his notion that civilisation has had effects upon man analogous to those of domestication upon animals, but he lacked logical persistency enough to enable him to adhere to his own idea, and work out conclusions from it.

It might further be pointed out in another direction that he takes for granted that the mode of advance into a social state has always been one and the same, a single and uniform process, marked by precisely the same set of several stages, following one another in precisely the same order. There is no evidence of this; on the contrary, evidence goes to show that civilisation varies in origin and process with race and other things, and that though in all cases starting from the prime factor of sociableness in man, yet the course of its development has depended on the particular sets of circumstances with which that factor has had to combine. These are full of variety, according to climate and racial predisposition, although, as has been justly said, the force of both these two elements diminishes as the influence of the past in giving consistency to our will becomes more definite, and our means of modifying climate and race become better known.   There is no sign that Rousseau, any more than many other inquirers, ever reflected whether the capacity for advance into the state of civil society in any highly developed form is universal throughout the species, or whether there are not races eternally incapable of advance beyond the savage state.   Progress would hardly be the exception which we know it to be in the history of communities if there were not fundamental diversities in the civilisable quality of races.   Why do some bodies of men get on to the high roads of civilisation, while others remain in the jungle and thicket of savagery; and why do some races advance along one of these roads, and others advance by different roads?

Considerations of this sort disclose the pinched frame of trim theory with which Rousseau advanced to set in order a huge mass of boundlessly varied, intricate, and unmanageable facts.   It is not, however, at all worth while to extend such criticism further than suffices to show how little his piece can stand the sort of questions which may be put to it from a scientific point of view.   Nothing that Rousseau had to say about the state of nature was seriously meant for scientific exposition, any more than the Sermon on the Mount was meant for political economy.   The importance of the Discourse on Inequality lay in its vehement denunciation of the existing social state.

To the writer the question of the origin of inequality is evidently far less a matter at heart, than the question of its results.   It is the natural inclination of one deeply moved by a spectacle of depravation in his own time and country, to extol some other time or country, of which he is happily ignorant enough not to know the drawbacks.   Rousseau wrote about the savage state in something of the same spirit in which Tacitus wrote the Germania.   And here, as in the Discourse on the influence of science and art upon virtue, there is a positive side.   To miss this in resentment of the unscientific paradox that lies about it, is to miss the force of the piece, and to render its enormous influence for a generation after it was written incomprehensible.   We may always be quite sure that no set of ideas ever produced this resounding effect on opinion, unless they contained something which the social or spiritual condition of the men whom they inflamed made true for the time, and true in an urgent sense.   Is it not tenable that the state of certain savage tribes is more normal, offers a better balance between desire and opportunity, between faculty and performance, than the permanent state of large classes in western countries, the broken wreck of civilisation ?[1]   To admit this is not to conclude, as

[1] "I have lived with communities of savages in South America and in the East, who have no laws or law courts but the public opinion of the village freely expressed.   Each man scrupulously respects the rights of his fellow, and any infraction of those rights rarely or never takes place.   In such a community all are nearly equal.   There are none of those wide distinctions

Rousseau so rashly concluded, that the movement away from the primitive stages has been productive only of evil and misery even to the masses of men, the hewers of wood and the drawers of water; or that it was occasioned, and has been carried on by the predominance of the lower parts and principles of human nature. Our provisional acquiescence in the straitness and blank absence of outlook or hope of the millions who come on to the earth that greets them with no smile, and then stagger blindly under dull burdens for a season, and at last are shovelled silently back under the ground,—our acquiescence can only be justified in the sight of humanity by the conviction

of education and ignorance, wealth and poverty, master and servant, which are the products of our civilisation ; there is none of that widespread division of labour which, while it in-creases wealth, produces also conflicting interests ; there is not that severe competition and struggle for existence, or for wealth, which the dense population of civilised countries inevitably creates.   All incitements to great crimes are thus wanting, and petty ones are repressed, partly by the influence of public opinion, but chiefly by that natural sense of justice and of his neighbour's right, which seems to be in some degree inherent in every race of man.   Now, although we have progressed vastly beyond the savage state in intellectual achievements, we have not advanced equally in morals.   It is true that among those classes who have no wants that cannot be easily supplied, and among whom public opinion has great influence, the rights of others are fully respected.   It is true, also, that we have vastly extended the sphere of those rights, and include within them all the brother-hood of man.   But it is not too much to say, that the mass of our populations have not at all advanced beyond the savage code of morals, and have in many cases sunk below it."   Wal-lace's *Malay Archipelago*, vol. ii. pp. 460-461.

that this is one of the temporary conditions of a vast
process, working forwards through the impulse and
agency of the finer human spirits, but needing much
blood, many tears, uncounted myriads of lives, and
immeasurable geologic periods of time, for its high
and beneficent consummation.   There is nothing surprising, perhaps nothing deeply condemnable, in the
burning anger for which this acquiescence is often
changed in the more impatient natures.   As against
the ignoble host who think that the present ordering
of men, with all its prodigious inequalities, is in
foundation and substance the perfection of social
blessedness, Rousseau was almost in the right.   If
the only alternative to the present social order remaining in perpetuity were a retrogression to some such
condition as that of the islanders of the South Sea,
a lover of his fellow-creatures might look upon the
result, so far as it affected the happiness of the bulk
of them, with tolerably complete indifference.   It is
only the faith that we are moving slowly away from
the existing order, as our ancestors moved slowly
away from the old want of order, that makes the
present endurable, and makes any tenacious effort to
raise the future possible.

An immense quantity of nonsense has been talked
about the equality of man, for which those who deny
that doctrine and those who assert it may divide the
responsibility.   It is in reality true or false, according
to the doctrines with which it is confronted.   As

against the theory that the existing way of sharing the laboriously acquired fruits and delights of the earth is a just representation and fair counterpart of natural inequalities among men in merit and capacity, the revolutionary theory is true, and the passionate revolutionary cry for equality of external chance most righteous and unanswerable. But the issues do not end here. Take such propositions as these:— there are differences in the capacity of men for serving the community; the well-being of the community demands the allotment of high function in proportion to high faculty; the rights of man in politics are confined to a right of the same protection for his own interests as is given to the interests of others. As against these principles, the revolutionary deductions from the equality of man are false. And such pretensions as that every man could be made equally fit for every function, or that not only each should have an equal chance, but that he who uses his chance well and sociably should be kept on a level in common opinion and trust with him who uses it ill and unsociably, or does not use it at all,—the whole of this is obviously most illusory and most disastrous, and in whatever degree any set of men have ever taken it up, to that degree they have paid the penalty.

What Rousseau's Discourse meant, what he intended it to mean, and what his first direct disciples understood it as meaning, is not that all men are born equal. He never says this, and his recognition of natural inequality implies the contrary proposition.

His position is that the artificial differences, springing
from the conditions of the social union, do not coincide
with the differences in capacity springing from original
constitution ; that the tendency of the social union as
now organised is to deepen the artificial inequalities,
and make the gulf between those endowed with privileges and wealth and those not so endowed ever
wider and wider. It would have been very difficult
a hundred years ago to deny the truth of this way of
stating the case. If it has to some extent already
ceased to be entirely true, and if violent popular
forces are at work making it less and less true, we
owe the origin of the change, among other causes and
influences, not least to the influence of Rousseau himself, and those whom he inspired. It was that
influence which, though it certainly did not produce,
yet did as certainly give a deep and remarkable bias,
first to the American Revolution, and a dozen years
afterwards to the French Revolution.

It would be interesting to trace the different
fortunes which awaited the idea of the equality of
man in America and in France. In America it has
always remained strictly within the political order,
and perhaps with the considerable exception of the
possible share it may have had, along with Christian
notions of the brotherhood of man, and statesmanlike
notions of national prosperity, in leading to the abolition of slavery, it has brought forth no strong moral
sentiment against the ethical and economic bases of
any part of the social order. In France, on the other

hand, it was the starting-point of movements that
have had all the fervour and intensity of religions,
and have made men feel about social inequalities the
burning shame and wrath with which a Christian saw
the flourishing temples of unclean gods.   This difference in the interpretation and development of the
first doctrine may be explained in various ways,—by
difference of material circumstance between America
and France; difference of the political and social level
from which the principle of equality had to start;
and not least by difference of intellectual temperament.   This last was itself partly the product of
difference in religion, which makes the English dread
the practical enforcement of logical conclusions, while
the French have hitherto been apt to dread and
despise any tendency to stop short of that.

Let us notice, finally, the important fact that the
appearance of Rousseau's Discourses was the first sign
of reaction against the historic mode of inquiry into
society that had been initiated by Montesquieu.   The
Spirit of Laws was published in 1748, with a truly
prodigious effect.   It coloured the whole of the social
literature in France during the rest of the century.
A history of its influence would be a history of one
of the most important sides of speculative activity.
In the social writings of Rousseau himself there is
hardly a chapter which does not contain tacit reference
to Montesquieu's book.   The Discourses were the
beginning of a movement in an exactly opposite

direction; that is, away from patient collection of
wide multitudes of facts relating to the conditions of
society, towards the promulgation of arbitrary systems
of absolute social dogmas. Mably, the chief dogmatic
socialist of the century, and one of the most dignified
and austere characters, is an important example of
the detriment done by the influence of Rousseau to
that of Montesquieu, in the earlier stages of the conflict between the two schools. Mably (1709-1785),
of whom the remark is to be made that he was for
some years behind the scenes of government as De
Tencin's secretary and therefore was versed in affairs,
began his inquiries with Greece and Rome. "You
will find everything in ancient history," he said.[1]
And he remained entirely in this groove of thought
until Rousseau appeared. He then gradually left
Montesquieu. "To find the duties of a legislator,"
he said, "I descend into the abysses of my heart, I
study my sentiments." He opposed the Economists,
the other school that was feeling its way imperfectly
enough to a positive method. "As soon as I see
landed property established," he wrote, "then I see

[1] So too Bougainville, a brother of the navigator, said in
1760, "For an attentive observer who sees nothing in events of
the utmost diversity of appearance but the natural effects of a
certain number of causes differently combined, Greece is the
universe in small, and the history of Greece an excellent
epitome of universal history." (Quoted in Egger's *Hellénisme
en France*, ii. 272.) The revolutionists of the next generation,
who used to appeal so unseasonably to the ancients, were only
following a literary fashion set by their fathers.

unequal fortunes; and from these unequal fortunes must there not necessarily result different and opposed interests, all the vices of riches, all the vices of poverty, the brutalisation of intelligence, the corruption of civil manners?" and so forth.[1] In his most important work, published in 1776, we see Rousseau's notions developed, with a logic from which their first author shrunk, either from fear, or more probably from want of firmness and consistency as a reasoner. "It is to equality that nature has attached the preservation of our social faculties and happiness: and from this I conclude that legislation will only be taking useless trouble, unless all its attention is first of all directed to the establishment of equality in the fortune and condition of citizens."[2] That is to say not only political equality, but economic communism. "What miserable folly, that persons who pass for philosophers should go on repeating after one another that without property there can be no society. Let us leave illusion. It is property that divides us into two classes, rich and poor; the first will alway prefer their fortune to that of the state, while the second will never love a government or laws that leave them in misery."[3] This was the kind of opinion for which Rousseau's diffuse and rhetorical exposition of social necessity had prepared France some twenty years before. After powerfully helping the process of general dis-

---

[1] *Doutes sur l'Ordre Naturel; Œuv.*, xi. 80. (Ed. 1794, 1795.)

[2] *La Législation*, I. i.   [3] *Ibid.*

solution, it produced the first fruits specifically after
its own kind some twenty years later in the system
of Babœuf.[1]

The unflinching application of principles is seldom
achieved by the men who first launch them. The
labour of the preliminary task seems to exhaust one
man's stock of mental force. Rousseau never thought
of the subversion of society or its reorganisation on a
communistic basis. Within a few months of his profession of profound lament that the first man who
made a claim to property had not been instantly
unmasked as the arch foe of the race, he speaks most
respectfully of property as the pledge of the engage-
ments of citizens and the foundation of the social
pact, while the first condition of that pact is that
every one should be maintained in peaceful enjoyment
of what belongs to him.[2] We need not impute the
apparent discrepancy to insincerity. Rousseau was
always apt to think in a slipshod manner. He sensibly though illogically accepted wholesome practical
maxims, as if they flowed from theoretical premisses
that were in truth utterly incompatible with them.

[1] It is not within our province to examine the vexed question
whether the Convention was fundamentally socialist, and not
merely political. That socialist ideas were afloat in the minds
of some members, one can hardly doubt. See Von Sybel's *Hist.
of the French Revolution*, Bk. II. ch. iv., on one side, and
Quinet's *La Révolution*, ii. 90-107, on the other.

[2] *Economie Politique*, pp. 41, 53, etc.

CHAPTER VI.

PARIS.

I.

By what subtle process did Rousseau, whose ideal had been a summer life among all the softnesses of sweet gardens and dappled orchards, turn into panegyrist of the harsh austerity of old Cato and grim Brutus's civic devotion? The amiability of eighteenth century France—and France was amiable in spite of the atrocities of White Penitents at Toulouse, and black Jansenists at Paris, and the men and women who dealt in *lettres-de-cachet* at Versailles—was revolted by the name of the cruel patriot who slew his son for the honour of discipline.[1] How came Rousseau of all men, the great humanitarian of his time, to rise to the height of these unlovely rigours?

The answer is that he was a citizen of Geneva transplanted. He had been bred in puritan and republican tradition, with love of God and love of law and freedom and love of country all penetrating it, and then he had been accidentally removed to a strange city that was in active ferment with ideas that were the direct abnegation of all these. In

[1] *Rép. à M. Bordes*, 163.

Paris the idea of a God was either repudiated along
with many other ancestral conceptions, or else it was
fatally entangled with the worst superstition and not
seldom with the vilest cruelties.   The idea of freedom
was unknown, and the idea of law was benumbed by
abuses and exceptions.   The idea of country was
enfeebled in some and displaced in others by a growing passion for the captivating something styled
citizenship of the world. If Rousseau could have
ended his days among the tranquil lakes and hills of
Savoy, Geneva might possibly never have come back
to him.   For it depends on circumstance, which of
the chances that slumber within us shall awake, and
which shall fall unroused with us into the darkness.
The fact of Rousseau ranking among the greatest of
the writers of the French language, and the yet more
important fact that his ideas found their most ardent
disciples and exploded in their most violent form in
France, constantly make us forget that he was not a
Frenchman, but a Genevese deeply imbued with the
spirit of his native city.   He was thirty years old
before he began even temporarily to live in France :
he had only lived there some five or six years when
he wrote his first famous piece, so un-French in all its
spirit ; and the ideas of the Social Contract were in
germ before he settled in France at all.

   There have been two great religious reactions, and
the name of Geneva has a fundamental association
with each of them.   The first was that against the
paganised catholicism of the renaissance, and of this

Calvin was a prime leader; the second was that against the materialism of the eighteenth century, of which the prime leader was Rousseau. The diplomatist was right who called Geneva the fifth part of the world. At the congress of Vienna, some one, wearied at the enormous place taken by the hardly visible Geneva in the midst of negotiations involving momentous issues for the whole habitable globe, called out that it was after all no more than a grain of sand. But he was not wrong who made bold to reply, "Geneva is no grain of sand; 'tis a grain of musk that perfumes all Europe."[1] We have to remember that it was at all events as a grain of musk ever pervading the character of Rousseau. It happened in later years that he repudiated his allegiance to her, but however bitterly a man may quarrel with a parent, he cannot change blood, and Rousseau ever remained a true son of the city of Calvin. We may perhaps conjecture without excessive fancifulness that the constant spectacle and memory of a community, free, energetic, and prosperous, whose institutions had been shaped and whose political temper had been inspired by one great lawgiver, contributed even more powerfully than what he had picked up about Lycurgus and Lacedæmon, to give him a turn for utopian speculation, and a conviction of the artificiality and easy modifiableness of the social structure. This, however, is less certain than that he unconsciously received impressions in his youth from the circum-

[1] Pictet de Sergy., i. 18.

stances of Geneva, both as to government and religion,
as to freedom, order, citizenship, manners, which
formed the deepest part of him on the reflective side,
and which made themselves visible whenever he exchanged the life of beatified sense for moods of speculative energy, "Never, he says, "did I see the
walls of that happy city, I never went into it, without
feeling a certain faintness at my heart, due to excess
of tender emotion. At the same time that the noble
image of freedom elevated my soul, those of equality,
of union, of gentle manners, touched me even to
tears." [1] His spirit never ceased to haunt city and
lake to the end, and he only paid the debt of an
owed acknowledgment in the dedication of his Discourse on Inequality to the republic of Geneva. [2] It
was there it had its root. The honour in which
industry was held in Geneva, the democratic phrases
that constituted the dialect of its government, the
proud tradition of the long battle which had won
and kept its independence, the severity of its manners,
the simplicity of its pleasures,—all these things awoke
in his memory as soon as ever occasion drew him to
serious thought. More than that, he had in a peculiar
manner drawn in with the breath of his earliest days
in this theocratically constituted city, the vital idea
that there are sacred things and objects of reverence
among men. And hence there came to him, though
with many stains and much misdirection, the most
priceless excellence of a capacity for devout veneration.

[1] *Conf.*, iv. 248.   [2] *Ib.* ix. 279.   Also *Economie Politique.*

There is certainly no real contradiction between the quality of reverence and the more equivocal quality of a sensuous temperament, though a man may well seem on the surface, as the first succeeds the second in rule over him, to be the contradiction to his other self. The objects of veneration and the objects of sensuous delight are externally so unlike and so incongruous, that he who follows both in their turns is as one playing the part of an ironical chorus in the tragi-comic drama of his own life. You may perceive these two to be mere imperfect or illusory opposites, when you confront a man like Rousseau with the true opposite of his own type; with those who are from their birth analysts and critics, keen, restless, urgent, inexorably questioning. That energetic type, though not often dead or dull on the side of sense, yet is incapable of steeping itself in the manifold delights of eye and ear, of nostril and touch, with the peculiar intensity of passive absorption that seeks nothing further nor deeper than unending continuance of this profound repose of all filled sensation, just as it is incapable of the kindred mood of elevated humility and joyful unmasking devoutness in the presence of emotions and dim thoughts that are beyond the compass of words.

The citizen of Geneva with this unseen fibre of Calvinistic veneration and austerity strong and vigorous within him, found a world that had nothing sacred and took nothing for granted; that held the past in contempt, and ever like old Athenians asked

for some new thing; that counted simplicity of life
an antique barbarism, and literary curiousness the
master virtue. There were giants in this world,
like the panurgic Diderot. There were industrious,
worthy, disinterested men, who used their minds
honestly and actively with sincere care for truth,
like D'Holbach. There was poured around the whole,
like a high stimulating atmosphere to the stronger,
and like some evil mental aphrodisiac to the weaker,
the influence of Voltaire, the great indomitable chief-
tain of them all. Intellectual size half redeems want
of perfect direction by its generous power and fulness.
It was not the strong men, atheists and philosophisers
as they were, who first irritated Rousseau into revolt
against their whole system of thought in all its
principles. The dissent between him and them was
fundamental and enormous, and in time it flamed out
into open war. Conflict of theory, however, was
brought home to him first by slow-growing exasperation at the follies in practice of the minor disciples of
the gospel of knowing and acting, as distinguished
from his own gospel of placid being. He craved
beliefs that should uphold men in living their lives,
substantial helps on which they might lean without
examination and without mistrust: his life in Paris was
thrown among people who lived in the midst of open
questions, and revelled in a reflective and didactic
morality, which had no root in the heart and so
made things easy for the practical conscience. He
sought tranquillity and valued life for its own sake,

not as an arena and a theme for endless argument
and debate : he found friends who knew no higher
pleasure than the futile polemics of mimic philosophy
over dessert, who were as full of quibble as the wrong-
headed interlocutors in a Platonic dialogue, and who
babbled about God and state of nature, about virtue
and the spirituality of the soul, much as Boswell
may have done when Johnson complained of him for
asking questions that would make a man hang himself. The highest things were thus brought down to
the level of the cheapest discourse, and subjects which
the wise take care only to discuss with the wise, were
here everyday topics for all comers.

The association with such high themes of those
light qualities of tact, gaiety, complaisance, which
are the life of the superficial commerce of men and
women of the world, probably gave quite as much
offence to Rousseau as the doctrines which some of
his companions had the honest courage or the heedless fatuity to profess. It was an outrage to all the
serious side of him to find persons of quality introducing materialism as a new fashion, and atheism as
the liveliest of condiments. The perfume of good
manners only made what he took for bad principles
the worse, and heightened his impatience at the
flippancy of pretensions to overthrow the beliefs of a
world between two wines.

Doctrine and temperament united to set him
angrily against the world around him. The one was
austere and the other was sensuous, and the sensuous

temperament in its full strength is essentially solitary.
The play of social intercourse, its quick transitions,
and incessant demands, are fatal to free and uninter-
rupted abandonment to the flow of soft internal
emotions. Rousseau, dreaming, moody, indolently,
meditative, profoundly enwrapped in the brooding
egoism of his own sensations, had to mix with men
and women whose egoism took the contrary form of
an eager desire to produce flashing effects on other
people. We may be sure that as the two sides of
his character—his notions of serious principle, and his
notions of personal comfort—both went in the same
direction, the irritation and impatience with which
they inspired him towards society did not lessen with
increased communication, but naturally deepened with
a more profoundly settled antipathy.

Rousseau lived in Paris for twelve years, from his
return from Venice in 1744 until his departure in
1756 for the rustic lodge in a wood which the good-
will of Madame d'Epinay provided for him. We
have already seen one very important side of his
fortunes during these years, in the relations he formed
with Theresa, and the relations which he repudiated
with his children. We have heard too the new
words with which during these years he first began
to make the hearts of his contemporaries wax hot
within them. It remains to examine the current of
daily circumstance on which his life was embarked,
and the shores to which it was bearing him.

His patrons were at present almost exclusively in

the circle of finance. Richelieu, indeed, took him for
a moment by the hand, but even the introduction to
him was through the too frail wife of one of the
greatest of the farmers general.[1] Madame Dupin
and Madame d'Epinay, his two chief patronesses,
were also both of them the wives of magnates of the
farm. The society of the great people of this world
was marked by all the glare, artificiality, and senti-
mentalism of the epoch, but it had also one or two
specially hollow characteristics of its own. As is
always the case when a new rich class rises in the
midst of a community possessing an old caste, the circle
of Parisian financiers made it their highest social aim
to thrust and strain into the circle of the Versailles
people of quality. They had no normal life of their
own, with independent traditions and self-respect;
and for the same reason that an essentially worn-out
aristocracy may so long preserve a considerable degree
of vigour and even of social utility under certain circumstances by means of tenacious pride in its own
order, a new plutocracy is demoralised from the very
beginning of its existence by want of a similar kind
of pride in itself, and by the ignoble necessity of
craving the countenance of an upper class that loves
to despise and humiliate it. Besides the more obvious
evils of a position resting entirely on material opulence,
and maintaining itself by coarse and glittering osten-

---

[1] Madame de la Popelinière, whose adventures and the mis-
adventures of her husband are only too well known to the
reader of Marmontel's Memoirs.

tation, there is a fatal moral hollowness which infects
both serious conduct and social diversion. The result
is seen in imitative manners, affected culture, and a
mixture of timorous self-consciousness within and
noisy self-assertion without, which completes the most
distasteful scene that any collected spirit can witness.

Rousseau was, as has been said, the secretary of
Madame Dupin and her stepson Francueil. He
occasionally went with them to Chenonceaux in
Touraine, one of Henry the Second's castles built for
Diana of Poitiers, and here he fared sumptuously
every day. In Paris his means, as we know, were
too strait. For the first two years he had a salary of
nine hundred francs ; then his employers raised it to
as much as fifty louis. For the first of the Discourses
the publisher gave him nothing, and for the second
he had to extract his fee penny by penny, and after
long waiting. His comic opera, the Village Soothsayer, was a greater success ; it brought him the
round sum of two hundred louis from the court, and
some five and twenty more from the bookseller, and
so, he says, " the interlude, which cost me five or six
weeks of work, produced nearly as much money as
Emilius afterwards did, which had cost me twenty
years of meditation and three years of composition."[1]

[1] The passages relating to income during his first residence in
Paris (1744-1756) are at pp. 119, 145, 153, 165, 200, 227, in
Books vii.-ix. of the *Confessions*. Rousseau told Bernardin
de St. Pierre (*Œuv.*, xii. 74) that Emile was sold for 7000 livres.
In the *Confessions* (xi. 126), he says 6000 livres, and one or two
hundred copies. It may be worth while to add that Diderot

Before the arrival of this windfall, M. Francueil, who was receiver-general, offered him the post of cashier in that important department, and Rousseau attended for some weeks to receive the necessary instructions. His progress was tardy as usual, and the complexities of accounts were as little congenial to him as notarial complexities had been three and twenty years previously. It is, however, one of the characteristics of times of national break-up not to be peremptory in exacting competence, and Rousseau gravely sat at the receipt of custom, doing the day's duty with as little skill as liking. Before he had been long at his post, his official chief going on a short journey left him in charge of the chest, which happened at the moment to contain no very portentous amount. The disquiet with which the watchful custody of this moderate treasure harassed and afflicted Rousseau, not only persuaded him that nature had never designed him to be the guardian of money chests, but also threw him into a fit of very painful illness. The surgeons let him understand that within six months he would be in the pale kingdoms. The effect of such a hint on a man of his temper, and the train of reflections which it would be sure to set aflame, are to be foreseen by us who know Rousseau's fashion of dealing with the irksome. Why sacrifice the peace and charm of the little fragment of days

and D'Alembert received 1200 livres a year apiece for editing the Encyclopædia. Sterne received £650 for two volumes of *Tristram Shandy* in 1760. Walpole's *Letters*, iii. 298.

left to him, to the bondage of an office for which he
felt nothing but disgust? How reconcile the austere
principles which he had just adopted in his denunciation of sciences and arts, and his panegyric on the
simplicity of the natural life, with such duties as he
had to perform? And how preach disinterestedness
and frugality from amid the cashboxes of a receiver-
general? Plainly it was his duty to pass in independence and poverty the little time that was yet left to
him, to bring all the forces of his soul to bear in
breaking the fetters of opinion, and to carry out
courageously whatever seemed best to himself, without suffering the judgment of others to interpose the
slightest embarrassment or hindrance.[1]

With Rousseau, to conceive a project of this kind
for simplifying his life was to hasten urgently towards
its realisation, because such projects harmonised with
all his strongest predispositions. His design mastered
and took whole possession of him. He resolved to
earn his living by copying music, as that was conform-
able to his taste, within his capacity, and compatible
with entire personal freedom. His patron did as the
world is so naturally ready to do with those who
choose the stoic's way ; he declared that Rousseau was
gone mad.[2] Talk like this had no effect on a man
whom self-indulgence led into a path that others
would only have been forced into by self-denial. Let
it be said, however, that this is a form of self-indulgence of which society is never likely to see an excess,

[1] *Conf.*, viii. 154-157.   [2] *Ib.* viii. 160.

and meanwhile we may continue to pay it some
respect as assuredly leaning to virtue's side. Rousseau's many lapses from grace perhaps deserve a certain
gentleness of treatment, after the time when with
deliberation and collected effort he set himself to the
hard task of fitting his private life to his public principles. Anything that heightens the self-respect of
the race is good for us to behold, and it is a permanent
source of comfort to all who thirst after reality in
teachers, whether their teaching happens to be our
own or not, to find that the prophet of social equality
was not a fine gentleman, nor the teacher of demo-
cracy a hanger-on to the silly skirts of fashion.

Rousseau did not merely throw up a post which
would one day have made him rich. Stoicism on the
heroic, peremptory scale is not so difficult as the
application of the same principle to trifles. Besides
this greater sacrifice, he gave up the pleasant things
for which most men value the money that procures
them, and instituted an austere sumptuary reform in
truly Genevese spirit. His sword was laid aside ; for
flowing peruke was substituted the small round wig ;
he left off gilt buttons and white stockings, and he
sold his watch with the joyful and singular thought
that he would never again need to know the time.
One sacrifice remained to be made. Part of his
equipment for the Venetian embassy had been a large
stock of fine linen, and for this he retained a particular affection, for both now and always Rousseau had
a passion for personal cleanliness, as he had for cor-

poreal wholesomeness. He was seasonably delivered
from bondage to his fine linen by aid from without.
One Christmas Eve it lay drying in a garret in the
rather considerable quantity of forty-two shirts, when
a thief, always suspected to be the brother of Theresa,
broke open the door and carried off the treasure, leaving Rousseau henceforth to be the contented wearer
of coarser stuffs.[1]

We may place this reform towards the end of the
year 1750, or the beginning of 1751, when his mind was
agitated by the busy discussion which his first Discourse excited, and by the new ideas of literary power
which its reception by the public naturally awakened
in him. "It takes," wrote Diderot, "right above the
clouds ; never was such a success."[2] We can hardly
have a surer sign of a man's fundamental sincerity than
that his first triumph, the first revelation to him of his
power, instead of seducing him to frequent the mischievous and disturbing circle of his applauders, should
throw him inwards upon himself and his own principles with new earnestness and refreshed independence. Rousseau very soon made up his mind what the
world was worth to him ; and this, not as the ordinary sentimentalist or satirist does, by way of set-off
against the indulgence of personal foibles, but from
recognition of his own qualities, of the bounds set to
our capacity of life, and of the limits of the world's
power to satisfy us. "When my destiny threw me
into the whirlpool of society," he wrote in his last

[1] *Conf.*, viii. 160, 161.   [2] *Ib.* viii. 159.

meditation on the course of his own life, "I found nothing there to give a moment's solace to my heart. Regret for my sweet leisure followed me everywhere; it shed indifference or disgust over all that might have been within my reach, leading to fortune and honours. Uncertain in the disquiet of my desires, I hoped for little, I obtained less, and I felt even amid gleams of prosperity that if I obtained all that I supposed myself to be seeking, I should still not have found the happiness for which my heart was greedily athirst, though without distinctly knowing its object. Thus everything served to detach my affections from society, even before the misfortunes which were to make me wholly a stranger to it. I reached the age of forty, floating between indigence and fortune, between wisdom and disorder, full of vices of habit without any evil tendency at heart, living by hazard, distracted as to my duties without despising them, but often without much clear knowledge what they were."[1]

A brooding nature gives to character a connectedness and unity that is in strong contrast with the dispersion and multiformity of the active type. The attractions of fame never cheated Rousseau into forgetfulness of the commanding principle that a man's life ought to be steadily composed to oneness with itself in all its parts, as by mastery of an art of moral counterpoint, and not crowded with a wild mixture of aim and emotion like distracted masks in high carnival. He complains of the philosophers with

[1] *Rêveries*, iii. 168.

whom he came into contact, that their philosophy was
something foreign to them and outside of their own
lives. They studied human nature for the sake of
talking learnedly about it, not for the sake of self-
knowledge; they laboured to instruct others, not to
enlighten themselves within. When they published
a book, its contents only interested them to the extent
of making the world accept it, without seriously troub-
ling themselves whether it were true or false, provided
only that it was not refuted. "For my own part,
when I desired to learn, it was to know things myself,
and not at all to teach others. I always believed that
before instructing others it was proper to begin by
knowing enough for one's self; and of all the studies
that I have tried to follow in my life in the midst of
men, there is hardly one that I should not have followed equally if I had been alone, and shut up in a
desert island for the rest of my days "[1]

When we think of Turgot, whom Rousseau occasionally met among the society which he denounces,
such a denunciation sounds a little outrageous. But
then Turgot was perhaps the one sane Frenchman of
the first eminence in the eighteenth century. Voltaire
chose to be an exile from the society of Paris and
Versailles as pertinaciously as Rousseau did, and he
spoke more bitterly of it in verse than Rousseau ever
spoke bitterly of it in prose.[2] It was, as has been so

---

[1] *Rêveries*, iii. 166.
[2] See the *Epître à Mdme. la Marquise du Châtelet, sur la
Calomnie.*

often said, a society dominated by women, from the
king's mistress who helped to ruin France, down to
the financier's wife who gave suppers to flashy men
of letters. The eighteenth century salon has been
described as having three stages; the salon of 1730,
still retaining some of the stately domesticity, elegance, dignity of the age of Lewis XIV. ; that of
1780, grave, cold, dry, given to dissertation ; and
between the two, the salon of 1750, full of intellectual
stir, brilliance, frivolous originality, glittering waste-
fulness.[1] Though this division of time must not
be pressed too closely, it is certain that the era of
Rousseau's advent in literature with his Discourses
fell in with the climax of social unreality in the surface intercourse of France, and that the same date
marks the highest point of feminine activity and
power.

The common mixture of much reflective morality
in theory with much light-hearted immorality in
practice, never entered so largely into manners. We
have constantly to wonder how they analysed and
defined the word Virtue, to which they so constantly
appealed in letters, conversation, and books, as the
sovereign object for our deepest and warmest adoration.
A whole company of transgressors of the marriage
law would melt into floods of tears over a hymn to
virtue, which they must surely have held of too sacred
an essence to mix itself with any one virtue in particular, except that very considerable one of charitably

[1] *La Femme au* 18*ième siècle*, par MM. de Goncourt, p. 40.

letting all do as they please. It is much, however, that these tears, if not very burning, were really honest. Society, though not believing very deeply in the supernatural, was not cursed with an arid, parching, and hardened scepticism about the genuineness of good emotions in a man, and so long as people keep this baleful poison out of their hearts, their lives remain worth having.

It is true that cynicism in the case of some women of this time occasionally sounded in a diabolic key, as when one said, "It is your lover to whom you should never say that you don't believe in God; to one's husband that does not matter, because in the case of a lover one must reserve for one's self some door of escape, and devotional scruples cut everything short."[1] Or here: "I do not distrust anybody, for that is a deliberate act; but I do not trust anybody, and there is no trouble in this."[2] Or again in the word thrown to a man vaunting the probity of some one: "What! can a man of intelligence like you accept the prejudice of *meum* and *tuum ?*"[3] Such speech, however, was probably most often a mere freak of the tongue, a mode and fashion, as who should go to a masked ball in guise of Mephistopheles, without anything more Mephistophelian about him than red apparel and peaked toes. "She was absolutely charming," said one of a new-comer; "she did

[1] Madame d'Epinay's *Mém.*, i. 295.
[2] Quoted in Goncourt's *Femme au* 18*ième siècle*, p. 376.
[3] *Ib.*, p. 337.

not utter one single word that was not a paradox."[1]
This was the passing taste. Human nature is able
to keep itself wholesome in fundamentals even under
very great difficulties, and it is as wise as it is charitable in judging a sharp and cynical tone to make
large allowances for mere costume and assumed
character.

In respect of the light companionship of common
usage, however, it is exactly the costume which comes
closest to us, and bad taste in that is most jarring
and least easily forgiven. There is a certain stage in
an observant person's experience of the heedlessness,
indolence, and native folly of men and women—and
if his observation be conducted in a catholic spirit,
he will probably see something of this not merely in
others—when the tolerable average sanity of human
arrangements strikes him as the most marvellous of
all the fortunate accidents in the universe. Rousseau
could not even accept the fact of this miraculous result,
the provisional and temporary sanity of things, and
he confronted society with eyes of angry chagrin. A
great lady asked him how it was that she had not seen
him for an age. "Because when I wish to see you,
I wish to see no one but you. What do you want
me to do in the midst of your society? I should cut
a sorry figure in a circle of mincing tripping coxcombs;
they do not suit me." We cannot wonder that on
some occasion when her son's proficiency was to be
tested before a company of friends, Madame d'Epinay

---

[1] Mdlle. L'Espinasse's *Letters*, ii. 89.

prayed Rousseau to be of them, on the ground that
he would be sure to ask the child outrageously absurd
questions, which would give gaiety to the affair.[1]
As it happened, the father was unwise. He was a
man of whom it was said that he had devoured two
million francs, without either saying or doing a single
good thing. He rewarded the child's performance
with the gift of a superb suit of cherry-coloured
velvet, extravagantly trimmed with costly lace; the
peasant from whose sweat and travail the money had
been wrung, went in heavy rags, and his children
lived as the beasts of the field. The poor youth was
ill dealt with. "That is very fine," said rude Duclos,
"but remember that a fool in lace is still a fool."
Rousseau, in reply to the child's importunity, was
still blunter: "Sir, I am no judge of finery, I am
only a judge of man; I wished to talk with you a
little while ago, but I wish so no longer."[2]

Marmontel, whose account may have been coloured
by retrospection in later years, says that before the
success of the first Discourse, Rousseau concealed his
pride under the external forms of a politeness that
was timid even to obsequiousness; in his uneasy
glance you perceived mistrust and observant jealousy;
there was no freedom in his manner, and no one ever
observed more cautiously the hateful precept to live
with your friends as though they were one day to be
your enemies.[3] Grimm's description is different and

---

[1] Madame d'Epinay's *Mém.*, ii. 47, 48.   [2] *Ib.*, ii. 55.

[3] *Mém.*, Bk. iv. 327.

more trustworthy.   Until he began to affect singularity, he says, Rousseau had been gallant and over-
flowing with artificial compliment, with manners that
were honeyed and even wearisome in their soft
elaborateness.   All at once he put on the cynic's
cloak, and went to the other extreme.   Still in spite
of an abrupt and cynical tone he kept much of his
old art of elaborate fine speeches, and particularly in
his relations with women.[1]   Of his abruptness, he
tells a most displeasing tale.   "One day Rousseau
told us with an air of triumph, that as he was coming
out of the opera where he had been seeing the first
representation of the Village Soothsayer, the Duke
of Zweibrücken had approached him with much
politeness, saying, 'Will you allow me to pay you a
compliment?' and that he replied, 'Yes, if it be very
short.'   Everybody was silent at this, until I said to
him laughingly, 'Illustrious citizen and co-sovereign
of Geneva, since there resides in you a part of the
sovereignty of the republic, let me represent to you
that, for all the severity of your principles, you should
hardly refuse to a sovereign prince the respect due to
a water-carrier, and that if you had met a word of
good-will from a water-carrier with an answer as
rough and brutal as that, you would have had to
reproach yourself with a most unseasonable piece of
impertinence.'"[2]

There were still more serious circumstances when
exasperation at the flippant tone about him carried

---

[1] *Corr. Lit.*, iii. 58.   [2] *Ib.*, 54.

him beyond the ordinary bounds of that polite time. A guest at table asked contemptuously what was the use of a nation like the French having reason, if they did not use it. "They mock the other nations of the earth, and yet are the most credulous of all." ROUSSEAU : "I forgive them for their credulity, but not for condemning those who are credulous in some other way." Some one said that in matters of religion everybody was right, but that everybody should remain in that in which he had been born. ROUSSEAU, with warmth : "Not so, by God, if it is a bad one, for then it can do nothing but harm." Then some one contended that religion always did some good, as a kind of rein to the common people who had no other morality. All the rest cried out at this in indignant remonstrance, one shrewd person remarking that the common people had much livelier fear of being hanged than of being damned. The conversation was broken off for a moment by the hostess calling out, "After all, one must nourish the tattered affair we call our body, so ring and let them bring us the joint." This done, the servants dismissed, and the door shut, the discussion was resumed with such vehemence by Duclos and Saint Lambert, that, says the lady who tells us the story, "I feared they were bent on destroying all religion, and I prayed for some mercy to be shown at any rate to natural religion." There was not a whit more sympathy for that than for the rest. Rousseau declared himself *paullo infirmior*, and clung to the morality of the

gospel as the natural morality which in old times
constituted the whole and only creed. "But what
is a God," cried one impetuous disputant, "who gets
angry and is appeased again?" Rousseau began to
murmur between grinding teeth, and a tide of
pleasantries set in at his expense, to which came this:
"If it is a piece of cowardice to suffer ill to be spoken
of one's friend behind his back, 'tis a crime to suffer
ill to be spoken of one's God, who is present; and
for my part, sirs, I believe in God." "I admit," said
the atheistic champion, "that it is a fine thing to see
this God bending his brow to earth and watching
with admiration the conduct of a Cato. But this
notion is, like many others, very useful in some great
heads, such as Trajan, Marcus Aurelius, Socrates,
where it can only produce heroism, but it is the germ
of all madnesses." ROUSSEAU: "Sirs, I leave the
room if you say another word more," and he was
rising to fulfil his threat, when the entry of a new-
comer stopped the discussion.[1]

His words on another occasion show how all that
he saw helped to keep up a fretted condition of mind,
in one whose soft tenacious memory turned daily back
to simple and unsophisticated days among the green
valleys, and refused to acquiesce in the conditions of
changed climate. So terrible a thing is it to be the
bondsman of reminiscence. Madame d'Epinay was
suspected, wrongfully as it afterwards proved, of

[1] Madame d'Epinay's *Mém.*, i. 378-381. Saint Lambert
formulated his atheism afterwards in the *Catéchisme Universel.*

having destroyed some valuable papers belonging to
a dead relative. There was much idle and cruel
gossip in an ill-natured world. Rousseau, her friend,
kept steadfast silence : she challenged his opinion.
"What am I to say?" he answered; "I go and come,
and all that I hear outrages and revolts me. I see
the one so evidently malicious and so adroit in their
injustice ; the other so awkward and so stupid in
their good intentions, that I am tempted (and it is
not the first time) to look on Paris as a cavern of
brigands, of whom every traveller in his turn is the
victim. What gives me the worst idea of society is
to see how eager each person is to pardon himself,
by reason of the number of the people who are
like him."[1]

Notwithstanding his hatred of this cavern of
brigands, and the little pains he took to conceal his
feelings from any individual brigand, whether male
or female, with whom he had to deal, he found out
that "it is not always so easy as people suppose to
be poor and independent." Merciless invasion of his
time in every shape made his life weariness. Sometimes he had the courage to turn and rend the
invader, as in the letter to a painter who sent him
the same copy of verses three times, requiring immediate acknowledgment. "It is not just," at length
wrote the exasperated Rousseau, "that I should be
tyrannised over for your pleasure ; not that my time
is precious, as you say ; it is either passed in suffering

[1] Madame d'Epinay's *Mém.*, i. 443.

or it is lost in idleness; but when I cannot employ it
usefully for some one, I do not wish to be hindered
from wasting it in my own fashion. A single minute
thus usurped is what all the kings of the universe
could not give me back, and it is to be my own
master that I flee from the idle folk of towns,—people
as thoroughly wearied as they are thoroughly wearisome,—who, because they do not know what to do
with their own time, think they have a right to waste
that of others."[1] The more abruptly he treated
visitors, persecuting dinner-givers, and all the tribe
of the importunate, the more obstinate they were in
possessing themselves of his time. In seizing the
hours they were keeping his purse empty, as well as
keeping up constant irritation in his soul. He appears
to have earned forty sous for a morning's work, and
to have counted this a fair fee, remarking modestly
that he could not well subsist on less.[2] He had one
chance of a pension, which he threw from him in a
truly characteristic manner.

When he came to Paris he composed his musical
diversion of the Muses Galantes, which was performed
(1745) in the presence of Rameau, under the patronage of M. de la Popelinière. Rameau apostrophised
the unlucky composer with much violence, declaring
that one-half of the piece was the work of a master,
while the other was that of a person entirely ignorant
of the musical rudiments; the bad work therefore

---

[1] *Corr.*, i. 317. Sept. 14, 1756.
[2] Letter to Madame de Créqui, 1752. *Corr.*, i. 171.

was Rousseau's own, and the good was a plagiarism.[1]
This repulse did not daunt the hero. Five or six
years afterwards on a visit to Passy, as he was lying
awake in bed, he conceived the idea of a pastoral
interlude after the manner of the Italian comic operas.
In six days the Village Soothsayer was sketched, and
in three weeks virtually completed. Duclos procured
its rehearsal at the Opera, and after some debate it
was performed before the court at Fontainebleau. The
Plutarchian stoic, its author, went from Paris in a
court coach, but his Roman tone deserted him, and
he felt shamefaced as a schoolboy before the great
world, such divinity doth hedge even a Lewis xv.,
and even in a soul of Genevan temper. The piece
was played with great success, and the composer was
informed that he would the next day have the honour
of being presented to the king, who would most probably mark his favour by the bestowal of a pension.[2]
Rousseau was tossed with many doubts. He would
fain have greeted the king with some word that
should show sensibility to the royal graciousness,
without compromising republican severity, "clothing
some great and useful truth in a fine and deserved
compliment." This moral difficulty was heightened
by a physical one, for he was liable to an infirmity
which, if it should overtake him in presence of king

[1] *Conf.*, vii. 104.

[2] The *Devin du Village* was played at Fontainebleau on
October 18, 1752, and at the Opera in Paris in March 1753.
Madame de Pompadour took a part in it in a private perform-
ance. See Rousseau's note to her, *Corr.*, i. 178.

and courtiers, would land him in an embarrassment worse than death. What would become of him if mind or body should fail, if either he should be driven into precipitate retreat, or else there should escape him, instead of the great truth wrapped delicately round in veracious panegyric, a heavy, shapeless word of foolishness? He fled in terror, and flung up the chance of pension and patronage. We perceive the born dreamer with a phantasmagoric imagination, seizing nothing in just proportion and true relation, and paralysing the spirit with terror of unrealities; in short, with the most fatal form of moral cowardice, which perhaps it is a little dangerous to try to analyse into finer names.

When Rousseau got back to Paris he was amazed to find that Diderot spoke to him of this abandonment of the pension with a fire that he could never have expected from a philosopher, Rousseau plainly sharing the opinion of more vulgar souls that philosopher is but fool writ large. "He said that if I was disinterested on my own account, I had no right to be so on that of Madame Le Vasseur and her daughter, and that I owed it to them not to let pass any possible and honest means of giving them bread. . . . This was the first real dispute I had with him, and all our quarrels that followed were of the same kind; he laying down for me what he insisted that I should do, and I refusing because I thought that I ought not to do it."[1]

[1] *Conf.*, viii. 190.

Let us abstain, at this and all other points, from
being too sure that we easily see to the bottom of
our Rousseau. When we are most ready to fling up
the book and to pronounce him all selfishness and
sophistry, some trait is at hand to revive moral
interest in him, and show him unlike common men,
reverent of truth and human dignity. There is a
slight anecdote of this kind connected with his visit
to Fontainebleau. The day after the representation
of his piece, he happened to be taking his breakfast
in some public place. An officer entered, and, proceeding to describe the performance of the previous
day, told at great length all that had happened,
depicted the composer with much minuteness, and
gave a circumstantial account of his conversation. In
this story, which was told with equal assurance and
simplicity, there was not a word of truth, as was
clear from the fact that the author of whom he spoke
with such intimacy sat unknown and unrecognised
before his eyes. The effect on Rousseau was singular
enough. "The man was of a certain age; he had no
coxcombical or swaggering air; his expression bespoke
a man of merit, and his cross of St. Lewis showed
that he was an old officer. While he was retailing
his untruths, I grew red in the face, I lowered my
eyes, I sat on thorns; I tried to think of some means
of believing him to have made a mistake in good
faith. At length trembling lest some one should
recognise me and confront him, I hastened to finish
my chocolate without saying a word; and stooping

down as I passed in front of him, I went out as fast
as possible, while the people present discussed his
tale. I perceived in the street that I was bathed in
sweat, and I am sure that if any one had recognised
me and called me by name before I got out, they
would have seen in me the shame and embarrassment
of a culprit, simply from a feeling of the pain the
poor man would have had to suffer if his lie had been
discovered."[1] One who can feel thus vividly humi-
liated by the meanness of another, assuredly has in
himself the wholesome salt of respect for the erectness
of his fellows ; he has the rare sentiment that the
compromise of integrity in one of them is as a stain
on his own self-esteem, and a lowering of his own
moral stature.   There is more deep love of humanity
in this than in giving many alms, and it was not the
less deep for being the product of impulse and sympathetic emotion, and not of a logical sorites.

Another scene in a café is worth referring to,
because it shows in the same way that at this time
Rousseau's egoism fell short of the fatuousness to
which disease or vicious habit eventually depraved it.
In 1752 he procured the representation of his comedy
of Narcisse, which he had written at the age of
eighteen, and which is as well worth reading or playing as most comedies by youths of that amount of
experience of the ways of the world and the heart of
man.   Rousseau was amazed and touched by the
indulgence of the public, in suffering without any sign

[1] *Conf.*, viii. 183.

of impatience even a second representation of his piece.
For himself, he could not so much as sit out the first;
quitting the theatre before it was over, he entered the
famous café de Procope at the other side of the street,
where he found critics as wearied as himself. Here
he called out, "The new piece has fallen flat, and it
deserved to fall flat; it wearied me to death. It is
by Rousseau of Geneva, and I am that very Rousseau."[1]
The relentless student of mental pathology is very
likely to insist that even this was egoism standing on
its head and not on its feet, choosing to be noticed for
an absurdity, rather than not be noticed at all. It
may be so, but this inversion of the ordinary form of
vanity is rare enough to be not unrefreshing, and we
are very loth to hand Rousseau wholly over to the
pathologist before his hour has come.

II.

In the summer of 1754 Rousseau, in company
with his Theresa, went to revisit the city of his birth,
partly because an exceptionally favourable occasion
presented itself, but in yet greater part because he
was growing increasingly weary of the uncongenial
world in which he moved. On his road he turned
aside to visit her who had been more than even his
birth-place to him. He felt the shock known to all

[1] *Conf.*, viii. 202; and Musset-Pathay, ii. 439. When in
Strasburg, in 1765, he could not bring himself to be present at
its representation. *Œuv. et Corr. Inéd.*, p. 434.

who cherish a vision for a dozen years, and then suddenly front the changed reality. He had not prepared
himself by recalling the commonplace which we only
remember for others, how time wears hard and ugly
lines into the face that recollection at each new energy
makes lovelier with an added sweetness. "I saw her,"
he says, "but in what a state, O God, in what debase-
ment! Was this the same Madame de Warens, in
those days so brilliant, to whom the priest of Pontverre
had sent me! How my heart was torn by the sight!"
Alas, as has been said with a truth that daily experience proves to those whom pity and self-knowledge
have made most indulgent, as to those whom pinched
maxims have made most rigorous,—*morality is the
nature of things.*[1] We may have a humane tenderness
for our Manon Lescaut, but we have a deep presenti
ment all the time that the poor soul must die in a
penal settlement. It is partly a question of time;
whether death comes fast enough to sweep you out of
reach of the penalties which the nature of things may
appoint, but which in their fiercest shape are mostly
of the loitering kind. Death was unkind to Madame
de Warens, and the unhappy creature lived long
enough to find that morality does mean something
after all; that the old hoary world has not fixed on
prudence in the outlay of money as a good thing, out
of avarice or pedantic dryness of heart; nor on some
continence and order in the relations of men and

---

[1] Madame de Stael insisted that her father said this, and
Necker insisted that it was his daughter's.

women as a good thing, out of cheerless grudge to the
body, but because the breach of such virtues is ever
in the long run deadly to mutual trust, to strength,
to freedom, to collectedness, which are the reserve of
humanity against days of ordeal.

Rousseau says that he tried hard to prevail upon
his fallen benefactress to leave Savoy, to come and
take up her abode peacefully with him, while he and
Theresa would devote their days to making her happy.
He had not forgotten her in the little glimpse of
prosperity ; he had sent her money when he had it.[1]
She was sunk in indigence, for her pension had long
been forestalled, but still she refused to change her
home.   While Rousseau was at Geneva she came to
see him. " She lacked money to complete her journey ;
I had not enough about me ; I sent it to her an hour
afterwards by Theresa.   Poor Maman !   Let me
relate this trait of her heart.   The only trinket she
had left was a small ring ; she took it from her finger
to place it on Theresa's, who instantly put it back, as
she kissed the noble hand and bathed it with her
tears."   In after years he poured bitter reproaches
upon himself for not quitting all to attach his lot to
hers until her last hour, and he professes always to
have been haunted by the liveliest and most enduring
remorse.[2]   Here is the worst of measuring duty by
sensation instead of principle ; if the sensations happen
not to be in right order at the critical moment, the
chance goes by, never to return, and then, as memory

[1] *Corr.*, i. 176.   Feb. 13, 1753.   [2] *Conf.*, viii. 208-210.

in the best of such temperaments is long though not
without intermittence, old sentiment revives and drags
the man into a burning pit.   Rousseau appears not to
have seen her again, but the thought of her remained
with him to the end, like a soft vesture fragrant with
something of the sweet mysterious perfume of many-
scented night in the silent garden at Charmettes.
She died in a hovel eight years after this, sunk in
disease, misery, and neglect, and was put away in the
cemetery on the heights above Chambéri.[1]   Rousseau
consoled himself with thoughts of another world that
should reunite him to her and be the dawn of new
happiness ; like a man who should illusorily confound
the last glistening of a wintry sunset seen through
dark yew-branches, with the broad-beaming strength
of the summer morning.   "If I thought," he said,
"that I should not see her in the other life, my poor
imagination would shrink from the idea of perfect
bliss, which I would fain promise myself in it."[2]   To
pluck so gracious a flower of hope on the edge of the
sombre unechoing gulf of nothingness into which our
friend has slid silently down, is a natural impulse of
the sensitive soul, numbing remorse and giving a
moment's relief to the hunger and thirst of a tenderness that has been robbed of its object.   Yet would

[1] She died on July 30, 1762, aged "about sixty-three years."
Arthur Young, visiting Chambéri in 1789, with some trouble
procured the certificate of her death, which may be found in his
Travels, i. 272.   See a letter of M. de Conzié to Rousseau, in
M. Streckeisen-Moultou's collection, ii. 445.

[2] *Conf.*, xii. 233.

not men be more likely to have a deeper love for those
about them, and a keener dread of filling a house with
aching hearts, if they courageously realised from the
beginning of their days that we have none of this
perfect companionable bliss to promise ourselves in
other worlds, that the black and horrible grave is
indeed the end of our communion, and that we know
one another no more?

The first interview between Rousseau and Madame
de Warens was followed by his ludicrous conversion to
Catholicism (1728); the last was contemporary with his
re-conversion to the faith in which he had been reared.
The sight of Geneva gave new fire to his Republican
enthusiasm; he surrendered himself to transports of
patriotic zeal. The thought of the Parisian world
that he had left behind, its frivolity, its petulance,
its disputation over all things in heaven and on the
earth, its profound deadness to all civic activity,
quickened his admiration for the simple, industrious,
and independent community from which he never
forgot that he was sprung. But no Catholic could
enjoy the rights of citizenship. So Rousseau proceeded
to reflect that the Gospel is the same for all Christians,
and the substance of dogma only differs, because
people interposed with explanations of what they
could not understand; that therefore it is in each
country the business of the sovereign to fix both the
worship and the amount and quality of unintelligible
dogma; that consequently it is the citizen's duty to
admit the dogma, and follow the worship by law

appointed. "The society of the Encyclopædists, far from shaking my faith, had confirmed it by my natural aversion for partisanship and controversy. The reading of the Bible, especially of the Gospel, to which I had applied myself for several years, had made me despise the low and childish interpretation put upon the words of Christ by the people who were least worthy to understand him. In a word, philosophy by drawing me towards the essential in religion, had drawn me away from that stupid mass of trivial formulas with which men had overlaid and darkened it."[1] We may be sure that if Rousseau had a strong inclination towards a given course of action, he would have no difficulty in putting his case in a blaze of the brightest light, and surrounding it with endless emblems and devices of superlative conviction. In short, he submitted himself faithfully to the instruction of the pastor of his parish; was closely catechised by a commission of members of the consistory; received from them a certificate that he had satisfied the requirements of doctrine in all points; was received to partake of the Communion, and finally restored to all his rights as a citizen.[1]

This was no farce, such as Voltaire played now and again at the expense of an unhappy bishop or unhappier parish priest; nor such as Rousseau himself had played six-and-twenty years before, at the expense of those honest Catholics of Turin whose helpful dona-

[1] *Conf.*, viii. 210.
[2] Gaberel's *Rousseau et les Genevois*, p. 62.   *Conf.*, viii. 212.

tion of twenty francs had marked their enthusiasm
over a soul that had been lost and was found again.
He was never a Catholic, any more than he was ever
an atheist, and if it might be said in one sense that
he was no more a Protestant than he was either of
these two, yet he was emphatically the child of
Protestantism. It is hardly too much to say that one
bred in Catholic tradition and observance, accustomed
to think of the whole life of men as only a manifestation of the unbroken life of the Church, and of all the
several communities of men as members of that great
organisation which binds one order to another, and
each generation to those that have gone before and
those that come after, would never have dreamed that
monstrous dream of a state of nature as a state of
perfection. He would never have held up to ridicule
and hate the idea of society as an organism with
normal parts and conditions of growth, and never
have left the spirit of man standing in bald isolation
from history, from his fellows, from a Church, from
a mediator, face to face with the great vague phantasm.
Nor, on the other hand, is it likely that one born and
reared in the religious school of authority with its
elaborately disciplined hierarchy, would have conceived that passion for political freedom, that zeal for
the rights of peoples against rulers, that energetic
enthusiasm for a free life, which constituted the fire
and essence of Rousseau's writing. As illustration of
this, let us remark how Rousseau's teaching fared
when it fell upon a Catholic country like France : so

many of its principles were assimilated by the revolutionary schools as were wanted for violent dissolvents,
while the rest dropped away, and in this rejected
portion was precisely the most vital part of his system.
In other words, in no country has the power of collec-
tive organisation been so pressed and exalted as in
revolutionised France, and in no country has the free
life of the individual been made to count for so little.
With such force does the ancient system of temporal
and spiritual organisation reign in the minds of those
who think most confidently that they have cast it
wholly out of them. The use of reason may lead a
man far, but it is the past that has cut the groove.

In re-embracing the Protestant confession, therefore, Rousseau was not leaving Catholicism, to which
he had never really passed over ; he was only under-
going in entire gravity of spirit a formality which
reconciled him with his native city, and reunited those
strands of spiritual connection with it which had never
been more than superficially parted. There can be
little doubt that the four months which he spent in
Geneva in 1754 marked a very critical time in the
formation of some of the most memorable of his
opinions. He came from Paris full of inarticulate and
smouldering resentment against the irreverence and
denial of the materialistic circle which used to meet
at the house of D'Holbach. What sort of opinions
he found prevailing among the most enlightened of
the Genevese pastors we know from an abundance of
sources. D'Alembert had three or four years later

than this to suffer a bitter attack from them, but the account of the creed of some of the ministers which he gave in his article on Geneva in the Encyclopædia, was substantially correct. "Many of them," he wrote, "have ceased to believe in the divinity of Jesus Christ. Hell, one of the principal points in our belief, is no longer one with many of the Genevese pastors, who contend that it is an insult to the Divinity to imagine that a being full of goodness and justice can be capable of punishing our faults by an eternity of torment. In a word, they have no other creed than pure Socinianism, rejecting everything that they call mysteries, and supposing the first principle of a true religion to be that it shall propose nothing for belief which clashes with reason. Religion here is almost reduced to the adoration of one single God, at least among nearly all who do not belong to the common people ; and a certain respect for Jesus Christ and the Scriptures is nearly the only thing that distin- guishes the Christianity of Geneva from pure Deism."[1] And it would be easy to trace the growth of these rationalising tendencies. Throughout the seventeenth century men sprang up who anticipated some of the rationalistic arguments of the eighteenth, in denying

[1] The venerable Company of Pastors and Professors of the Church and Academy of Geneva appointed a committee, as in duty bound, to examine these allegations, and the committee, equally in duty bound, reported (Feb. 10, 1758) with mild in- dignation, that they were unfounded, and that the flock was untainted by unseasonable use of its mind. See on this Rous- seau's *Lettres écrites de la Montagne,* ii. 231.

the Trinity, and so forth,[1] but the time was not then
ripe. The general conditions grew more favourable.
Burnet, who was at Geneva in 1685-6, says that though
there were not many among the Genevese of the first
form of learning, "yet almost everybody here has a
good tincture of a learned education."[2] The pacification of civic troubles in 1738 was followed by a
quarter of a century of extreme prosperity and contentment, and it is in such periods that the minds of
men previously trained are wont to turn to the great
matters of speculation. There was at all times a
constant communication, both public and private,
going on between Geneva and Holland, as was only
natural between the two chief Protestant centres of
the Continent. The controversy of the seventeenth
century between the two churches was as keenly
followed in Geneva as at Leyden, and there is more
than one Genevese writer who deserves a place in the
history of the transition in the beginning of the
eighteenth century from theology proper to that
metaphysical theology, which was the first marked
dissolvent of dogma within the Protestant bodies.
To this general movement of the epoch, of course,
Descartes supplied the first impulse. The leader of
the movement in Geneva, that is of an attempt to
pacify the Christian churches on the basis of some
such Deism as was shortly to find its passionate ex-

[1] See Picot's *Hist. de Genève*, ii. 415.
[2] *Letters containing an account of Switzerland, Italy, etc., in*
1685-86. By G. Burnet, p. 9.

pression in the Savoyard Vicar's Confession of Faith, was John Alphonse Turretini (1661-1737). He belonged to a family of Italian refugees from Lucca, and his grandfather had been sent on a mission to Holland for aid in defence of Geneva against Catholic Savoy. He went on his travels in 1692; he visited Holland, where he saw Bayle, and England, where he saw Newton, and France, where he saw Bossuet. Chouet initiated him into the mysteries of Descartes. All this bore fruit when he returned home, and his eloquent exposition of rationalistic ideas aroused the usual cry of heresy from the people who justly insist that Deism is not Christianity. There was much stir for many years, but he succeeded in holding his own and in finding many considerable followers.[1] For example, some three years or so after his death, a work appeared in Geneva under the title of *La Religion Essentielle a l'Homme*, showing that faith in the existence of a God suffices, and treating

[1] J. A. Turretini's complete works were published as late as 1776, including among much besides that no longer interests men, an *Oratio de Scientiarum Vanitate et Præstantia* (vol. iii. 437), not at all in the vein of Rousseau's Discourse, and a treatise in four parts, *De Legibus Naturalibus*, in which, among other matters, he refutes Hobbes and assails the doctrine of Utility (i. 173, etc.), by limiting its definition to τὸ πρὸς ἑαυτὸν in its narrowest sense. He appears to have been a student of Spinoza (i. 326). Francis Turretini, his father, took part in the discussion as to the nature of the treaty or contract between God and man, in a piece entitled *Fœdus Naturæ a primo homine ruṭ tum, ejusque Prævaricationem posteris imputatam* (1675).

with contempt the belief in the inspiration of the Gospels.[1]

Thus we see what vein of thought was running through the graver and more active minds of Geneva about the time of Rousseau's visit. Whether it be true or not that the accepted belief of many of the preachers was a pure Deism, it is certain that the theory was fully launched among them, and that those who could not accept it were still pressed to refute it, and in refuting, to discuss. Rousseau's friendships were according to his own account almost entirely among the ministers of religion and the professors of the academy, precisely the sort of persons who would be most sure to familiarise him, in the course of frequent conversations, with the current religious ideas and the arguments by which they were opposed or upheld. We may picture the effect on his mind of the difference in tone and temper in these grave, candid, and careful men, and the tone of his Parisian friends in discussing the same high themes; how this difference would strengthen his repugnance, and corroborate his own inborn spirit of veneration; how he would here feel himself in his own world. For as wise men have noticed, it is not so much difference of opinion that stirs resentment in us, at least in great subjects where the difference is not trivial but profound, as difference in gravity of humour and manner of moral approach. He returned to Paris (Oct. 1754) warm with the resolution to give up his concerns

[1] Gaberel's *Eglise de Genève*, iii. 188.

there, and in the spring go back once and for all to
the city of liberty and virtue, where men revered
wisdom and reason instead of wasting life in the
frivolities of literary dialectic.[1]

The project, however, grew cool. The dedication
of his Discourse on Inequality to the Republic was
received with indifference by some and indignation
by others.[2] Nobody thought it a compliment, and
some thought it an impertinence. This was one
reason which turned his purpose aside. Another was
the fact that the illustrious Voltaire now also signed
himself Swiss, and boasted that if he shook his wig
the powder flew over the whole of the tiny Republic.
Rousseau felt certain that Voltaire would make a
revolution in Geneva, and that he should find in his
native country the tone, the air, the manners which
were driving him from Paris. From that moment he
counted Geneva lost. Perhaps he ought to make
head against the disturber, but what could he do
alone, timid and bad talker as he was, against a man
arrogant, rich, supported by the credit of the great,
of brilliant eloquence, and already the very idol of
women and young men?[3] Perhaps it would not be
uncharitable to suspect that this was a reason after
the event, for no man was ever so fond as Rousseau,
or so clever a master in the art, of covering an accident
in a fine envelope of principle, and, as we shall see,

---

[1] *Corr.*, i. 223 (to Vernes, April 5, 1755).
[2] *Conf.*, viii. 215, 216.   *Corr.*, i. 218 (to Perdriau, Nov. 28,
1754).   [3] *Conf.*, viii. 218.

he was at this time writing to Voltaire in strains of
effusive panegyric.   In this case he almost tells us
that the one real reason why he did not return to
Geneva was that he found a shelter from Paris close
at hand.   Even before then he had begun to conceive
characteristic doubts whether his fellow-citizens at
Geneva would not be nearly as hostile to his love of
living solitarily and after his own fashion as the good
people of Paris.

Rousseau has told us a pretty story, how one day
he and Madame d'Epinay wandering about the park
came upon a dilapidated lodge surrounded by fruit
gardens, in the skirts of the forest of Montmorency ;
how he exclaimed in delight at its solitary charm
that here was the very place of refuge made for him ;
and how on a second visit he found that his good
friend had in the interval had the old lodge pulled
down, and replaced by a pretty cottage exactly
arranged for his own household.   "My poor bear,"
she said, "here is your place of refuge ; it was you
who chose it, 'tis friendship offers it ; I hope it will
drive away your cruel notion of going from me." [1]

---

[1] *Conf.*, viii. 217. It is worth noticing as bearing on the
accuracy of the Confessions, that Madame d'Epinay herself
(*Mém.*, ii. 115) says that when she began to prepare the Hermitage for Rousseau he had never been there, and that she was
careful to lead him to believe that the expense had not been
incurred for him.   Moreover her letter to him describing it
could only have been written to one who had not seen it, and
though her Memoirs are full of sheer imagination and romance,
the documents in them are substantially authentic, and this
letter is shown to be so by Rousseau's reply to it.

Though moved to tears by such kindness, Rousseau did not decide on the spot, but continued to waver for some time longer between this retreat and return to Geneva.

In the interval Madame d'Epinay had experience of the character she was dealing with. She wrote to Rousseau pressing him to live at the cottage in the forest, and begging him to allow her to assist him in assuring the moderate annual provision which he had once accidentally declared to mark the limit of his wants.[1] He wrote to her bitterly in reply, that her proposition struck ice into his soul, and that she could have but sorry appreciation of her own interests in thus seeking to turn a friend into a valet. He did not refuse to listen to what she proposed, if only she would remember that neither he nor his sentiments were for sale.[2] Madame d'Epinay wrote to him patiently enough in return, and then Rousseau hastened to explain that his vocabulary needed special appreciation, and that he meant by the word valet "the degradation into which the repudiation of his principles would throw his soul. The independence I seek is not immunity from work; I am firm for winning my own bread, I take pleasure in it; but I mean not to subject myself to any other duty, if I can help it. I will never pledge any portion of my liberty, either for my own subsistence or that of any one else. I intend to work, but at my own will and pleasure, and even to do nothing, if it happens to

[1] *Mém.*, ii. 116.   [2] *Corr.* (1755), i. 242.

suit me, without any one finding fault except my
stomach."[1]   We may call this unamiable, if we please,
but in a frivolous world amiability can hardly go with
firm resolve to live an independent life after your own
fashion.   The many distasteful sides of Rousseau's
character ought not to hinder us from admiring his
steadfastness in refusing to sacrifice his existence to
the first person who spoke him civilly.   We may
wish there had been more of rugged simplicity in his
way of dealing with temptations to sell his birthright
for a mess of pottage; less of mere irritability.   But
then this irritability is one side of soft temperament.
The soft temperament is easily agitated, and this un-
pleasant disturbance does not stir up true anger nor
lasting indignation, but only sends quick currents of
eager irritation along the sufferer's nerves   Rousseau,
quivering from head to foot with self-consciousness,
is sufficiently unlike our plain Johnson, the strong-
armoured; yet persistent withstanding of the patron
is as worthy of our honour in one instance as in the
other.   Indeed, resistance to humiliating pressure is
harder for such a temper as Rousseau's, in which
deliberate endeavour is needed, than it is for the
naturally stoical spirit which asserts itself spontaneously and rises without effort.

    When our born solitary, wearied of Paris and half
afraid of the too friendly importunity of Geneva, at
length determined to accept Madame d'Epinay's offer
of the Hermitage on conditions which left him an

[1] *Corr.*, i. 245.

entire sentiment of independence of movement and
freedom from all sense of pecuniary obligation, he
was immediately exposed to a very copious torrent of
pleasantry and remonstrance from the highly social
circle who met round D'Holbach's dinner-table. They
deemed it sheer midsummer madness, or even a sign
of secret depravity, to quit their cheerful world for
the dismal solitude of woods and fields. "Only the
bad man is alone," wrote Diderot in words which
Rousseau kept resentfully in his memory as long as
he lived. The men and women of the eighteenth
century had no comprehension of solitude, the strength
which it may impart to the vigorous, the poetic graces
which it may shed about the life of those who are
less than vigorous; and what they did not comprehend, they dreaded and abhorred, and thought monstrous in the one man who did comprehend it. They
were all of the mind of Socrates when he said to
Phædrus, "Knowledge is what I love, and the men
who dwell in the town are my teachers, not trees
and landscape."[1] Sarcasms fell on him like hail, and
the prophecies usual in cases where a stray soul does
not share the common tastes of the herd. He would
never be able to live without the incense and the
amusements of the town; he would be back in a
fortnight; he would throw up the whole enterprise
within three months.[2] Amid a shower of such words,
springing from men's perverse blindness to the binding propriety of keeping all propositions as to what

[1] *Phædrus*, 230.   [2] *Conf.*, viii. 221, etc.

is the best way of living in respect of place, hours,
companionship, strictly relative to each individual
case, Rousseau stubbornly shook the dust of the city
from off his feet, and sought new life away from the
stridulous hum of men. Perhaps we are better pleased
to think of the unwearied Diderot spending laborious
days in factories and quarries and workshops and
forges, while friendly toilers patiently explained to
him the structure of stocking looms and velvet looms,
the processes of metal-casting and wire-drawing and
slate-cutting, and all the other countless arts and
ingenuities of fabrication, which he afterwards reproduced to a wondering age in his spacious and magnificent repertory of human thought, knowledge, and
practical achievement. And it is yet more elevating
to us to think of the true stoic, the great high-souled
Turgot, setting forth a little later to discharge beneficent duty in the hard field of his distant Limousin
commissionership, enduring many things and toiling
late and early for long years, that the burden of
others might be lighter, and the welfare of the land
more assured. But there are many paths for many
men, and if only magnanimous self-denial has the
power of inspiration, and can move us with the deep
thrill of the heroic, yet every truthful protest, even
of excessive personality, against the gregarious trifling
of life in the social groove, has a side which it is not
ill for us to consider, and perhaps for some men and
women in every generation to seek to imitate.

CHAPTER VII.

THE HERMITAGE.

IT would have been a strange anachronism if the decade of the the Encyclopædia and the Seven Years' War had reproduced one of those scenes which are as still resting-places amid the ceaseless forward tramp of humanity, where some holy man turned away from the world, and with adorable seriousness sought communion with the divine in mortification of flesh and solitude of spirit. Those were the retreats of firm hope and beatified faith. The hope and faith of the eighteenth century were centred in action, not in contemplation, and the few solitaries of that epoch, as well as of another nearer to our own, fled away from the impotence of their own will, rather than into the haven of satisfied conviction and clear-eyed acceptance. Only one of them——Wordsworth, the poetic hermit of our lakes—impresses us in any degree like one of the great individualities of the ages when men not only craved for the unseen, but felt the closeness of its presence over their heads and about their feet. The modern anchorite goes forth in the spirit of the preacher who declared all

the things that are under the sun to be vanity, not
in the transport of the saint who knew all the things
that are under the sun to be no more than the shadow
of a dream in the light of a celestial brightness to come.

Rousseau's mood, deeply tinged as it was by bitterness against society and circumstance, still contained
a strong positive element in his native exultation in
all natural objects and processes, which did not leave
him vacantly brooding over the evil of the world he
had quitted. The sensuousness that penetrated him
kept his sympathy with life extraordinarily buoyant,
and all the eager projects for the disclosure of a
scheme of wisdom became for a time the more vividly
desired, as the general tide of desire flowed more
fully within him. To be surrounded with the simplicity of rural life was with him not only a stimulus,
but an essential condition to free intellectual energy.
Many a time, he says, when making excursions into
the country with great people, "I was so tired of
fine rooms, fountains, artificial groves and flower beds,
and the still more tiresome people who displayed all
these; I was so worn out with pamphlets, card-play-
ing, music, silly jokes, stupid airs, great suppers, that
as I spied a poor hawthorn copse, a hedge, a farm-
stead, a meadow, as in passing through a hamlet I
snuffed the odour of a good chervil omelette, as I heard
from a distance the rude refrain of the shepherd's
songs, I used to wish at the devil the whole tale of
rouge and furbelows."[1]   He was no anchorite proper,

[1] *Conf.*, ix. 247.

one weary of the world and waiting for the end, but a man with a strong dislike for one kind of life and a keen liking for another kind. He thought he was now about to reproduce the old days of the Charmettes, true to his inveterate error that one may efface years and accurately replace a past. He forgot that instead of the once vivacious and tender benefactress who was now waiting for slow death in her hovel, his house-mates would be a poor dull drudge and her vile mother. He forgot, too, that since those days the various processes of intellectual life had expanded within him, and produced a busy fermentation which makes a man's surroundings very critical. Finally, he forgot that in proportion as a man suffers the smooth course of his thought to depend on anything external, whether on the greenness of the field or the gaiety of the street or the constancy of friends, so comes he nearer to chance of making shipwreck. Hence his tragedy, though the very root of the tragedy lay deeper,—in temperament.

L.

Rousseau's impatience drove him into the country almost before the walls of his little house were dry (April 9, 1756). "Although it was cold, and snow still lay upon the ground, the earth began to show signs of life; violets and primroses were to be seen; the buds on the trees were beginning to shoot; and the very night of my arrival was marked by the first

song of the nightingale. I heard it close to my
window in a wood that touched the house. After a
light sleep I awoke, forgetting that I was transplanted;
I thought myself still in the Rue de Grenelle, when
in an instant the warbling of the birds made me thrill
with delight. My very first care was to surrender
myself to the impression of the rustic objects about
me. Instead of beginning by arranging things inside
my quarters, I first set about planning my walks,
and there was not a path nor a copse nor a grove
round my cottage which I had not found out before
the end of the next day. The place, which was lonely
rather than wild, transported me in fancy to the end
of the world, and no one could ever have dreamed
that we were only four leagues from Paris."[1]

This rural delirium, as he justly calls it, lasted for
some days, at the end of which he began seriously to
apply himself to work. But work was too soon
broken off by a mood of vehement exaltation, produced by the stimulus given to all his senses by the
new world of delight in which he found himself.
This exaltation was in a different direction from that
which had seized him half a dozen years before, when
he had discarded the usage and costume of politer

---

[1] *Conf.*, ix. 230. Madame d'Epinay (*Mém.*, ii. 132) has given
an account of the installation, with a slight discrepancy of date.
When Madame d'Epinay's son-in-law emigrated at the Revolution, the Hermitage—of which nothing now stands—along with
the rest of the estate became national property, and was bought
after other purchasers by Robespierre, and afterwards by Grétry
the composer, who paid 10,000 livres for it.

society, and had begun to conceive an angry contempt
for the manners, prejudices, and maxims of his time.
Restoration to a more purely sensuous atmosphere
softened this austerity.   No longer having the vices
of a great city before his eyes, he no longer cherished
the wrath which they had inspired in him.   " When
I did not see men, I ceased to despise them ; and
when I had not the bad before my eyes, I ceased to
hate them.   My heart, little made as it is for hate,
now did no more than deplore their wretchedness,
and made no distinction between their wretchedness
and their badness.   This state, so much more mild, if
much less sublime, soon dulled the glowing enthusiasm
that had long transported me." [1]   That is to say, his
nature remained for a moment not exalted but fairly
balanced.   It was only for a moment.   And in study-
ing the movements of impulse and reflection in him
at this critical time of his life, we are hurried rapidly
from phase to phase.   Once more we are watching
a man who lived without either intellectual or spiritual
direction, swayed by a reminiscence, a passing mood,
a personality accidentally encountered, by anything
except permanent aim and fixed objects, and who
would at any time have surrendered the most
deliberately pondered scheme of persistent effort to
the fascination of a cottage slumbering in a bounteous
landscape.   Hence there could be no normally composed state for him ; the first soothing effect of the
rich life of forest and garden on a nature exasperated

[1] *Conf.*, ix. 255.

by the life of the town passed away, and became
transformed into an exaltation that swept the stoic
into space, leaving sensuousness to sovereign and
uncontrolled triumph, until the delight turned to its
inevitable ashes and bitterness.

At first all was pure and delicious. In after times
when pain made him gloomily measure the length of
the night, and when fever prevented him from having
a moment of sleep, he used to try to still his suffering
by recollection of the days that he had passed in
the woods of Montmorency, with his dog, the birds,
the deer, for his companions. " As I got up with the
sun to watch his rising from my garden, if I saw the
day was going to be fine, my first wish was that neither
letters nor visits might come to disturb its charm.
After having given the morning to divers tasks which
I fulfilled with all the more pleasure that I could put
them off to another time if I chose, I hastened to eat
my dinner, so as to escape from the importunate and
make myself a longer afternoon. Before one o'clock,
even on days of fiercest heat, I used to start in the
blaze of the sun, along with my faithful Achates,
hurrying my steps lest some one should lay hold of
me before I could get away. But when I had once
passed a certain corner, with what beating of the
heart, with what radiant joy, did I begin to breathe
freely, as I felt myself safe and my own master for
the rest of the day ! Then with easier pace I went
in search of some wild and desert spot in the forest,
where there was nothing to show the hand of man,

or to speak of servitude and domination ; some refuge
where I could fancy myself its discoverer, and where
no inopportune third person came to interfere between
nature and me.   She seemed to spread out before my
eyes a magnificence that was always new.   The gold
of the broom and the purple of the heather struck
my eyes with a glorious splendour that went to my
very heart; the majesty of the trees that covered me
with their shadow, the delicacy of the shrubs that
surrounded me, the astonishing variety of grasses and
flowers that I trod under foot, kept my mind in a
continual alternation of attention and delight. . . . .
My imagination did not leave the earth thus superbly
arrayed without inhabitants.   I formed a charming
society, of which I did not feel myself unworthy ; I
made a golden age to please my own fancy, and filling
up these fair days with all those scenes of my life that
had left sweet memories behind, and all that my
heart could yet desire or hope in scenes to come, I
waxed tender even to shedding tears over the true
pleasures of humanity, pleasures so delicious, so pure,
and henceforth so far from the reach of men.   Ah, if
in such moments any ideas of Paris, of the age, of my
little aureole as author, came to trouble my dreams,
with what disdain did I drive them out, to deliver
myself without distraction to the exquisite sentiments
of which I was so full.   Yet in the midst of it all,
the nothingness of my chimeras sometimes broke
sadly upon my mind.   Even if every dream had
suddenly been transformed into reality, it would not

have been enough ; I should have dreamed, imagined, yearned still." Alas, this deep insatiableness of sense, the dreary vacuity of soul that follows fulness of animal delight, the restless exactingness of un-directed imagination, was never recognised by Rous-seau distinctly enough to modify either his conduct or his theory of life. He filled up the void for a short space by that sovereign aspiration, which changed the dead bones of old theology into the living figure of a new faith. "From the surface of the earth I raised my ideas to all the existences in nature, to the universal system of things, to the incompre-hensible Being who embraces all. Then with mind lost in that immensity, I did not think, I did not reason, I did not philosophise ; with a sort of pleasure I felt overwhelmed by the weight of the universe, I surrendered myself to the ravishing confusion of these vast ideas. I loved to lose myself in imagination in immeasurable space ; within the limits of real exist-ences my heart was too tightly compressed ; in the universe I was stifled ; I would fain have launched myself into the infinite. I believe that if I had un-veiled all the mysteries of nature, I should have found myself in a less delicious situation than that bewilder-ing ecstasy to which my mind so unreservedly delivered itself, and which sometimes transported me until I cried out, 'O mighty Being! O mighty Being!' without power of any other word or thought." [1]

It is not wholly insignificant that though he could

[1] Third letter to Malesherbes, 364-368.

thus expand his soul with ejaculatory delight in something supreme, he could not endure the sight of one of his fellow-creatures. "If my gaiety lasted the whole night, that showed that I had passed the day alone; I was very different after I had seen people, for I was rarely content with others and never with myself. Then in the evening I was sure to be in taciturn or scolding humour." It is not in every condition that effervescent passion for ideal forms of the religious imagination assists sympathy with the real beings who surround us. And to this let us add that there are natures in which all deep emotion is so entirely associated with the ideal, that real and particular manifestations of it are repugnant to them as something alien; and this without the least insincerity, though with a vicious and disheartening inconsistency. Rousseau belonged to this class, and loved man most when he saw men least. Bad as this was, it does not justify us in denouncing his love of man as artificial; it was one side of an ideal exaltation, which stirred the depths of his spirit with a force as genuine as that which is kindled in natures of another type by sympathy with the real and concrete, with the daily walk and conversation and actual doings and sufferings of the men and women whom we know.

The fermentation which followed his arrival at the Hermitage, in its first form produced a number of literary schemes. The idea of the Political Institutions, first conceived at Venice, pressed upon his meditations. He had been earnestly requested to

compose a treatise on education. Besides this, his
thoughts wandered confusedly round the notion of a
treatise to be called Sensitive Morality, or the
Materialism of the Sage, the object of which was to
examine the influence of external agencies, such as
light, darkness, sound, seasons, food, noise, silence,
motion, rest, on our corporeal machine, and thus indirectly upon the soul also. By knowing these and
acquiring the art of modifying them according to our
individual needs, we should become surer of ourselves
and fix a deeper constancy in our lives. An external
system of treatment would thus be established, which
would place and keep the soul in the condition most
favourable to virtue.[1] Though the treatise was never
completed, and the sketch never saw the light, we
perceive at least that Rousseau would have made the
means of access to character wide enough, and the
material influences that impress it and produce its
caprices, multitudinous enough, instead of limiting
them with the medical specialist to one or two organs,
and one or two of the conditions that affect them.
Nor, on the other hand, do the words in which he
sketches his project in the least justify the attribution
to him of the doctrine of the absolute power of the
physical constitution over the moral habits, whether
that doctrine would be a credit or a discredit to his
philosophical thoroughness of perception. No one
denies the influence of external conditions on the
moral habits, and Rousseau says no more than that he

[1] *Conf.*, ix. 239.

proposed to consider the extent and the modifiableness of this influence. It was not then deemed essential
for a spiritualist thinker to ignore physical organisation.

A third undertaking of a more substantial sort was
to arrange and edit the papers and printed works of
the Abbé de Saint Pierre (1658-1743), confided to
him through the agency of Saint Lambert, and partly
also of Madame Dupin, the warm friend of that singular
and good man.[1] This task involved reading, considering, and picking extracts from twenty-three diffuse
and chaotic volumes, full of prolixity and repetition.
Rousseau, dreamer as he was, yet had quite keenness
of perception enough to discern the weakness of a
dreamer of another sort; and he soon found out that
the Abbé de Saint Pierre's views were impracticable,
in consequence of the author's fixed idea that men are
guided rather by their lights than by their passions. In
fact, Saint Pierre was penetrated with the eighteenth-
century faith to a peculiar degree. As with Condorcet
afterwards, he was led by his admiration for the
extent of modern knowledge to adopt the principle
that perfected reason is capable of being made the
base of all institutions, and would speedily terminate
all the great abuses of the world. "He went wrong,"
says Rousseau, "not merely in having no other passion
but that of reason, but by insisting on making all men
like himself, instead of taking them as they are and
as they will continue to be." The critic's own error

_____

[1] *Conf.*, ix. 237, 238, and 263, etc.

in later days was not very different from this, save
that it applied to the medium in which men live,
rather than to themselves, by refusing to take complex
societies as they are, even as starting-points for higher
attempts at organisation. Rousseau had occasionally
seen the old man, and he preserved the greatest
veneration for his memory, speaking of him as the
honour of his age and race, with a fulness of enthusiasm very unusual towards men, though common
enough towards inanimate nature. The sincerity of
this respect, however, could not make the twenty-
three volumes which the good man had written, either
fewer in number or lighter in contents, and after
dealing as well as he could with two important parts
of Saint Pierre's works, he threw up the task.[1] It
must not be supposed that Rousseau would allow that
fatigue or tedium had anything to do with a resolve
which really needed no better justification. As we
have seen before, he had amazing skill in finding a
certain ingeniously contrived largeness for his motives.
Saint Pierre's writings were full of observations on
the government of France, some of them remarkably
bold in their criticism, but he had not been punished
for them because the ministers always looked upon

---

[1] The extract from the Project for Perpetual Peace and the
Polysynodia, together with Rousseau's judgments on them, are
found at the end of the volume containing the Social Contract.
The first, but without the judgment, was printed separately
without Rousseau's permission, in 1761, by Bastide, to whom
he had sold it for twelve louis for publication in his journal
only. *Conf.*, xi. 107. *Corr.*, ii. 110, 128.

him as a kind of preacher rather than a genuine politician, and he was allowed to say what he pleased, because it was observed that no one listened to what he said. Besides, he was a Frenchman, and Rousseau was not, and hence the latter, in publishing Saint Pierre's strictures on French affairs, was exposing himself to a sharp question why he meddled with a country that did not concern him. "It surprised me," says Rousseau, "that the reflection had not occurred to me earlier," but this coincidence of the discovery that the work was imprudent, with the discovery that he was weary of it, will surprise nobody versed in study of a man who lives in his sensations, and yet has vanity enough to dislike to admit it.

The short remarks which Rousseau appended to his abridgment of Saint Pierre's essays on Perpetual Peace, and on a Polysynodia, or Plurality of Councils, are extremely shrewd and pointed, and would suffice to show us, if there were nothing else to do so, the right kind of answer to make to the more harmful dreams of the Social Contract. Saint Pierre's fault is said, with entire truth, to be a failure to make his views relative to men, to times, to circumstances; and there is something that startles us when we think whose words we are reading, in the declaration that, "whether an existing government be still that of old times, or whether it have insensibly undergone a change of nature, it is equally imprudent to touch it: if it is the same, it must be respected, and if it has degenerated, that is due to the force of time and

circumstance, and human sagacity is powerless."
Rousseau points to France, asking his readers to judge
the peril of once moving by an election the enormous
masses comprising the French monarchy; and in
another place, after a wise general remark on the
futility of political machinery without men of a
certain character, he illustrates it by this scornful
question : When you see all Paris in a ferment about
the rank of a dancer or a wit, and the affairs of the
academy or the opera making everybody forget the
interest of the ruler and the glory of the nation, what
can you hope from bringing political affairs close to
such a people, and removing them from the court to
the town ?[1]   Indeed, there is perhaps not one of these
pages which Burke might not well have owned.[2]

A violent and prolonged crisis followed this not
entirely unsuccessful effort after sober and laborious
meditation.   Rousseau was now to find that if society
has its perils, so too has solitude, and that if there is
evil in frivolous complaisance for the puppet-work of
a world that is only a little serious, so there is evil in
a passionate tenderness for phantoms of an imaginary
world that is not serious at all.   To the pure or
stoical soul the solitude of the forest is strength, but
then the imagination must know the yoke.   Rousseau's
imagination, in no way of the strongest either as

[1] P. 485.
[2] For a sympathetic account of the Abbé de Saint Pierre's
life and speculations, see M. Léonce de Lavergne's *Economistes
français du* 18*ième siècle* (Paris : 1870).   Also Comte's *Lettres
à M. Valat*, p. 73.

receptive or inventive, was the free accomplice of his
sensations. The undisciplined force of animal sensibility gradually rose within him, like a slowly welling
flood. The spectacle does not either brighten or
fortify the student's mind, yet if there are such states,
it is right that those who care to speak of human
nature should have an opportunity of knowing its
less glorious parts. They may be presumed to exist,
though in less violent degree, in many people whom
we meet in the street and at the table, and there can
be nothing but danger in allowing ourselves to be so
narrowed by our own virtuousness, viciousness being
conventionally banished to the remoter region of
the third person, as to forget the presence of "the
brute brain within the man's." In Rousseau's case,
at any rate, it was no wicked broth nor magic potion
that "confused the chemic labour of the blood," but
the too potent wine of the joyful beauty of nature
herself, working misery in a mental structure that no
educating care nor envelope of circumstance had ever
hardened against her intoxication. Most of us are
protected against this subtle debauch of sensuous
egoism by a cool organisation, while even those who
are born with senses and appetites of great strength
and keenness, are guarded by accumulated discipline
of all kinds from without, especially by the necessity
for active industry which brings the most exaggerated
native sensibility into balance. It is the constant
and rigorous social parade which keeps the eager
regiment of the senses from making furious rout

Rousseau had just repudiated all social obligation, and he had never gone through external discipline. He was at an age when passion that has never been broken in has the beak of the bald vulture, tearing and gnawing a man ; but its first approach is in fair shapes.

Wandering and dreaming "in the sweetest season of the year, in the month of June, under the fresh groves, with the song of the nightingale and the soft murmuring of the brooks in his ear," he began to wonder restlessly why he had never tasted in their plenitude the vivid sentiments which he was conscious of possessing in reserve, or any of that intoxicating delight which he felt potentially existent in his soul. Why had he been created with faculties so exquisite, to be left thus unused and unfruitful ? The feeling of his own quality, with this of a certain injustice and waste superadded, brought warm tears which he loved to let flow. Visions of the past, from girl play-mates of his youth down to the Venetian courtesan, thronged in fluttering tumult into his brain. He saw himself surrounded by a seraglio of houris whom he had known, until his blood was all aflame and his head in a whirl. His imagination was kindled into deadly activity. "The impossibility of reaching to the real beings plunged me into the land of chimera ; and seeing nothing actual that rose to the height of my delirium, I nourished it in an ideal world, which my creative imagination had soon peopled with beings after my heart's desire. In my continual ecstasies, I

made myself drunk with torrents of the most delicious
sentiments that ever entered the heart of man. Forgetting absolutely the whole human race, I invented
for myself societies of perfect creatures, as heavenly
for their virtues as their beauties ; sure, tender, faithful friends, such as I never found in our nether world.
I had such a passion for haunting this empyrean with
all its charming objects, that I passed hours and days
in it without counting them as they went by ; and
losing recollection of everything else, I had hardly
swallowed a morsel in hot haste, before I began to
burn to run off in search of my beloved groves. If,
when I was ready to start for the enchanted world, I
saw unhappy mortals coming to detain me on the
dull earth, I could neither moderate nor hide my
spleen, and, no longer master over myself, I used to
give them greeting so rough that it might well be
called brutal."[1]

This terrific malady was something of a very
different kind from the tranquil sensuousness of the
days in Savoy, when the blood was young, and life
was not complicated with memories, and the sweet
freshness of nature made existence enough. Then
his supreme expansion had been attended with a kind
of divine repose, and had found edifying voice in
devout acknowledgment in the exhilaration of the
morning air of the goodness and bounty of a beneficent master. In this later and more pitiable time
the beneficent master hid himself, and creation was

---

[1] *Conf.*, ix. 270-274.

only not a blank because it was veiled by troops of
sirens not in the flesh.   Nature without the association of some living human object, like Madame de
Warens, was a poison to Rousseau, until the advancing
years which slowly brought decay of sensual force
thus brought the antidote.   At our present point we
see one stricken with an ugly disease.   It was almost
mercy when he was laid up with a sharp attack of
the more painful, but far less absorbing and frightful
disorder, to which Rousseau was subject all his life
long.   It gave pause to what he misnames his angelic
loves.   "Besides that one can hardly think of love
when suffering anguish, my imagination, which is
animated by the country and under the trees,
languishes and dies in a room and under roof-beams."
This interval he employed with some magnanimity,
in vindicating the ways and economy of Providence,
in the letter to Voltaire which we shall presently
examine.   The moment he could get out of doors
again into the forest, the transport returned, but this
time accompanied with an active effort in the creative
faculties of his mind to bring the natural relief to
these over-wrought paroxysms of sensual imagination.
He soothed his emotions by associating them with the
life of personages whom he invented, and by introducing into them that play and movement and changing relation which prevented them from bringing his
days to an end in malodorous fever.   The egoism of
persistent invention and composition was at least
better than the egoism of mere unreflecting ecstasy

in the charm of natural objects, and took off something from the violent excess of sensuous force.   His
thought became absorbed in two female figures, one
dark and the other fair, one sage and the other yielding, one gentle and the other quick, analogous in
character but different, not handsome but animated
by cheerfulness and feeling.   To one of these he gave
a lover, to whom the other was a tender friend.   He
planted them all, after much deliberation and some
changes, on the shores of his beloved lake at Vevay,
the spot where his benefactress was born, and which
he always thought the richest and loveliest in all
Europe.

This vicarious or reflected egoism, accompanied as
it was by a certain amount of productive energy,
seemed to mark a return to a sort of moral con-
valescence.   He walked about the groves with pencil
and tablets, assigning this or that thought or expression to one or other of the three companions of his
fancy.   When the bad weather set in, and he was
confined to the house (the winter of 1756-7), he tried
to resume his ordinary indoor labour, the copying of
music and the compilation of his Musical Dictionary.
To his amazement he found that this was no longer
possible.   The fever of that literary composition of
which he had always such dread had strong possession of him.   He could see nothing on any side but
the three figures and the objects about them made
beautiful by his imagination.   Though he tried hard
to dismiss them, his resistance was vain, and he set

himself to bringing some order into his thoughts "so as to produce a kind of romance." We have a glimpse of his mental state in the odd detail, that he could not bear to write his romance on anything but the very finest paper with gilt edges; that the powder with which he dried the ink was of azure and sparkling silver; and that he tied up the quires with delicate blue riband.[1] The distance from all this to the state of nature is obviously very great indeed. It must not be supposed that he forgot his older part as Cato, Brutus, and the other Plutarchians. "My great embarrassment," he says honestly, "was that I should belie myself so clearly and thoroughly. After the severe principles I had just been laying down with so much bustle, after the austere maxims I had preached so energetically, after so many biting invectives against the effeminate books that breathed love and soft delights, could anything be imagined more shocking, more unlooked-for, than to see me inscribe myself with my own hand among the very authors on whose books I had heaped this harsh censure? I felt this inconsequence in all its force, I taxed myself with it, I blushed over it, and was overcome with mortification; but nothing could restore me to reason."[2] He adds that perhaps on the whole the composition of the New Heloïsa was turning his madness to the best account. That may be true, but does not all this make the bitter denunciation, in the Letter to D'Alembert, of love and of all who make its repre-

sentation a considerable element in literature or the
drama, at the very time when he was composing one
of the most dangerously attractive romances of his
century, a rather indecent piece of invective ? We may
forgive inconsistency when it is only between two of a
man's theories, or two self-concerning parts of his conduct, but hardly when it takes the form of reviling in
others what the reviler indulgently permits to himself.

We are more edified by the energy with which
Rousseau refused connivance with the public outrages
on morality perpetrated by a patron. M. d'Epinay
went to pay him a visit at the Hermitage, taking with
him two ladies with whom his relations were less than
equivocal, and for whom among other things he had
given Rousseau music to copy. "They were curious
to see the eccentric man," as M. d'Epinay afterwards
told his scandalised wife, for it was in the manners
of the day on no account to parade even the most
notorious of these unblessed connections. "He was
walking in front of the door; he saw me first; he
advanced cap in hand ; he saw the ladies ; he saluted
us, put on his cap, turned his back, and stalked off
as fast as he could. Can anything be more mad ?"[1]
In the miserable and intricate tangle of falsity, weakness, sensuality, and quarrel, which make up this
chapter in Rousseau's life, we are glad of even one
trait of masculine robustness. We should perhaps
be still more glad if the unwedded Theresa were not
visible in the background of this scene of high morals.

[1] D'Epinay, ii. 153.

II.

The New Heloïsa was not to be completed without a further extension of morbid experience of a still more burning kind than the sufferings of compressed passion. The feverish torment of mere visions of the air swarming impalpable in all his veins, was replaced when the earth again began to live and the sap to stir in plants, by the more concentred fire of a consuming passion for one who was no dryad nor figure of a dream. In the spring of 1757 he received a visit from Madame d'Houdetot, the sister-in-law of Madame d'Epinay.[1] Her husband had gone to the war (we are in the year of Rossbach), and so had her lover, Saint Lambert, whose passion had been so fatal to Voltaire's Marquise du Châtelet eight years before. She rode over in man's guise to the Hermitage from a house not very far off, where she was to pass her retreat during the absence of her two natural protectors. Rousseau had seen her before on various occasions ; she had been to the Hermitage the previous year, and had partaken of its host's homely fare.[2] But the time was not ripe ; the

[1] Madame d'Houdetot, (b. 1730—d. 1813) was the daughter of M. de Bellegarde, the father of Madame d'Epinay's husband. Her marriage with the Count d'Houdetot, of high Norman stock, took place in 1748. The circumstances of the marriage, which help to explain the lax view of the vows common among the great people of the time, are given with perhaps a shade too much dramatic colouring in Madame d'Epinay's Mém., i. 101.

[2] Conf., ix. 281.

force of a temptation is not from without but within.
Much, too, depended with our hermit on the temperature ; one who would have been a very ordinary
mortal to him in cold and rain, might grow to
Aphrodite herself in days when the sun shone hot
and the air was aromatic. His fancy was suddenly
struck with the romantic guise of the female cavalier,
and this was the first onset of a veritable intoxication,
which many men have felt, but which no man before
or since ever invited the world to hear the story of.
He may truly say that after the first interview with
her in this disastrous spring, he was as one who had
thirstily drained a poisoned bowl. A sort of palsy
struck him. He lay weeping in his bed at night, and
on days when he did not see the sorceress he wept
in the woods.[1] He talked to himself for hours, and
was of a black humour to his house-mates. When
approaching the object of this deadly fascination, his
whole organisation seemed to be dissolved. He walked
in a dream that filled him with a sense of sickly torture, commixed with sicklier delight.

People speak with precisely marked division of
mind and body, of will, emotion, understanding ; the
division is good in logic, but its convenient lines are
lost to us as we watch a being with soul all blurred,
body all shaken, unstrung, poisoned, by erotic mania,
rising in slow clouds of mephitic steam from suddenly
heated stagnancies of the blood, and turning the
reality of conduct and duty into distant unmeaning

[1] D'Epinay, ii. 246.

shadows. If such a disease were the furious mood of
the brute in spring-time, it would be less dreadful,
but shame and remorse in the ever-struggling reason
of man or woman in the grip of the foul thing, produces an aggravation of frenzy that makes the
mental healer tremble. Add to all this lurking
elements of hollow rage that his passion was not
returned; of stealthy jealousy of the younger man
whose place he could not take, and who was his friend
besides; of suspicion that he was a little despised for
his weakness by the very object of it, who saw that
his hairs were sprinkled with gray,—and the whole
offers a scene of moral humiliation that half sickens,
half appals, and we turn away with dismay as from a
vision of the horrid loves of heavy-eyed and scaly
shapes that haunted the warm primeval ooze.

Madame d'Houdetot, the unwilling enchantress
bearing in an unconscious hand the cup of defilement,
was not strikingly singular either in physical or
mental attraction. She was now seven-and-twenty.
Small-pox, the terrible plague of the country, had
pitted her face and given a yellowish tinge to her
complexion; her features were clumsy and her brow
low; she was short-sighted, and in old age at any
rate was afflicted by an excessive squint. This homeliness was redeemed by a gentle and caressing expression, and by a sincerity, a gaiety of heart, and free
sprightliness of manner, that no trouble could restrain.
Her figure was very slight, and there was in all her
movements at once awkwardness and grace. She was

natural and simple, and had a fairly good judgment
of a modest kind, in spite of the wild sallies in which
her spirits sometimes found vent.   Capable of chagrin,
she was never prevented by it from yielding to any
impulse of mirth.   "She weeps with the best faith
in the world, and breaks out laughing at the same
moment; never was anybody so happily born," says
her much less amiable sister-in-law.[1]   Her husband
was indifferent to her.   He preserved an attachment
to a lady whom he knew before his marriage, whose
society he never ceased to frequent, and who finally
died in his arms in 1793.   Madame d'Houdetot
found consolation in the friendship of Saint Lambert.
"We both of us," said her husband, "both Madame
d'Houdetot and I, had a vocation for fidelity, only
there was a mis-arrangement."   She occasionally
composed verses of more than ordinary point, but
she had good sense enough not to write them down,
nor to set up on the strength of them for poetess and
wit.[2]   Her talk in her later years, and she lived
down to the year of Leipsic, preserved the pointed
sententiousness of earlier time.   One day, for instance,
in the era of the Directory, a conversation was going
on as to the various merits and defects of women;
she heard much, and then with her accustomed suavity
of voice contributed this light summary :—"Without

[1] D'Epinay, ii. 269.

[2] Musset-Pathay has collected two or three trifles of her
composition, ii. 136-138.   Heal so quotes Madame d'Allard's
account of her, pp. 140, 141.

women, the life of man would be without aid at the beginning, without pleasure in the middle, and without solace at the end."[1]

We may be sure that it was not her power of saying things of this sort that kindled Rousseau's flame, but rather the sprightly naturalness, frankness, and kindly softness of a character which in his opinion united every virtue except prudence and strength, the two which Rousseau would be least likely to miss. The bond of union between them was subtle. She found in Rousseau a sympathetic listener while she told the story of her passion for Saint Lambert, and a certain contagious force produced in him a thrill which he never felt with any one else before or after. Thus, as he says, there was equally love on both sides, though it was not reciprocal. "We were both of us intoxicated with passion, she for her lover, I for her; our sighs and sweet tears mingled. Tender confidants, each of the other, our sentiments were of such close kin that it was impossible for them not to mix; and still she never forgot her duty for a moment, while for myself, I protest, I swear, that if sometimes drawn astray by my senses, still "—still he was a paragon of virtue, subject to rather new definition. We can appreciate the author of the New Heloïsa; we can appreciate the author of Emilius; but this strained attempt to confound those two very different persons by combining tearful erotics with

[1] Quoted by M. Girardin, *Rev. des Deux Mondes*, Sept. 1853, p. 1080.

high ethics, is an exhibition of self-delusion that the
most patient analyst of human nature might well find
hard to suffer. "The duty of privation exalted my
soul. The glory of all the virtues adorned the idol
of my heart in my sight; to soil its divine image
would have been to annihilate it," and so forth.[1]
Moon-lighted landscape gave a background for the
sentimentalist's picture, and dim groves, murmuring
cascades, and the soft rustle of the night air, made
up a scene which became for its chief actor "an
immortal memory of innocence and delight." "It
was in this grove, seated with her on a grassy bank,
under an acacia heavy with flowers, that I found
expression for the emotions of my heart in words
that were worthy of them. 'Twas the first and single
time of my life; but I was sublime, if you can use
the word of all the tender and seductive things that
the most glowing love can bring into the heart of a
man. What intoxicating tears I shed at her knees,
what floods she shed in spite of herself! At length
in an involuntary transport, she cried out, 'Never
was man so tender, never did man love as you do!
But your friend Saint Lambert hears us, and my
heart cannot love twice.'"[2] Happily, as we learn
from another source, a breath of wholesome life from
without brought the transcendental to grotesque end.
In the climax of tears and protestations, an honest
waggoner at the other side of the park wall, urging

---

[1] *Conf.*, ix. 304.
[2] *Ib.* ix. 305. Slightly modified version in *Corr.*, i. 377.

on a lagging beast launched a round and far-sounding
oath out into the silent night. Madame d'Houdetot
answered with a lively continuous peal of young
laughter, while an angry chill brought back the dis-
comfited lover from an ecstasy that was very full of
peril.[1]

Rousseau wrote in the New Heloïsa very sagely
that you should grant to the senses nothing when
you mean to refuse them anything. He admits that
the saying was falsified by his relations with Madame
d'Houdetot. Clearly the credit of this happy falsifi-
cation was due to her rather than to himself. What
her feelings were, it is not very easy to see. Honest
pity seems to have been the strongest of them. She
was idle and unoccupied, and idleness leaves the soul
open for much stray generosity of emotion, even
towards an importunate lover. She thought him
mad, and she wrote to Saint Lambert to say so.
"His madness must be very strong," said Saint
Lambert, "since she can perceive it."[2]

Character is ceaselessly marching, even when we
seem to have sunk into a fixed and stagnant mood.
The man is awakened from his dream of passion by
inexorable event; he finds the house of the soul not
swept and garnished for a new life, but possessed by
demons who have entered unseen. In short, such
profound disorder of spirit, though in its first stage
marked by ravishing delirium, never escapes a bitter

---

[1] M. Boiteau's note to Madame d'Epinay, ii. 273.

[2] Grimm, to Madame d'Epinay, ii. 305.

sequel.   When a man lets his soul be swept away
from the narrow track of conduct appointed by his
relations with others, still the reality of such relations
survives.   He may retreat to rural lodges ; that will
not save him either from his own passion, or from
some degree of that kinship with others which instantly
creates right and wrong like a wall of brass around
him.   Let it be observed that the natures of finest
stuff suffer most from these forced reactions, and it
was just because Rousseau had innate moral sensitive-
ness, and a man like Diderot was without it, that the
first felt his fall so profoundly, while the second was
unconscious of having fallen at all.

One day in July Rousseau went to pay his accustomed visit.   He found Madame d'Houdetot dejected,
and with the flush of recent weeping on her cheeks.
A bird of the air had carried the matter.   As usual,
the matter was carried wrongly, and apparently all
that Saint Lambert suspected was that Rousseau's
high principles had persuaded Madame d'Houdetot
of the viciousness of her relations with her lover.[1]
"They have played us an evil turn," cried Madame
d'Houdetot ; "they have been unjust to me, but that
is no matter.   Either let us break off at once, or be
what you ought to be." [2]   This was Rousseau's first

[1] This is shown partly by Saint Lambert's letter to Rousseau,
to which we come presently, and partly by a letter of Madame
d'Houdetot to Rousseau in May, 1758 (Streckeisen-Moultou,
i. 411-413), where she distinctly says that she concealed his
mad passion for her from Saint Lambert, who first heard of it in
common conversation.   [2] *Conf.*, ix. 311.

taste of the ashes of shame into which the lusciousness of such forbidden fruit, plucked at the expense of others, is ever apt to be transformed. Mortification of the considerable spiritual pride that was yet alive after this lapse, was a strong element in the sum of his emotion, and it was pointed by the reflection which stung him so incessantly, that his monitress was younger than himself. He could never master his own contempt for the gallantry of grizzled locks.[1] His austerer self might at any rate have been consoled by knowing that this scene was the beginning of the end, though the end came without any seeking on his part and without violence. To his amazement, one day Saint Lambert and Madame d'Houdetot came to the Hermitage, asking him to give them dinner, and much to the credit of human nature's elasticity, the three passed a delightful afternoon. The wronged lover was friendly, though a little stiff, and he passed occasional slights which Rousseau would surely not have forgiven, if he had not been disarmed by consciousness of guilt. He fell asleep, as we can well imagine that he might do, while Rousseau read aloud his very inadequate justification of Providence against Voltaire.[2]

In time he returned to the army, and Rousseau began to cure himself of his mad passion. His method, however, was not unsuspicious, for it in-

---

[1] Besides the many hints of reference to this in the Confessions, see the phrenetic Letters to Sarah, printed in the *Mélanges*, pp. 347-360.　　　　　[2] *Conf.*, ix. 337.

volved the perilous assistance of Madame d'Houdetot.
Fortunately her loyalty and good sense forced a more
resolute mode upon him.   He found, or thought he
found her distracted, embarrassed, indifferent.   In
despair at not being allowed to heal his passionate
malady in his own fashion, he did the most singular
thing that he could have done under the circumstances.
He wrote to Saint Lambert.[1]   His letter is a prodigy
of plausible duplicity, though Rousseau in some of his
mental states had so little sense of the difference between the actual and the imaginary, and was moreover
so swiftly borne away on a flood of fine phrases, that
it is hard to decide how far this was voluntary, and
how far he was his own dupe.   Voluntary or not, it
is detestable.   We pass the false whine about "being
abandoned by all that was dear to him," as if he had
not deliberately quitted Paris against the remonstrance of every friend he had ; about his being "solitary and sad," as if he was not ready at this very time
to curse any one who intruded on his solitude, and
hindered him of a single half-hour in the desert spots
that he adored.   Remembering the scenes in moon-
lighted groves and elsewhere, we read this :—" Whence
comes her coldness to me ?   Is it possible that you
can have suspected me of wronging you with her,
and of turning perfidious in consequence of an unseasonably rigorous virtue ?   A passage in one of your
letters shows a glimpse of some such suspicion.   No,
no, Saint Lambert, the breast of J. J. Rousseau never

[1] *Corr.*, i. 398.   Sept. 4, 1757.

held the heart of a traitor, and I should despise myself more than you suppose, if I had ever tried to rob you of her heart. . . . Can you suspect that her friendship for me may hurt her love for you ? Surely natures endowed with sensibility are open to all sorts of affections, and no sentiment can spring up in them which does not turn to the advantage of the dominant passion. Where is the lover who does not wax the more tender as he talks to his friend of her whom he loves ? And is it not sweeter for you in your banishment that there should be some sympathetic creature to whom your mistress loves to talk of you, and who loves to hear ?"

Let us turn to another side of his correspondence. The way in which the sympathetic creature in the present case loved to hear his friend's mistress talk of him, is interestingly shown in one or two passages from a letter to her; as when he cries, "Ah, how proud would even thy lover himself be of thy constancy, if he only knew how much it has surmounted. . . . I appeal to your sincerity. You, the witness and the cause of this delirium, these tears, these ravishing ecstasies, these transports which were never made for mortal, say, have I ever tasted your favours in such a way that I deserve to lose them ? . . . Never once did my ardent desires nor my tender supplications dare to solicit supreme happiness, without my feeling stopped by the inner cries of a sorrow-stricken soul. . . . O Sophie, after moments so sweet, the idea of eternal privation is too frightful for one who groans

that he cannot identify himself with thee. What, are
thy tender eyes never again to be lowered with a
delicious modesty, intoxicating me with pleasure?
What, are my burning lips never again to lay my
very soul on thy heart along with my kisses? What,
may I never more feel that heavenly shudder, that
rapid and devouring fire, swifter than lightning?"[1]
. . . We see a sympathetic creature assuredly, and
listen to the voice of a nature endowed with sensibility
even more than enough, but with decency, loyalty,
above all with self-knowledge, far less than enough.

One more touch completes the picture of the fallen
desperate man. He takes great trouble to persuade
Saint Lambert that though the rigour of his principles
constrains him to frown upon such breaches of social
law as the relations between Madame d'Houdetot and
her lover, yet he is so attached to the sinful pair that
he half forgives them. "Do not suppose," he says,
with superlative gravity, "that you have seduced me
by your reasons; I see in them the goodness of your
heart, not your justification. I cannot help blaming
your connection : you can hardly approve it yourself ;
and so long as you both of you continue dear to me,
I will never leave you in careless security as to the
innocence of your state. Yet love such as yours
deserves considerateness. . . . I feel respect for a
union so tender, and cannot bring myself to attempt
to lead it to virtue along the path of despair'
(p. 401).

[1] To Madame d'Houdetot. *Corr.*, i. 376-387. June 1757.

Ignorance of the facts of the case hindered Saint Lambert from appreciating the strange irony of a man protesting about leading to virtue along the path of despair a poor woman whom he had done as much as he could to lead to vice along the path of highly stimulated sense. Saint Lambert was as much a sentimentalist as Rousseau was, but he had a certain manliness, acquired by long contact with men, which his correspondent only felt in moods of severe exaltation. Saint Lambert took all the blame on himself. He had desired that his mistress and his friend should love one another; then he thought he saw some coolness in his mistress, and he set the change down to his friend, though not on the true grounds. "Do not suppose that I thought you perfidious or a traitor; I knew the austerity of your principles; people had spoken to me of it; and she herself did so with a respect that love found hard to bear." In short, he had suspected Rousseau of nothing worse than being over-virtuous, and trying in the interest of virtue to break off a connection sanctioned by contemporary manners, but not by law or religion. If Madame d'Houdetot had changed, it was not that she had ceased to honour her good friend, but only that her lover might be spared a certain chagrin, from suspecting the excess of scrupulosity and conscience in so austere an adviser.[1]

It is well known how effectively one with a germ

[1] Saint Lambert to Rousseau, from Wolfenbuttel, Oct. 11, 1757. Streckeisen-Moultou, i. 415.

of good principle in him is braced by being thought
better than he is. With this letter in his hands and
its words in his mind, Rousseau strode off for his last
interview with Madame d'Houdetot. Had Saint
Lambert, he says, been less wise, less generous, less
worthy, I should have been a lost man. As it was,
he passed four or five hours with her in a delicious
calm, infinitely more delightful than the accesses of
burning fever which had seized him before. They
formed the project of a close companionship of three,
including the absent lover ; and they counted on the
project coming more true than such designs usually
do, "since all the feelings that can unite sensitive and
upright hearts formed the foundation of it, and we
three united talents enough as well as knowledge
enough to suffice to ourselves, without need of aid or
supplement from others." What happened was this.
Madame d'Houdetot for the next three or four months,
which were among the most bitter in Rousseau's life,
for then the bitterness which became chronic was new
and therefore harder to be borne, wrote him the wisest,
most affectionate, and most considerate letters that a
sincere and sensible woman ever wrote to the most
petulant, suspicious, perverse, and irrestrainable of
men. For patience and exquisite sweetness of friendship some of these letters are matchless, and we can
only conjecture the wearing querulousness of the
letters to which they were replies. If through no
fault of her own she had been the occasion of the
monstrous delirium of which he never shook off the

consequences, at least this good soul did all that wise counsel and grave tenderness could do, to bring him out of the black slough of suspicion and despair into which he was plunged.[1] In the beginning of 1758 there was a change. Rousseau's passion for her some- how became known to all the world; it reached the ears of Saint Lambert, and was the cause of a passing disturbance between him and his mistress. Saint Lambert throughout acted like a man who is thoroughly master of himself. At first, we learn, he ceased for a moment to see in Rousseau the virtue which he sought in him, and which he was persuaded that he found in him. "Since then, however," wrote Madame d'Houdetot, "he pities you more for your weakness than he reproaches you, and we are both of us far from joining the people who wish to blacken your character; we have and always shall have the courage to speak of you with esteem."[2] They saw one another a few times, and on one occasion the Count and Countess d'Houdetot, Saint Lambert, and Rousseau all sat at table together, happily without breach of the peace.[3] One curious thing about this meeting was that it took place some three weeks after Rous- seau and Saint Lambert had interchanged letters on the subject of the quarrel with Diderot, in which each promised the other contemptuous oblivion.[4] Per-

---

[1] These letters are given in M. Streckeisen-Moultou's first volume (pp. 354-414). The thirty-second of them (Jan. 10, 1758) is perhaps the one best worth turning to.

[2] Streckeisen-Moultou, i. 412. May 6, 1768. *Conf.*, x. 15.

[3] *Ib.* x. 22.   [4] *Ib.* x. 18. Streckeisen, i. 422.

petuity of hate is as hard as perpetuity of love for our poor short-spanned characters, and at length the three who were once to have lived together in self-sufficing union, and then in their next mood to have forgotten one another instantly and for ever, held to neither of the extremes, but settled down into an easier middle path of indifferent good-will. The conduct of all three, said the most famous of them, may serve for an example of the way in which sensible people separate, when it no longer suits them to see one another.[1] It is at least certain that in them Rousseau lost two of the most unimpeachably good friends that he ever possessed.

III.

The egoistic character that loves to brood and hates to act, is big with catastrophe. We have now to see how the inevitable law accomplished itself in the case of Rousseau. In many this brooding egoism produces a silent and melancholy insanity; with him it was developed into something of acridly corrosive quality. One of the agents in this disastrous process was the wearing torture of one of the most painful of disorders. This disorder, arising from an internal malformation, harassed him from his infancy to the day of his death. Our fatuous persistency in reducing man to the spiritual, blinds the biographer to the circumstance that the history of a life is the history of

[1] *Conf.*, x. 24.

a body no less than that of a soul. Many a piece of conduct that divides the world into two factions of moral assailants and moral vindicators, provoking a thousand ingenuities of ethical or psychological analysis, ought really to have been nothing more than an item in a page of a pathologist's case-book. We are not to suspend our judgment on action; right and wrong can depend on no man's malformations. In trying to know the actor, it is otherwise; here it is folly to underestimate the physical antecedents of mental phenomena. In firm and lofty character, pain is mastered; in a character so little endowed with cool tenacious strength as Rousseau's, pain such as he endured was enough to account, not for his unsociality, which flowed from temperament, but for the bitter, irritable, and suspicious form which this unsociality now first assumed. Rousseau was never a saintly nature, but far the reverse, and in reading the tedious tale of his quarrels with Grimm and Madame d'Epinay and Diderot—a tale of labyrinthine nightmares—let us remember that we may even to this point explain what happened, without recourse to the too facile theory of insanity, unless one defines that misused term so widely as to make many sane people very uncomfortable.

His own account was this: "In my quality of solitary, I am more sensitive than another; if I am wrong with a friend who lives in the world, he thinks of it for a moment, and then a thousand distractions make him forget it for the rest of the day; but there

is nothing to distract me as to his wrong towards me;
deprived of my sleep, I busy myself with him all night
long; solitary in my walks, I busy myself with him
from sunrise until sunset; my heart has not an
instant's relief, and the harshness of a friend gives
me in one day years of anguish. In my quality of
invalid, I have a title to the considerateness that
humanity owes to the weakness or irritation of a man
in agony. Who is the friend, who is the good man,
that ought not to dread to add affliction to an unfortunate wretch tormented with a painful and incurable malady?"[1] We need not accept this as an
adequate extenuation of perversities, but it explains
them without recourse to the theory of uncontrollable
insanity. Insanity came later, the product of intellectual excitation, public persecution, and moral reaction
after prolonged tension. Meanwhile he may well be
judged by the standards of the sane; knowing his
temperament, his previous history, his circumstances,
we have no difficulty in accounting for his conduct.
Least of all is there any need for laying all the blame
upon his friends. There are writers whom enthusiasm
for the principles of Jean Jacques has driven into
fanatical denigration of every one whom he called
his enemy, that is to say, nearly every one whom
he ever knew.[2] Diderot said well, "Too many

[1] To Madame d'Epinay, 1757. *Corr.*, i. 362, 353. See also
Conf., ix. 307.

[2] One of the most unflinching in this kind is an *Essai sur la
vie et le caractère de J. J. Rousseau*, by G. H. Morin (Paris:
1851): the laborious production of a bitter advocate, who

honest people would be wrong, if Jean Jacques were right."

The first downright breach was with Grimm, but there were angry passages during the year 1757, not only with him, but with Diderot and Madame d'Epinay as well. Diderot, like many other men of energetic nature unchastened by worldly wisdom, was too interested in everything that attracted his attention to keep silence over the indiscretion of a friend. He threw as much tenacity and zeal into a trifle, if it had once struck him, as he did into the Encyclopædia. We have already seen how warmly he rated Jean Jacques for missing the court pension. Then he scolded and laughed at him for turning hermit. With still more seriousness he remonstrated with him for remaining in the country through the winter, thus endangering the life of Theresa's aged mother. This stirred up hot anger in the Hermitage, and two or three bitter letters were interchanged,[1] those of Diderot being pronounced by a person who was no partisan of Rousseau decidedly too harsh.[2] Yet there is copious warmth of friendship in these very letters, if only the man to whom they were written had not hated interference in his affairs as the worst of injuries. "I loved Diderot tenderly, I esteemed him sincerely," says Rousseau, "and I counted with entire confidence accepts the Confessions, Dialogues, Letters, etc., with the reverence due to verbal inspiration, and writes of everybody who offended his hero, quite in the vein of Marat towards aristocrats.

[1] *Corr.*, i. 327-335.   D'Epinay, ii. 165-182.
[2] D'Epinay, ii. 173.

upon the same sentiments in him. But worn out by his unwearied obstinacy in everlastingly thwarting my tastes, my inclinations, my ways of living, every-thing that concerned myself only; revolted at seeing a younger man than myself insist with all his might on governing me like a child; chilled by his readiness in giving his promise and his negligence in keeping it; tired of so many appointments which he made and broke, and of his fancy for repairing them by new ones to be broken in their turn; provoked at waiting for him to no purpose three or four times a month on days which he had fixed, and of dining alone in the evening, after going on as far as St. Denis to meet him and waiting for him all day,—I had my heart already full of a multitude of grievances." [1] This irritation subsided in presence of the storms that now rose up against Diderot. He was in the thick of the dangerous and mortifying distractions stirred up by the foes of the Encyclopædia. Rous-seau in friendly sympathy went to see him; they embraced, and old wrongs were forgotten until new arose. [2]

There is a less rose-coloured account than this. Madame d'Epinay assigns two motives to Rousseau: a desire to find an excuse for going to Paris, in order to avoid seeing Saint Lambert; secondly, a wish to hear Diderot's opinion of the two first parts of the New Heloïsa. She says that he wanted to borrow a portfolio in which to carry the manuscripts to Paris;

[1] *Conf.*, ix. 325.   [2] *Ib.*, ix. 334.

Rousseau says that they had already been in Diderot's
possession for six months.[1]   As her letters containing
this very circumstantial story were written at the
moment, it is difficult to uphold the Confessions as
valid authority against them.   Thirdly, Rousseau
told her that he had not taken his manuscripts to
Paris (p. 302), whereas Grimm writing a few days
later (p. 309) mentions that he has received a letter
from Diderot, to the effect that Rousseau's visit had
no other object than the revision of these manuscripts.
The scene is characteristic.   "Rousseau kept him
pitilessly at work from Saturday at ten o'clock in the
morning till eleven at night on Monday, hardly giving
him time to eat and drink.   The revision at an end,
Diderot chats with him about a plan he has in his
head, and begs Rousseau to help him in contriving
some incident which he cannot yet arrange to his
taste.   'It is too difficult,' replies the hermit coldly,
'it is late, and I am not used to sitting up.   Good
night; I am off at six in the morning, and 'tis time
for bed.'   He rises from his chair, goes to bed, and
leaves Diderot petrified at his behaviour.   The day
of his departure, Diderot's wife saw that her husband
was in bad spirits, and asked the reason.   'It is that
man's want of delicacy,' he replied, 'which afflicts
me; he makes me work like a slave, but I should
never have found that out, if he had not so drily

[1] *Mém.*, ii. 297.   She also places the date many months
later than Rousseau, and detaches the reconciliation from the
quarrel in the winter of 1756-1757.

refused to take an interest in me for a quarter of an hour.' ' You are surprised at that,' his wife answered ; ' do you not know him ? He is devoured with envy ; he goes wild with rage when anything fine appears that is not his own. You will see him one day commit some great crime rather than let himself be ignored. I declare I would not swear that he will not join the ranks of the Jesuits, and undertake their vindication.'"

Of course we cannot be sure that Grimm did not manipulate these letters long after the event, but there is nothing in Rousseau's history to make us perfectly sure that he was incapable either of telling a falsehood to Madame d'Epinay, or of being shamelessly selfish in respect of Diderot. I see no reason to refuse substantial credit to Grimm's account, and the points of coincidence between that and the Confessions make its truth probable.[1]

Rousseau's relations with Madame d'Epinay were more complex, and his sentiments towards her underwent many changes. There was a prevalent opinion that he was her lover, for which no real foundation seems to have existed.[2] Those who disbelieved that he had reached this distinction, yet made sure that he had a passion for her, which may or may not have been true.[3]

[1] The same story is referred to in Madame de Vandeul's *Mém. de Diderot*, p. 61.

[2] *Conf.*, ix. 245, 246.

[3] Grimm to Madame d'Epinay, ii. 259, 269, 313, 326. *Conf.*, x. 17.

Madame d'Epinay herself was vain enough to be willing that this should be generally accepted, and it is certain that she showed a friendship for him which, considering the manners of the time, was invitingly open to misconception. Again, she was jealous of her sister-in-law, Madame d'Houdetot, if for no other reason than that the latter, being the wife of a Norman noble, had access to the court, and this was unattainable by the wife of a farmer-general. Hence Madame d'Epinay's barely-concealed mortification when she heard of the meetings in the forest, the private suppers, the moonlight rambles in the park. When Saint Lambert first became uneasy as to the relations between Rousseau and his mistress, and wrote to her to say that he was so, Rousseau instantly suspected that Madame d'Epinay had been his informant. Theresa confirmed the suspicion by tales of baskets and drawers ransacked by Madame d'Epinay in search of Madame d'Houdetot's letters to him. Whether these tales were true or not, we can never know ; we can only say that Madame d'Epinay was probably not incapable of these meannesses, and that there is no reason to suppose that she took the pains to write directly to Saint Lambert a piece of news which she was writing to Grimm, knowing that he was then in communication with Saint Lambert. She herself suspected that Theresa had written to Saint Lambert,[1] but it may be doubted whether Theresa's imagination could have risen to such feat

---

[1] *Mém.*, ii. 318.

as writing to a marquis, and a marquis in what would
have seemed to her to be remote and inaccessible
parts of the earth. All this, however, has become
ghostly for us; a puzzle that can never be found out,
nor be worth finding out. Rousseau was persuaded
that Madame d'Epinay was his betrayer, and was
seized by one of his blackest and most stormful
moods. In reply to an affectionate letter from her,
inquiring why she had not seen him for so long, he
wrote thus: "I can say nothing to you yet. I wait
until I am better informed, and this I shall be sooner
or later. Meanwhile, be certain that accused innocence will find a champion ardent enough to make
calumniators repent, whoever they may be." It is
rather curious that so strange a missive as this, instead
of provoking Madame d'Epinay to anger, was answered
by a warmer and more affectionate letter than the
first. To this Rousseau replied with increased
vehemence, charged with dark and mysteriously
worded suspicion. Still Madame d'Epinay remained
willing to receive him. He began to repent of his
imprudent haste, because it would certainly end by
compromising Madame d'Houdetot, and because,
moreover, he had no proof after all that his suspicions
had any foundation. He went instantly to the
house of Madame d'Epinay; at his approach she
threw herself on his neck and melted into tears.
This unexpected reception from so old a friend
moved him extremely; he too wept abundantly.
She showed no curiosity as to the precise nature of

his suspicions or their origin, and the quarrel came
to an end.[1]

Grimm's turn followed.   Though they had been
friends for many years, there had long been a certain
stiffness in their friendship.   Their characters were
in fact profoundly antipathetic.   Rousseau we know,
—sensuous, impulsive, extravagant, with little sense of
the difference between reality and dreams.   Grimm
was exactly the opposite ; judicious, collected, self-
seeking, coldly upright.   He was a German (born at
Ratisbon), and in Paris was first a reader to the Duke
of Saxe Gotha, with very scanty salary.   He made
his way, partly through the friendship of Rousseau,
into the society of the Parisian men of letters, rapidly
acquired a perfect mastery of the French language,
and with the inspiring help of Diderot, became an
excellent critic.   After being secretary to sundry high
people, he became the literary correspondent of various
German sovereigns, keeping them informed of what

[1] *Conf.*, ix. 322.   Madame d'Epinay (*Mém.*, ii. 326), writing
to Grimm, gives a much colder and stiffer colour to the scene of
reconciliation, but the nature of her relations with him would
account for this.   The same circumstance, as M. Girardin
has pointed out (*Rev. des Deux Mondes*, Sept. 1853), would explain the discrepancy between her letters as given in the Confessions, and the copies of them sent to Grimm, and printed in
her Memoirs.   M. Sainte Beuve, who is never perfectly master
of himself in dealing with the chiefs of the revolutionary schools,
as might indeed have been expected in a writer with his pre-
dilections for the seventeenth century, rashly hints (*Causeries*,
vii. 301) that Rousseau was the falsifier.   The publication from
the autograph originals sets this at rest.

was happening in the world of art and letters, just as
an ambassador keeps his government informed of what
happens in politics.   The sobriety, impartiality, and
discrimination of his criticism make one think highly
of his literary judgment; he had the courage, or shall
we say he preserved enough of the German, to defend
both Homer and Shakespeare against the unhappy
strictures of Voltaire.[1]   This is not all, however; his
criticism is conceived in a tone which impresses us
with the writer's integrity.   And to this internal
evidence we have to add the external corroboration
that in the latter part of his life he filled various
official posts, which implied a peculiar confidence in
his probity on the part of those who appointed him.
At the present moment (1756-57), he was acting as
secretary to Marshal d'Estrées, commander of the
French army in Westphalia at the outset of the Seven
Years' War.   He was an able and helpful man, in
spite of his having a rough manner, powdering his
face, and being so monstrously scented as to earn the
name of the musk-bear.   He had that firmness and
positivity which are not always beautiful, but of which
there is probably too little rather than too much in
the world, certainly in the France of his time, and of
which there was none at all in Rousseau.   Above all
things he hated declamation.   Apparently cold and
reserved, he had sensibility enough underneath the
surface to go nearly out of his mind for love of a singer
at the opera who had a thrilling voice.   As he did

[1] For Shakespeare, see *Corr. Lit.*, iv. 143, etc.

not believe in the metaphysical doctrine about the
freedom of the will, he accepted from temperament
the necessity which logic confirmed, of guiding the
will by constant pressure from without. "I am surprised," Madame d'Epinay said to him, "that men
should be so little indulgent to one another." "Nay,
the want of indulgence comes of our belief in freedom;
it is because the established morality is false and bad,
inasmuch as it starts from this false principle of
liberty." "Ah, but the contrary principle, by making one too indulgent, disturbs order." "It does
nothing of the kind. Though man does not
wholly change, he is susceptible of modification;
you can improve him; hence it is not useless to
punish him. The gardener does not cut down a
tree that grows crooked; he binds up the branch
and keeps it in shape; that is the effect of public
punishment."[1] He applied the same doctrine, as we
shall see, to private punishment for social crooked-
ness.

It is easy to conceive how Rousseau's way of ordering himself would gradually estrange so hard a head
as this. What the one thought a weighty moral
reformation, struck the other as a vain desire to attract
attention. Rousseau on the other hand suspected
Grimm of intriguing to remove Theresa from him, as
well as doing his best to alienate all his friends. The
attempted alienation of Theresa consisted in the secret
allowance to her mother and her by Grimm and

[1] D'Epinay, ii. 188.

Diderot of some sixteen pounds a year.[1] Rousseau was unaware of this, but the whisperings and goings and comings to which it gave rise, made him darkly uneasy. That the suspicions in other respects were in a certain sense not wholly unfounded, is shown by Grimm's own letters to Madame d'Epinay. He dis-approved of her installing Rousseau in the Hermitage, and warned her in a very remarkable prophecy that solitude would darken his imagination.[2] "He is a poor devil who torments himself, and does not dare to confess the true subject of all his sufferings, which is in his cursed head and his pride; he raises up imagin-ary matters, so as to have the pleasure of complain-ing of the whole human race."[3] More than once he assures her that Rousseau will end by going mad, it being impossible that so hot and ill-organised a head should endure solitude.[4] Rousseauite partisans usually explain all this by supposing that Grimm was eager to set a woman for whom he had a passion, against a man who was suspected of having a passion for her; and it is possible that jealousy may have stimulated the exercise of his natural shrewdness. But this shrewdness, added to entire want of imagination and a very narrow range of sympathy, was quite enough to account for Grimm's harsh judgment, without the addition of any sinister sentiment. He was perfectly right in suspecting Rousseau of want of loyalty to

---

[1] D'Epinay, ii. 150.   Also Vandeul's *Mém. de Diderot*, p. 61.
[2] *Mém.* ii. 128.
[3] P. 258.   See also p. 146.   [4] Pp. 282, 336, etc.

Madame d'Epinay, for we find our hermit writing to
her in strains of perfect intimacy, while he was writing
of her to Madame d'Houdetot as "your unworthy
sister."[1]   On the other hand, while Madame d'Epinay
was overwhelming him with caressing phrases, she
was at the same moment describing him to Grimm as
a master of impertinence and intractableness.   As
usual where there is radical incompatibility of character, an attempted reconciliation between Grimm
and Rousseau (some time in the early part of October
1757) had only made the thinly veiled antipathy more
resolute.   Rousseau excused himself for wrongs of
which in his heart he never thought himself guilty.
Grimm replied by a discourse on the virtues of friendship and his own special aptitude for practising them.
He then conceded to the impetuous penitent the kiss
of peace, in a slight embrace which was like the
accolade given by a monarch to new knights.[2]   The
whole scene is ignoble.   We seem to be watching an
unclean cauldron, with Theresa's mother, a cringing
and babbling crone, standing witch-like over it and
infusing suspicion, falsehood, and malice.   When
minds are thus surcharged, any accident suffices to

---

[1] *Corr.*, i. 386.   June 1757.

[2] *Conf.*, ix. 355.   For Madame d'Epinay's equally credible
version, assigning all the stiffness and arrogance to Rousseau,
see *Mém.*, ii. 355-358.   Saint Lambert refers to the momentary
reconciliation in his letter to Rousseau of Nov. 21 (Streckeisen,
i. 418), repeating what he had said before (p. 417), that Grimm
always spoke of him in amicable terms, though complaining of
Rousseau's injustice.

release the evil creatures that lurk in an irritated imagination.

One day towards the end of the autumn of 1757, Rousseau learned to his unbounded surprise that Madame d'Epinay had been seized with some strange disorder, which made it advisable that she should start without any delay for Geneva, there to place herself under the care of Tronchin, who was at that time the most famous doctor in Europe. His surprise was greatly increased by the expectation which he found among his friends that he would show his gratitude for her many kindnesses to him, by offering to bear her company on her journey, and during her stay in a town which was strange to her and thoroughly familiar to him. It was to no purpose that he protested how unfit was one invalid to be the nurse of another; and how great an incumbrance a man would be in a coach in the bad season, when for many days he was absolutely unable to leave his chamber without danger. Diderot, with his usual eagerness to guide a friend's course, wrote him a letter urging that his many obligations, and even his grievances in respect of Madame d'Epinay, bound him to accompany her, as he would thus repay the one and console himself for the other. "She is going into a country where she will be like one fallen from the clouds. She is ill; she will need amusement and distraction. As for winter, are you worse now than you were a month back, or than you will be at the opening of the spring? For me, I confess that if I could not bear the coach, I

would take a staff and follow her on foot."[1]   Rousseau
trembled with fury, and as soon as the transport was
over, he wrote an indignant reply, in which he more
or less politely bade the panurgic one to attend to his
own affairs, and hinted that Grimm was making a tool
of him.   Next he wrote to Grimm himself a letter,
not unfriendly in form, asking his advice and promising
to follow it, but hardly hiding his resentment.   By
this time he had found out the secret of Madame
d'Epinay's supposed illness and her anxiety to pass
some months away from her family, and the share
which Grimm had in it.   This, however, does not make
many passages of his letter any the less ungracious
or unseemly.   "If Madame d'Epinay has shown friendship to me, I have shown more to her. . . . As for
benefits, first of all I do not like them, I do not want
them, and I owe no thanks for any that people may
burden me with by force.   Madame d'Epinay, being
so often left alone in the country, wished me for
company ; it was for that she had kept me.   After
making one sacrifice to friendship, I must now make
another to gratitude.   A man must be poor, must be
without a servant, must be a hater of constraint, and
he must have my character, before he can know what
it is for me to live in another person's house.   For all
that, I lived two years in hers, constantly brought into
bondage with the finest harangues about liberty, served
by twenty domestics, and cleaning my own shoes every
morning, overloaded with gloomy indigestion, and

[1] *Conf.*, ix. 372.

incessantly sighing for my homely porringer. . . . Consider how much money an hour of the life and the time of a man is worth; compare the kindnesses of Madame d'Epinay with the sacrifice of my native country and two years of serfdom; and then tell me whether the obligation is greater on her side or mine." He then urges with a torrent of impetuous eloquence the thoroughly sound reasons why it was unfair and absurd for him, a beggar and an invalid, to make the journey with Madame d'Epinay, rich and surrounded by attendants. He is particularly splenetic that the philosopher Diderot, sitting in his own room before a good fire and wrapped in a well-lined dressing-gown, should insist on his doing his five and twenty leagues a day on foot, through the mud in winter.[1]

The whole letter shows, as so many incidents in his later life showed, how difficult it was to do Rousseau a kindness with impunity, and how little such friends as Madame d'Epinay possessed the art of soothing this unfortunate nature. They fretted him by not leaving him sufficiently free to follow his own changing moods, while he in turn lost all self-control, and yielded in hours of bodily torment to angry and resentful fancies. But let us hasten to an end. Grimm replied to his eloquent manifesto somewhat drily, to the effect that he would think the matter over, and that meanwhile Rousseau had best keep quiet in his hermitage. Rousseau burning with excitement at once conceived a thousand suspicions, wholly unable to understand that

[1] *Corr.*, i. 404-416.   Oct. 19, 1757.

a cold and reserved German might choose to deliberate at length, and finally give an answer with brevity. "After centuries of expectation in the cruel uncertainty in which this barbarous man had plunged me"—that is after eight or ten days, the answer came, apparently not without a second direct application for one.[1] It was short and extremely pointed, not complaining that Rousseau had refused to accompany Madame d'Epinay but protesting against the horrible tone of the apology which he had sent to him for not accompanying her. "It has made me quiver with indignation ; so odious are the principles it contains, so full is it of blackness and duplicity.   You venture to talk to me of your slavery, to me who for more than two years have been the daily witness of all the marks of the tenderest and most generous friendship that you have received at the hands of that woman.   If I could pardon you, I should think myself unworthy of having a single friend. I will never see you again while I live, and I shall think myself happy if I can banish the recollection of your conduct from my mind."[2]   A flash of manly anger like this is very welcome to us, who have to thread a tedious way between morbid egoistic irritation on the one hand, and sly pieces of equivocal complais-ance on the other.   The effect on Rousseau was terrific.   In a paroxysm he sent Grimm's letter back to him, with three or four lines in the same key.   He

---

[1] Grimm to Diderot, in Madame d'Epinay's *Mém.* ii. 386. Nov. 3, 1757.

[2] D'Epinay, ii. 387.   Nov. 3.

wrote note after note to Madame d'Houdetot, in
shrieks. "Have I a single friend left, man or woman?
One word, only one word, and I can live." A day or
two later : "Think of the state I am in. I can bear
to be abandoned by all the world, but you ! You who
know me so well ! Great God ! am I a scoundrel ? a
scoundrel, I !"[1] And so on, raving. It was to no
purpose that Madame d'Houdetot wrote him soothing
letters, praying him to calm himself, to find something
to busy himself with, to remain at peace with Madame
d'Epinay, "who had never appeared other than the
most thoughtful and warm-hearted friend to him."[2]
He was almost ready to quarrel with Madame d'Houdetot
herself because she paid the postage of her letters,
which he counted an affront to his poverty.[3] To
Madame d'Epinay he had written in the midst of his
tormenting uncertainty as to the answer which Grimm
would make to his letter. It was an ungainly assertion
that she was playing a game of tyranny and intrigue
at his cost. For the first time she replied with spirit
and warmth. "Your letter is hardly that of a man
who, on the eve of my departure, swore to me that he
could never in his life repair the wrongs he had done

[1] *Corr.*, i. 425. Nov. 8. *Ib.* 426.

[2] Streckeisen-Moultou, i. 381-383.

[3] *Ib.* 387. Many years after, Rousseau told Bernardin de
St. Pierre (*Œuv.*, xii. 57) that one of the reasons which made
him leave the Hermitage was the indiscretion of friends who
insisted on sending him letters by some conveyance that cost 4
francs, when it might equally well have been sent for as many
sous.

me." She then tersely remarks that it is not natural
to pass one's life in suspecting and insulting one's
friends, and that he abuses her patience. To this he
answered with still greater terseness that friendship
was extinct between them, and that he meant to leave
the Hermitage, but as his friends desired him to
remain there until the spring he would with her permission follow their counsel. Then she, with a final
thrust of impatience, in which we perhaps see the hand
of Grimm : " Since you meant to leave the Hermitage,
and felt you ought to do so, I am astonished that your
friends could detain you. For me, I don't consult
mine as to my duties, and I have nothing more to say
to you as to yours." This was the end. Rousseau
returned for a moment from ignoble petulance to
dignity and self-respect. He wrote to her that if it is
a misfortune to make a mistake in the choice of friends,
it is one not less cruel to awake from so sweet an error,
and two days before he wrote, he left her house. He
found a cottage at Montmorency, and thither, nerved
with fury, through snow and ice he carried his scanty
household goods (Dec. 15, 1757).[1]

We have a picture of him in this fatal month.
Diderot went to pay him a visit (Dec. 5). Rousseau
was alone at the bottom of his garden. As soon as
he saw Diderot, he cried in a voice of thunder and

---

[1] The sources of all this are in the following places. *Corr.*,
i. 416. Oct. 29. Streckeisen, i. 349. Nov. 12. *Conf.*, ix.
377. *Corr.*, i. 427. Nov. 23. *Conf.*, ix. 381. Dec. 1. *Ib.*,
ix. 383. Dec. 17.

with his eyes all aflame : " What have you come here for?" "I want to know whether you are mad or malicious." " You have known me for fifteen years ; you are well aware how little malicious I am, and I will prove to you that I am not mad : follow me." He then drew Diderot into a room, and proceeded to clear himself, by means of letters, of the charge of trying to make a breach between Saint Lambert and Madame d'Houdetot. They were in fact letters that convicted him, as we know, of trying to persuade Madame d'Houdetot of the criminality of her relations with her lover, and at the same time to accept himself in the very same relation. Of all this we have heard more than enough already. He was stubborn in the face of Diderot's remonstrance, and the latter left him in a state which he described in a letter to Grimm the same night. "I throw myself into your arms, like one who has had a shock of fright : that man intrudes into my work ; he fills me with trouble, and I am as if I had a damned soul at my side. May I never see him again ; he would make me believe in devils and hell."[1] And thus the unhappy man who had begun this episode in his life with confident ecstasy in the glories and clear music of spring, ended it looking out from a narrow chamber upon the sullen crimson of the wintry twilight and over fields silent in snow, with the haggard desperate gaze of a lost spirit.

[1] Diderot to Grimm ; D'Epinay, ii. 397. Diderot's *Œuv.*, xix. 446. See also 449 and 210.

CHAPTER VIII

MUSIC.

SIMPLIFICATION has already been used by us as the key-word to Rousseau's aims and influence. The scheme of musical notation with which he came to try his fortune in Paris in 1741, his published vindication of it, and his musical compositions afterwards all fall under this term. Each of them was a plea for the extrication of the simple from the cumbrousness of elaborated pedantry, and for a return to nature from the unmeaning devices of false art. And all tended alike in the popular direction, towards the extension of enjoyment among the common people, and the glorification of their simple lives and moods, in the art designed for the great.

The Village Soothsayer was one of the group of works which marked a revolution in the history of French music, by putting an end to the tyrannical tradition of Lulli and Rameau, and preparing the way through a middle stage of freshness, simplicity, naturalism, up to the noble severity of Gluck (1714-1787). This great composer, though a Bohemian by birth, found his first appreciation in a public that

had been trained by the Italian pastoral operas, of
which Rousseau's was one of the earliest produced in
France.   Grétri, the Fleming (1741-1813), who had
a hearty admiration for Jean Jacques, and out of a
sentiment of piety lived for a time in his Hermitage,
came in point of musical excellence between the group
of Rousseau, Philidor, Duni, and the rest, and Gluck.
" I have not produced exaltation in people's heads by
tragical superlative," Grétri said, " but I have revealed
the accent of truth, which I have impressed deeper
in men's hearts."[1]   These words express sufficiently
the kind of influence which Rousseau also had.   Crude
as the music sounds to us who are accustomed to more
sumptuous schools, we can still hear in it the note
which would strike a generation weary of Rameau.
It was the expression in one way of the same mood
which in another way revolted against paint, false hair,
and preposterous costume as of savages grown opulent.
Such music seems without passion or subtlety or depth
or magnificence.   Thus it had hardly any higher than
a negative merit, but it was the necessary preparation
for the acceptance of a more positive style, that should
replace both the elaborate false art of the older
French composers and the too colourless realism of
the pastoral comic opera, by the austere loveliness
and elevation of *Orfeo* and *Alceste.*

"In 1752 an Italian company visited Paris, and
performed at the Opera a number of pieces by Per-
golese, and other composers of their country.   A

[1] Quoted in Martin's *Hist. de France,* xvi. 158.

violent war arose, which agitated Paris far more
intensely than the defeat of Rossbach and the loss of
Canada did afterwards.   The quarrel between the
Parliament and the Clergy was at its height.   The
Parliament had just been exiled, and the gravest
confusion threatened the State.   The operatic quarrel
turned the excitement of the capital into another
channel.   Things went so far that the censor was
entreated to prohibit the printing of any work containing the damnable doctrine and position that
Italian music is good.   Rousseau took part enthusi-
astically with the Italians.[1]   His Letter on French
Music (1753) proved to the great fury of the people
concerned, that the French had no national music,
and that it would be so much the worse for them if
they ever had any.   Their language, so proper to be
the organ of truth and reason, was radically unfit
either for poetry or music.   All national music must
derive its principal characteristics from the language.
Now if there is a language in Europe fit for music, it
is certainly the Italian, for it is sweet, sonorous, harmonious, and more accentuated than any other, and
these are precisely the four qualities which adapt a
language to singing.   It is sweet because the articu-
lations are not composite, because the meeting of
consonants is both infrequent and soft, and because
a great number of the syllables being only formed of
vowels, frequent elisions make its pronunciation more
flowing.   It is sonorous because most of the vowels

[1] *Conf.*, viii. 197.   Grimm, *Corr. Lit.*, i. 27.

are full, because it is without composite diphthongs, because it has few or no nasal vowels. Again, the inversions of the Italian are far more favourable to true melody than the didactic order of French. And so onwards, with much close grappling of the matter. French melody does not exist; it is only a sort of modulated plain-song which has nothing agreeable in itself, which only pleases with the aid of a few capricious ornaments, and then only pleases those who have agreed to find it beautiful.[1]

The letter contains a variety of acute remarks upon music, and includes a vigorous protest against fugues, imitations, double designs, and the like. Scarcely any one succeeds in them, and success even when obtained hardly rewards the labour. As for counterfugues, double fugues, and "other difficult fooleries that the ear cannot endure nor the reason justify," they are evidently relics of barbarism and bad taste which only remain, like the porticoes of our gothic churches, to the disgrace of those who had patience enough to construct them.[2] The last phrase —and both Voltaire and Turgot used gothic architecture as the symbol for the supreme of rudeness and barbarism—shows that even a man who seems to run counter to the whole current of his time yet does not escape its influence.

Grimm, after remarking on the singularity of a demonstration of the impossibility of setting melody

[1] *Lettre sur la Musique Française*, 178, etc., 187.
[2] P. 197.

to French words on the part of a writer who had just
produced the Village Soothsayer, informs us that the
letter created a furious uproar, and set all Paris in a
blaze.   He had himself taken the side of the Italians
in an amusing piece of pleasantry, which became a
sort of classic model for similar facetiousness in other
controversies of the century.   The French, as he said,
forgive everything in favour of what makes them
laugh, but Rousseau talked reason and demolished
the pretensions of French music with great sounding
strokes as of an axe.[1]   Rousseau expected to be
assassinated, and gravely assures us that there was a
plot to that effect, as well as a design to put him in
the Bastille.   This we may fairly surmise to have
been a fiction of his own imagination, and the only
real punishment that overtook him was the loss of
his right to free admission to the Opera.   After what
he had said of the intolerable horrors of French music,
the directors of the theatre can hardly be accused of
vindictiveness in releasing him from them.[2]   Some
twenty years after (1774), when Paris was torn asunder
by the violence of the two great factions of the Gluck-
ists and Piccinists, Rousseau retracted his opinion as to
the impossibility of wedding melody to French words.[3]

[1] *Corr. Lit.*, i. 92.   His own piece was *Le petit prophète de
Bœhmischbroda*, the style of which will be seen in a subsequent
footnote.

[2] He was burnt in effigy by the musicians of the Opera.
Grimm, *Corr. Lit.*, i. 113.

[3] This is Turgot's opinion on the controversy (Letter to
Caillard, *Œuv.*, ii. 827) :—" Vous avez donc vu Jean-Jacques ;

He went as often as he could to hear the works both of Grétri and Gluck, and *Orfeo* delighted him, while the *Fausse magie* of the former moved him to say to the composer, "Your music stirs sweet sensations to which I thought my heart had long been closed."[1] This being so, and life being as brief as art is long, we need not further examine the controversy. It may be worth adding that Rousseau wrote some of the articles on music for the Encyclopædia, and that in 1767 he published a not inconsiderable Musical Dictionary of his own.

His scheme of a new musical notation and the principles on which he defended it are worth attention, because some of the ideas are now accepted as the base of a well-known and growing system of musical instruction. The aim of the scheme, let us say to begin with, was at once practical and popular; to reduce the difficulty of learning music to the lowest possible point, and so to bring the most delightful of the arts within the reach of the largest possible number of people. Hence, although he maintains the fitness of his scheme for instrumental as well as vocal

la musique est un excellent passe-port auprès de lui. Quant à l'impossibilité de faire de la musique française, je ne puis y croire, et votre raison ne me paraît pas bonne ; car il n'est point vrai que l'essence de la langue française est d'être sans accent. Point de conversation animée sans beaucoup d'accent ; mais l'accent est libre et déterminé seulement par l'affection de celui qui parle, sans être fixé par des conventions sur certaines syllabes, quoique nous ayons aussi dans plusieurs mots des syllabes dominantes qui seules peuvent être accentuées."

[1] Musset-Pathay, i. 289.

performances, it is clearly the latter which he has
most at heart, evidently for the reason that this is
the kind of music most accessible to the thousands,
and it was always the thousands of whom Rousseau
thought. This is the true distinction of music, it is
for the people ; and the best musical notation is that
which best enables persons to sing at sight. The
difficulty of the old notation had come practically
before him as a teacher. The quantity of details
which the pupil was forced to commit to memory
before being able to sing from the open book, struck
him then as the chief obstacle to anything like facility
in performance, and without some of this facility he
rightly felt that music must remain a luxury for the
few. So genuine was his interest in the matter, that
he was not very careful to fight for the originality of
his own scheme. Our present musical signs, he said,
are so imperfect and so inconvenient that it is no
wonder that several persons have tried to re-cast or
amend them ; nor is it any wonder that some of them
should have hit upon the same device in selecting the
signs most natural and proper, such as numerical
figures. As much, however, depends on the way of
dealing with these figures, as with their adoption, and
here he submitted that his own plan was as novel as
it was advantageous.[1] Thus we have to bear in mind
that Rousseau's scheme was above all things a
practical device, contrived for making the teach-

[1] Preface to *Dissertation sur la Musique Moderne*, pp.
32, 33.

ing and the learning of musical elements an easier
process.[1]

The chief element of the project consists in the
substitution of a relative series of notes or symbols in
place of an absolute series. In the common notation
any given note, say the A of the treble clef, is uni-
formly represented by the same symbol, namely, the
position of second space in the clef, whatever key it
may belong to. Rousseau, insisting on the varying
quality impressed on any tone of a given pitch by the
key-note of the scale to which it belongs, protested
against the same name being given to the tone, however
the quality of it might vary. Thus Re or D, which
is the second tone in the key of C, ought, according
to him, to have a different name when found as the
fifth in the key of G, and in every case the name
should at once indicate the interval of a tone from its
key-note. His mode of effecting this change is as
follows. The names *ut, re,* and the rest, are kept for
the fixed order of the tones, C, D, E, and the rest.
The key of a piece is shown by prefixing one of these
symbols, and this determines the absolute quality of
the melody as to pitch. That settled, every tone is
expressed by a number bearing a relation to the key-
note. This tonic note is represented by one, the
other six tones of the scale are expressed by the
numbers from two to seven. In the popular Tonic

[1] I am indebted to Mr. James Sully, M.A., for furnishing me
with notes on a technical subject with which I have too little
acquaintance.

Sol-Fa notation, which corresponds so closely to Rousseau's in principle, the key-note is always styled Do, and the other symbols, *mi*, *la*, and the rest, indicate at once the relative position of these tones in their particular key or scale.   Here the old names were preserved as being easily sung ; Rousseau selected numbers because he supposed that they best expressed the generation of the sounds.[1]

Rousseau attempted to find a theoretic base for this symbolic establishment of the relational quality of tones, and he dimly guessed that the order of the harmonics or upper tones of a given tonic would furnish a principle for forming the familiar major scale,[2] but his knowledge of the order was faulty. He was perhaps groping after the idea by which Professor Helmholtz has accounted for the various mental effects of the several intervals in a key— namely, the degree of natural affinity, measured by means of the upper tones, existing between the given tone and its tonic.   Apart from this, however, the practical value of his ideas in instruction in singing is clearly shown by the circumstance that at any given time many thousands of young children are now being taught to read melody in the Sol-Fa notation in a few weeks.   This shows how right Rousseau was in continually declaring the ease of hitting a particular tone, when the relative position of the tone in respect to the key-note is clearly manifested.   A singer in trying to hit the tone is compelled to measure the interval

[1] *Dissertation*, p. 42.   [2] P. 52.

between it and the preceding tone, and the simplest
and easiest mode of doing this is to associate every
tone with the tonics, thus constituting it a term of a
relation with this fundamental tone.

Rousseau made a mistake when he supposed that
his ideas were just as applicable to instrumental as
they were to vocal music. The requirements of the
singer are not those of the player. To a performer
on the piano, who has to light rapidly and simultane-
ously on a number of tones, or to a violinist who has
to leap through several octaves with great rapidity,
the most urgent need is that of a definite and fixed
mark, by which the absolute pitch of each successive
tone may be at once recognised. Neither of these
has any time to think about the melodious relation of
the tones; it is quite as much as they can do to find
their place on the key-board or the string. Rousseau's
scheme, or any similar one, fails to supply the clear
and obvious index to pitch supplied by the old system.
Old Rameau pointed this out to Rousseau when the
scheme was laid before him, and Rousseau admitted
that the objection was decisive,[1] though his admission
was not practically deterrent.

His device for expressing change of octave by
means of points would render the rapid seizing of a
particular tone by the performer still more difficult,
and it is strange that he should have preferred this
to the other plan suggested, of indicating height of
octave by visible place above or below a horizontal

[1] *Conf.*, vii. 18, 19.   Also *Dissertation*, pp. 74, 75.

line. Again, his attempt to simplify the many
varieties of musical time by reducing them all to the
two modes of double and triple time, though laudable
enough, yet implies an imperfect recognition of the
full meaning of time, by omitting all reference to the
distribution of accent and to the average time value
of the tones in a particular movement.

CHAPTER IX.

VOLTAIRE AND D'ALEMBERT.

EVERYBODY in the full tide of the eighteenth century had something to do with Voltaire, from serious personages like Frederick the Great and Turgot, down to the sorriest poetaster who sent his verses to be corrected or bepraised. Rousseau's debt to him in the days of his unformed youth we have already seen, as well as the courtesies with which they approached one another, when Richelieu employed the struggling musician to make some modifications in the great man's unconsidered court-piece. Neither of them then dreamed that their two names were destined to form the great literary antithesis of the century. In the ten years that elapsed between their first interchange of letters and their first fit of coldness, it must have been tolerably clear to either of them, if either of them gave thought to the matter, that their dissidence was increasing and likely to increase. Their methods were different, their training different, their points of view different, and above all these things, their temperaments were different by a whole heaven's breadth.

A great number of excellent and pointed half-truths have been uttered by various persons in illustration of all these contrasts.   The philosophy of Voltaire, for instance, is declared to be that of the happy, while Rousseau is the philosopher of the unhappy.   Voltaire steals away their faith from those who doubt, while Rousseau strikes doubt into the mind of the unbeliever. The gaiety of the one saddens, while the sadness of the other consoles.   If we pass from the marked divergence in tendencies, which is imperfectly hinted at in such sayings as these, to the divergence between them in all the fundamental conditions of intellectual and moral life, then the variation which divided the revolutionary stream into two channels, flowing broadly apart through unlike regions and climates down to the great sea, is intelligible enough.   Voltaire was the arch-representative of all those elements in contemporary thought, its curiosity, irreverence, intrepidity, vivaciousness, rationality, to which, as we have so often had to say, Rousseau's temperament and his Genevese spirit made him profoundly antipathetic.   Voltaire was the great high priest, robed in the dazzling vestments of poetry and philosophy and history, of that very religion of knowledge and art which Rousseau declared to be the destroyer of the felicity of men.   The glitter has faded away from Voltaire's philosophic raiment since those days, and his laurel bough lies a little leafless.   Still this can never make us forget that he was in his day and generation one of the sovereign emancipators, because he awoke one dormant set of energies, just as Rousseau presently came to awake another set. Each was a power, not merely by virtue of some singular pre-eminence of understanding or mysterious unshared insight of his own, but for a far deeper reason. No partial and one-sided direction can permanently satisfy the manifold aspirations and faculties of the human mind in the great average of common men, and it is the common average of men to whom exceptional thinkers speak, whom they influence, and by whom they are in turn influenced, depressed, or buoyed up, just as a painter or a dramatist is affected. Voltaire's mental constitution made him eagerly objective, a seeker of true things, quivering for action, admirably sympathetic with all life and movement, a spirit restlessly traversing the whole world. Rousseau, far different from this, saw in himself a reflected micro-cosm of the outer world, and was content to take that instead of the outer world, and as its truest version. He made his own moods the premises from which he deduced a system of life for humanity, and so far as humanity has shared his moods or some parts of them, his system was true, and has been accepted. To him the bustle of the outer world was only a hind-rance to that process of self-absorption which was his way of interpreting life. Accessible only to interests of emotion and sense, he was saved from intellectual sterility, and made eloquent, by the vehemence of his emotion and the fire of his senses. He was a master example of sensibility,

as Voltaire was a master example of clear-eyed
penetration.

This must not be taken for a rigid piece of
mutually exclusive division, for the edges of character
are not cut exactly sharp, as words are. Especially
when any type is intense, it seems to meet and touch
its opposite. Just as Voltaire's piercing activity and
soundness of intelligence made him one of the humanest
of men, so Rousseau's emotional susceptibility endowed
him with the gift of a vision that carried far into the
social depths. It was a very early criticism on the
pair, that Voltaire wrote on more subjects, but that
Rousseau was the more profound. In truth one was
hardly much more profound than the other. Rousseau
had the sonorousness of speech which popular confusion of thought is apt to identify with depth.
And he had seriousness. If profundity means the
quality of seeing to the heart of subjects, Rousseau
had in a general way rather less of it than the
shrewd-witted crusher of the Infamous. What the
distinction really amounts to is that Rousseau had a
strong feeling for certain very important aspects of
human life, which Voltaire thought very little about,
or never thought about at all, and that while Voltaire
was concerned with poetry, history, literature, and the
more ridiculous parts of the religious superstition of
his time, Rousseau thought about social justice and
duty and God and the spiritual consciousness of men,
with a certain attempt at thoroughness and system.
As for the substance of his thinking, as we have

already seen in the Discourses, and shall soon have an opportunity of seeing still more clearly, it was often as thin and hollow as if he had belonged to the company of the epigrammatical, who, after all, have far less of a monopoly of shallow thinking than is often supposed. The prime merit of Rousseau, in comparing him with the brilliant chief of the rationalistic school of the time, is his reverence; reverence for moral worth in however obscure intellectual company, for the dignity of human character and the loftiness of duty, for some of those cravings of the human mind after the divine and incommensurable, which may indeed often be content with solutions proved by long time and slow experience to be inadequate, but which are closely bound up with the highest elements of nobleness of soul.

It was this spiritual part of him which made Rousseau a third great power in the century, between the Encyclopædic party and the Church. He recognised a something in men, which the Encyclopædists treated as a chimera imposed on the imagination by theologians and others for their own purposes. And he recognised this in a way which did not offend the rational feeling of the times, as the Catholic dogmas offended it. In a word he was religious. In being so, he separated himself from Voltaire and his school, who did passably well without religion. Again, he was a puritan. In being this, he was cut off from the intellectually and morally unreformed church, which was then the organ of religion in France. Nor is this

all. It was Rousseau, and not the feeble contro-
versialists put up from time to time by the Jesuits
and other ecclesiastical bodies, who proved the effective
champion of religion, and the only power who could
make head against the triumphant onslaught of the
Voltaireans. He gave up Christian dogmas and
mysteries, and, throwing himself with irresistible
ardour upon the emotions in which all religions have
their root and their power, he breathed new life into
them, he quickened in men a strong desire to have
them satisfied, and he beat back the army of emancipators with the loud and incessantly repeated cry
that they were not come to deliver the human mind,
but to root out all its most glorious and consolatory
attributes.   This immense achievement accomplished,
—the great framework of a faith in God and immortality and providential government of the world thus
preserved, it was an easy thing by and by for the
churchmen to come back, and once more unpack and
restore to their old places the temporarily discredited
paraphernalia of dogma and mystery.   How far all this
was good or bad for the mental elevation of France
and Europe, we shall have a better opportunity of
considering presently.

We have now only to glance at the first skirmishes
between the religious reactionist, on the one side,
and, on the other, the leader of the school who
believed that men are better employed in thinking
as accurately, and knowing as widely, and living as
humanely, as all those difficult processes are possible,

than in wearying themselves in futile search after
gods who dwell on inaccessible heights.

Voltaire had acknowledged Rousseau's gift of the
second Discourse with his usual shrewd pleasantry :
" I have received your new book against the human
race, and thank you for it. Never was such cleverness
used in the design of making us all stupid. One
longs in reading your book to walk on all fours. But
as I have lost that habit for more than sixty years, I
feel unhappily the impossibility of resuming it. Nor
can I embark in search of the savages of Canada,
because the maladies to which I am condemned render
a European surgeon necessary to me ; because war is
going on in those regions ; and because the example
of our actions has made the savages nearly as bad as
ourselves. So I content myself with being a very
peaceable savage in the solitude which I have chosen
near your native place, where you ought to be too."
After an extremely inadequate discussion of one or two
points in the essay,[1] he concludes :—" I am informed
that your health is bad ; you ought to come to set it
up again in your native air, to enjoy freedom, to drink
with me the milk of our cows and browse our grass."[2]
Rousseau replied to all this in a friendly way, recognising Voltaire as his chief, and actually at the very
moment when he tells us that the corrupting presence
of the arrogant and seductive man at Geneva helped

[1] See above p. 149.
[2] Voltaire to Rousseau. Aug. 30, 1755.

to make the idea of returning to Geneva odious to him, hailing him in such terms as these :—" Sensible of the honour you do my country, I share the gratitude of my fellow-citizens, and hope that it will increase when they have profited by the lessons that you of all men are able to give them. Embellish the asylum you have chosen ; enlighten a people worthy of your instruction ; and do you who know so well how to paint virtue and freedom, teach us to cherish them in our walls."[1]

Within a year, however, the bright sky became a little clouded. In 1756 Voltaire published one of the most sincere, energetic, and passionate pieces to be found in the whole literature of the eighteenth century, his poem on the great earthquake of Lisbon (November 1755). No such word had been heard in Europe since the terrible images in which Pascal had figured the doom of man. It was the reaction of one who had begun life by refuting Pascal with doctrines of cheerfulness drawn from the optimism of Pope and Leibnitz, who had done Pope's Essay on Man (1732-34) into French verse as late as 1751,[2] and whose imagination, already sombred by the triumphant cruelty and superstition which raged around him, was suddenly struck with horror by a catastrophe which, in a world where whatever is is best, destroyed hundreds of human creatures in the smoking ashes and engulfed wreck of their city. How, he cried, can you persist in talking of the deliberate will of a free

[1] *Corr.*, i. 237. Sept. 10, 1755.   [2] *La Loi Naturelle.*

and benevolent God, whose eternal laws necessitated
such an appalling climax of misery and injustice as
this? Was the disaster retributive? If so, why is
Lisbon in ashes, while Paris dances? The enigma is
desperate and inscrutable, and the optimist lives in
the paradise of the fool. We ask in vain what we
are, where we are, whither we go, whence we came.
We are tormented atoms on a clod of earth, whom
death at last swallows up, and with whom destiny
meanwhile makes cruel sport. The past is only a
disheartening memory, and if the tomb destroys the
thinking creature, how frightful is the present!

Whatever else we may say of Voltaire's poem, it
was at least the first sign of the coming reaction of
sympathetic imagination against the polished common
sense of the great Queen Anne school, which had for
more than a quarter of a century such influence in
Europe.[1] It is a little odd that Voltaire, the most
brilliant and versatile branch of this stock, should
have broken so energetically away from it, and that
he should have done so, shows how open and how
strong was the feeling in him for reality and actual
circumstance.

Rousseau was amazed that a man overwhelmed
as Voltaire was with prosperity and glory, should
declaim against the miseries of this life and pro-

[1] In 1754 the Berlin Academy proposed for a prize essay,
An Examination of Pope's System, and Lessing the next year
wrote a pamphlet to show that Pope had no system, but only
a patchwork. See Mr. Pattison's *Introduction to Pope's Essay
on Man*, p. 12. Sime's *Lessing*, i. 128.

nounce that all is evil and vanity.   "Voltaire in
seeming always to believe in God, never really believed
in anybody but the devil, since his pretended God is
a maleficent being who according to him finds all his
pleasure in working mischief.   The absurdity of this
doctrine is especially revolting in a man crowned
with good things of every sort, and who from the
midst of his own happiness tries to fill his fellow-
creatures with despair, by the cruel and terrible
image of the serious calamities from which he is himself free."[1]

As if any doctrine could be more revolting than
this which Rousseau so quietly takes for granted, that
if it is well with me and I am free from calamities,
then there must needs be a beneficent ruler of the
universe, and the calamities of all the rest of the
world, if by chance they catch the fortunate man's
eye, count for nothing in our estimate of the method
of the supposed divine government.   It is hard to
imagine a more execrable emotion than the complacent
religiosity of the prosperous.   Voltaire is more admirable in nothing than in the ardent humanity and far-
spreading lively sympathy with which he interested
himself in all the world's fortunes, and felt the catastrophe of Lisbon as profoundly as if the Geneva at
his gates had been destroyed.   He relished his own
prosperity keenly enough, but his prosperity became
ashes in his mouth when he heard of distress or wrong,
and he did not rest until he had moved heaven and

[1] *Conf.* ix. 276.

earth to soothe the distress and repair the wrong.   It
was his impatience in the face of the evils of the time
which wrung from him this desperate cry, and it is precisely because these evils did not touch him in his own
person, that he merits the greater honour for the sur-
passing energy and sincerity of his feeling for them.

Rousseau, however, whose biographer has no such
stories to tell as those of Calas and La Barre, Sirven
and Lally, but only tales of a maiden wrongfully
accused of theft, and a friend left senseless on the
pavement of a strange town, and a benefactress abandoned to the cruelty of her fate, still was moved in
the midst of his erotic visions in the forest of Montmorency to speak a jealous word in vindication of the
divine government of our world.   For him at any
rate life was then warm and the day bright and the
earth very fair, and he lauded his gods accordingly.
It was his very sensuousness, as we are so often saying, that made him religious.   The optimism which
Voltaire wished to destroy was to him a sovereign
element of comfort.   "Pope's poem," he says, "softens
my misfortunes and inclines me to patience, while
yours sharpens all my pains, excites me to murmuring,
and reduces me to despair.   Pope and Leibnitz exhort
me to resignation by declaring calamities to be a
necessary effect of the nature and constitution of the
universe.   You cry, Suffer for ever, unhappy wretch ;
if there be a God who created thee, he could have
stayed thy pains if he would : hope for no end to
them, for there is no reason to be discerned for thy

existence, except to suffer and to perish."[1] Rousseau then proceeds to argue the matter, but he says nothing really to the point which Pope had not said before, and said far more effectively. He begins, however, originally enough by a triumphant reference to his own great theme of the superiority of the natural over the civil state. Moral evil is our own work, the result of our liberty; so are most of our physical evils, except death, and that is mostly an evil only from the preparations that we make for it. Take the case of Lisbon. Was it nature who collected the twenty thousand houses, all seven stories high? If the people of Lisbon had been dispersed over the face of the country, as wild tribes are, they would have fled at the first shock, and they would have been seen the next day twenty leagues away, as gay as if nothing had happened. And how many of them perished in the attempt to rescue clothes or papers or money? Is it not true that the person of a man is now, thanks to civilisation, the least part of himself, and is hardly worth saving after loss of the rest? Again, there are some events which lose much of their horror when we look at them closely. A premature death is not always a real evil and may be a relative good; of the people crushed to death under the ruins of Lisbon, many no doubt thus escaped still worse calamities. And is it worse to be killed swiftly than to await death in prolonged anguish?[2]

[1] *Corr.*, i. 289-316.   Aug. 18, 1756.
[2] Joseph De Maistre put all this much more acutely; *Soirées*, iv.

The good of the whole is to be sought before the
good of the part. Although the whole material universe ought not to be dearer to its Creator than a
single thinking and feeling being, yet the system of
the universe which produces, preserves, and perpetuates
all thinking and feeling beings, ought to be dearer to
him than any one of them, and he may, notwithstanding his goodness, or rather by reason of his goodness,
sacrifice something of the happiness of individuals to
the preservation of the whole. "That the dead body
of a man should feed worms or wolves or plants is
not, I admit, a compensation for the death of such a
man; but if in the system of this universe, it is
necessary for the preservation of the human race that
there should be a circulation of substance between
men, animals, vegetables, then the particular mishap
of an individual contributes to the general good. I
die, I am eaten by worms; but my children, my
brothers, will live as I have lived; my body enriches
the earth of which they will consume the fruits; and
so I do, by the order of nature and for all men, what
Codrus, Curtius, the Decii, and a thousand others,
did of their own free will for a small part of men."
(p. 305.)

All this is no doubt very well said, and we are
bound to accept it as true doctrine. Although, however, it may make resignation easier by explaining
the nature of evil, it does not touch the point of Voltaire's outburst, which is that evil exists, and exists
in shapes which it is a mere mockery to associate with

the omnipotence of a benevolent controller of the
world's forces. According to Rousseau, if we go to
the root of what he means, there is no such thing as
evil, though much that to our narrow and impatient
sight has the look of it. This may be true if we use
that fatal word in an arbitrary and unreal sense, for
the avoidable, the consequent without antecedent, or
antecedent without consequent. If we consent to talk
in this way, and only are careful to define terms so
that there is no doubt as to their meaning, it is hardly
deniable that evil is a mere word and not a reality,
and whatever is is indeed right and best, because no
better is within our reach. Voltaire, however, like
the man of sense that he was, exclaimed that at any
rate relatively to us poor creatures the existence of
pain, suffering, waste, whether caused or uncaused,
whether in accordance with stern immutable law or
mere divine caprice, is a most indisputable reality :
from our point of view it is a cruel puerility to cry
out at every calamity and every iniquity that all is
well in the best of possible worlds, and to sing hymns
of praise and glory to the goodness and mercy of a
being of supreme might, who planted us in this evil
state and keeps us in it. Voltaire's is no perfect
philosophy ; indeed it is not a philosophy at all, but
a passionate ejaculation ; but it is perfect in comparison
with a cut and dried system like this of Rousseau's,
which rests on a mocking juggle with phrases, and
the substitution by dexterous sleight of hand of one
definition for another.

Rousseau really gives up the battle, by confessing frankly that the matter is beyond the light of reason, and that, "if the theist only founds his sentiment on probabilities, the atheist with still less precision only founds his on the alternative possibilities." The objections on both sides are insoluble, because they turn on things of which men can have no veritable idea; "yet I believe in God as strongly as I believe any other truth, because believing and not believing are the last things in the world that depend on me." So be it. But why take the trouble to argue in favour of one side of an avowedly insoluble question? It was precisely because he felt that the objections on both sides cannot be answered, that Voltaire, hastily or not, cried out that he faced the horrors of such a catastrophe as the Lisbon earthquake without a glimpse of consolation. The upshot of Rousseau's remonstrance only amounted to this, that he could not furnish one with any consolation out of the armoury of reason, that he himself found this consolation, but in a way that did not at all depend upon his own effort or will, and was therefore as incommunicable as the advantage of having a large appetite or being six feet high. The reader of Rousseau becomes accustomed to this way of dealing with subjects of discussion. We see him using his reason as adroitly as he knows how for three-fourths of the debate, and then he suddenly flings himself back with a triumphant kind of weariness into the buoyant waters of emotion and sentiment. "You sir, who are a poet," once said Madame d'Epinay

to Saint Lambert, "will agree with me that the existence of a Being, eternal, all powerful, and of sovereign
intelligence, is at any rate the germ of the finest
enthusiasm."[1]	To take this position and cleave to it
may be very well, but why spoil its dignity and repose
by an unmeaning and superfluous flourish of the
weapons of the reasoner?

With the same hasty change of direction Rousseau
says the true question is not whether each of us
suffers or not, but whether it is good that the universe
should be, and whether our misfortunes were inevit-
able in its constitution.	Then within a dozen lines
he admits that there can be no direct proof either
way ; we must content ourselves with settling it by
means of inference from the perfections of God.	Of
course, it is clear that in the first place what Rousseau
calls the true question consists of two quite distinct
questions.	Is the universe in its present ordering on
the whole good relatively either to men, or to all
sentient creatures?	Next was evil an inevitable
element in that ordering?	Second, this way of
putting it does not in the least advance the case
against Voltaire, who insisted that no fine phrases
ought to hide from us the dreadful power and crush-
ing reality of evil and the desolate plight in which
we are left.	This is no exhaustive thought, but a
deep cry of anguish at the dark lot of men, and of
just indignation against the philosophy which to creatures asking for bread gave the brightly polished

[1] Madame d'Epinay, *Mém.*, i. 380.

stone of sentimental theism. Rousseau urged that
Voltaire robbed men of their only solace. What
Voltaire really did urge was that the solace derived
from the attribution of humanity and justice to the
Supreme Being, and from the metaphysical account
of evil, rests on too narrow a base either to cover the
facts, or to be a true solace to any man who thinks
and observes. He ought to have gone on, if it had
only been possible in those times, to persuade his
readers that there is no solace attainable, except that
of an energetic fortitude, and that we do best to go
into life not in a softly lined silken robe, but with a
sharp sword and armour thrice tempered. As between
himself and Rousseau, he saw much the more keenly
of the two, and this was because he approached the
matter from the side of the facts, while the latter
approached it from the side of his own mental comfort
and the preconceptions involved in it.

The most curious part of this curious letter is the
conclusion, where Rousseau, loosely wandering from
his theme, separates Voltaire from the philosopher,
and beseeches him to draw up a moral code or profession of civil faith that should contain positively
the social maxims that everybody should be bound to
admit, and negatively the intolerant maxims that
everybody should be forced to reject as seditious.
Every religion in accord with the code should be
allowed, and every religion out of accord with it pro-
scribed, or a man might be free to have no other
religion but the code itself.

Voltaire was much too clear-headed a person to take any notice of nonsense like this. Rousseau's letter remained unanswered, nor is there any reason to suppose that Voltaire ever got through it, though Rousseau chose to think that *Candide* (1759) was meant for a reply to him.[1] He is careful to tell us that he never read that incomparable satire, for which one would be disposed to pity any one except Rousseau, whose appreciation of wit, if not of humour also, was probably more deficient than in any man who ever lived, either in Geneva or any other country fashioned after Genevan guise. Rousseau's next letter to Voltaire was four years later, and by that time the alienation which had no definitely avowed cause, and can be marked by no special date, had become complete. "I hate you, in fact," he concluded, "since you have so willed it; but I hate you like a man still worthier to have loved you, if you had willed it. Of all the sentiments with which my heart was full towards you, there only remains the admiration that we cannot refuse to your fine genius, and love for your writings. If there is nothing in you which I can honour but your talents, that is no fault of mine."[2] We know that Voltaire did not take reproach with serenity, and he behaved with bitter

---

[1] *Conf.*, ix. 277. Also *Corr.*, iii. 326. March 11, 1764. Tronchin's long letter, to which Rousseau refers in this passage, is given in M. Streckeisen-Moultou's collection, i. 323, and is interesting to people who care to know how Voltaire looked to a doctor who saw him closely.

[2] *Corr.*, ii. 132. June 17, 1760. Also *Conf.*, x. 91.

violence towards Rousseau in circumstances when
silence would have been both more magnanimous and
more humane. Rousseau occasionally, though not
very often, retaliated in the same vein.[1] On the
whole his judgment of Voltaire, when calmly given,
was not meant to be unkind. "Voltaire's first
impulse," he said, "is to be good; it is reflection that
makes him bad." [2] Tronchin had said in the same
way that Voltaire's heart was the dupe of his understanding. Rousseau is always trying to like him, he
always recognises him as the first man of the time,
and he subscribed his mite for the erection of a statue
to him. It was the satire and mockery in Voltaire
which irritated Rousseau more than the doctrines or
denial of doctrine which they cloaked; in his eyes
sarcasm was always the veritable dialect of the evil
power. It says something for the sincerity of his
efforts after equitable judgment, that he should have

---

[1] Some other interesting references to Voltaire in Rousseau's
letters are—ii. 170 (Nov. 29, 1760), denouncing Voltaire as "that
trumpet of impiety, that fine genius, and that low soul," and
so forth ; iii. 29 (Oct. 30, 1762), accusing Voltaire of malicious
intrigues against him in Switzerland ; iii. 168 (Mar. 21, 1763),
that if there is to be any reconciliation, Voltaire must make
first advances ; iii. 280 (Dec., 1763), described a trick played
by Voltaire ; iv. 40 (Jan. 31, 1765) 64 ; *Corr.*, v. 74 (Jan. 5,
1767), replying to Voltaire's calumnious account of his early
life ; note on this subject giving Voltaire the lie direct, iv. 150
(May 31, 1765) ; the *Lettre à D'Alembert*, p. 193, etc.

[2] Bernardin St. Pierre, xii. 96. In the same sense, in
Dusaulx, *Mes Rapports avec J. J. R.* (Paris : 1798), p. 101. See
also *Corr.*, iv. 254. Dec. 30, 1765. And again, iv. 276, Feb.
23, 1766, and p. 356.

had the patience to discern some of the fundamental merit of the most remorseless and effective mocker that ever made superstition look mean, and its doctors ridiculous.

II.

Voltaire was indirectly connected with Rousseau's energetic attack upon another great Encyclopædist leader, the famous Letter to D'Alembert on Stage Plays. "There," Rousseau said afterwards, "is my favourite book, my Benjamin, because I produced it without effort, at the first inspiration, and in the most lucid moments of my life." [1] Voltaire, who to us figures so little as a poet and dramatist, was to himself and to his contemporaries of this date a poet and dramatist before all else, the author of *Zaïre* and *Mahomet*, rather than of *Candide* and the *Philosophical Dictionary*. D'Alembert was Voltaire's staunchest henchman. He only wrote his article on Geneva for the Encyclopædia to gratify the master. Fresh from a visit to him when he composed it, he took occasion to regret that the austerity of the tradition of the city deprived it of the manifold advantages of a theatre. This suggestion had its origin partly in a desire to promote something that would please the eager vanity of the dramatist whom Geneva now had for so close a neighbour, and who had just set her the example by setting up a theatre of his own; and partly, also, because it gave the writer an opportunity

[1] Dusaulx, p. 102.

of denouncing the intolerant rigour with which the church nearer home treated the stage and all who appeared on it. Geneva was to set an example that could not be resisted, and France would no longer see actors on the one hand pensioned by the government, and on the other an object of anathema, excommunicated by priests and regarded with contempt by citizens.[1]

The inveterate hostility of the church to the theatre was manifested by the French ecclesiastics in the full eighteenth century as bitterly as ever. The circumstance that Voltaire was the great play-writer of the time would not tend to soften their traditional prejudice, and the persecution of players by priests was in some sense an episode of the war between the priest and the philosophers. The latter took up the cause of the stage partly because they hoped to make the drama an effective rival to the teaching of pulpit and confessional, partly from their natural sympathy with an elevated form of intellectual manifestation, and partly from their abhorrence of the practical inhumanity with which the officers of the church treated stage performers. While people of quality eagerly sought the society of those who furnished them as much diversion in private as in public, the church refused to all players the marriage blessing; when an actor or actress wished to marry, they were

---

[1] This part of D'Alembert's article is reproduced in Rousseau's preface, and the whole is given at the end of the volume in M. Auguis's edition, p. 409.

obliged to renounce the stage, and the Archbishop
of Paris diligently resisted evasion or subterfuge.[1]
The atrocities connected with the refusal of burial, as
well in the case of players as of philosophers, are
known to all readers in a dozen illustrious instances,
from Molière and Adrienne Lecouvreur downwards.

Here, as along the whole line of the battle between
new light and old prejudice, Rousseau took part, if
not with the church, at least against its adversaries.
His point of view was at bottom truly puritanical.
Jeremy Collier in his *Short View of the Profaneness and
Immorality of the English Stage* (1698) takes up quite
a different position.   This once famous piece was not
a treatment of the general question, but an attack on
certain specific qualities of the plays of his time—their
indecency of phrase, their oaths, their abuse of the
clergy, the gross libertinism of the characters.   One
can hardly deny that this was richly deserved by the
English drama of the Restoration, and Collier's strictures were not applicable, nor meant to apply, either
to the ancients, for he has a good word even for
Aristophanes, or to the French drama.   Bossuet's
loftier denunciation, like Rousseau's, was puritanical,
and it extended to the whole body of stage plays.   He
objected to the drama as a school of concupiscence, as
a subtle or gross debaucher of the gravity and purity
of the understanding, as essentially a charmer of the
senses, and therefore the most equivocal and untrust-

[1] Goncourt, *Femme au* 18*ième siècle*, p. 256.   Grimm, *Corr.
Lit.*, vi. 248.

worthy of teachers. He appeals to the fathers, to
Scripture, to Plato, and even to Christ, who cried,
Woe unto you that laugh.[1] There is a fine austerity
about Bossuet's energetic criticism ; it is so free from
breathless eagerness, and so severe without being thinly
bitter. The churchmen of a generation or two later
had fallen from this height into gloomy peevishness.

Rousseau's letter on the theatre, it need hardly be
said, is meant to be an appeal to the common sense
and judgment of his readers, and not conceived in the
ecclesiastical tone of unctuous anathema and fulgurant
menace. It is no bishop's pastoral, replete with sole-
cisms of thought and idiom, but a piece of firm dialectic
in real matter. His position is this : that the moral
effect of the stage can never be salutary in itself,
while it may easily be extremely pernicious, and that
the habit of frequenting the theatre, the taste for
imitating the style of the actors, the cost in money,
the waste in time, and all the other accessory conditions, apart from the morality of the matter represented, are bad things in themselves, absolutely and
in every circumstance. Secondly, these effects in all
kinds are specially bad in relation to the social condition and habits of Geneva.[2] The first part of the

---

[1] *Maximes sur la Comédie*, § 15, etc. They were written in
reply to a plea for Comedy by Caffaro, a Jesuit father.

[2] The letter may be conveniently divided into three parts :
I. pp. 1-89, II. pp. 90-145, III. pp. 146 to the end. Of course
if Rousseau in saying that tragedy leads to pity through terror,
was thinking of the famous passage in the sixth chapter of Aristotle's *Poetics*, he was guilty of a shocking mistranslation.

discussion is an ingenious answer to some of the now trite pleas for the morality of the drama, such as that tragedy leads to pity through terror, that comedy corrects men while amusing them, that both make virtue attractive and vice hateful.[1]   Rousseau insists with abundance of acutely chosen illustration that the pity that is awaked by tragedy is a fleeting emotion which subsides when the curtain falls; that comedy as often as not amuses men at the expense of old age, uncouth virtue, paternal carefulness, and other objects which we should be taught rather to revere than to ridicule; and that both tragedy and comedy, instead of making vice hateful, constantly win our sympathy for it.   Is not the French stage, he asks, as much the triumph of great villains, like Catilina, Mahomet, Atreus, as of illustrious heroes?

This rude handling of accepted commonplace is always one of the most interesting features in Rousseau's polemic.   It was of course a characteristic of the eighteenth century always to take up the ethical and high prudential view of whatever had to be justified, and Rousseau seems from this point to have been successful in demolishing arguments which might hold of Greek tragedy at its best, but which certainly do not hold of any other dramatic forms.   The childishness of the old criticism which attaches the label of some moral from the copybook to each piece, as its

[1] Some of the arguments seem drawn from Plato; see, besides the well-known passages in the *Republic*, the *Laws*, iv. 719, and still more directly, *Gorgias*, 502.

lesson and point of moral aim, is evident. In repudiating this Rousseau was certainly right.[1] Both the
assailants and the defenders of the stage, however,
commit the double error, first of supposing that the
drama is always the same thing, from the Agamemnon
down to the last triviality of a London theatre, and
next of pitching the discussion in too high a key, as
if the effect or object of a stage play in the modern
era, where grave sentiment clothes itself in other
forms, were substantially anything more serious than
an evening's amusement. Apart from this, and in so
far as the discussion is confined to the highest dramatic
expression, the true answer to Rousseau is now a very
plain one. The drama does not work in the sphere
of direct morality, though like everything else in the
world it has a moral or immoral aspect. It is an art
of ideal presentation, not concerned with the inculcation of immediate practical lessons, but producing a
stir in all our sympathetic emotions, quickening the
imagination, and so communicating a wider life to the
character of the spectator. This is what the drama
in the hands of a worthy master does ; it is just what
noble composition in music does, and there is no more
directly moralising effect in the one than in the other.
You must trust to the sum of other agencies to guide
the interest and sympathy thus quickened into channels

[1] Yet D'Alembert in his very cool and sensible reply (p. 245)
repeats the old saws, as that in *Catilina* we learn the lesson of
the harm which may be done to the human race by the abuse of
great talents, and so forth.

of right action.   Rousseau, like most other controver-
sialists, makes an attack of which the force rests on
the assumption that the special object of the attack
is the single influencing element and the one decisive
instrument in making men bad or good.   What he
says about the drama would only be true if the public
went to the play all day long, and were accessible to
no other moral force whatever, modifying and counteracting such lessons as they might learn at the theatre.
He failed here as in the wider controversy on the
sciences and arts, to consider the particular subject
of discussion in relation to the whole of the general
medium in which character moves, and by whose
manifold action and reaction it is incessantly affected
and variously shaped.

So when he passed on from the theory of dramatic
morality to the matter which he had more at heart,
namely, the practical effects of introducing the drama
into Geneva, he keeps out of sight all the qualities in
the Genevese citizen which would protect him against
the evil influence of the stage, though it is his anxiety
for the preservation of these very qualities that gives
all its fire to his eloquence.   If the citizen really was
what Rousseau insisted that he was, then his virtues
would surely neutralise the evil of the drama; if not,
the drama would do him no harm.   We need not
examine the considerations in which Rousseau pointed
out the special reasons against introducing a theatre
into his native town.   It would draw the artisans
away from their work, cause wasteful expenditure of

money in amusements, break up the harmless and inexpensive little clubs of men and the social gatherings of women. The town was not populous enough to support a theatre, therefore the government would have to provide one, and this would mean increased taxation. All this was the secondary and merely colourable support by argumentation, of a position that had been reached and was really held by sentiment. Rousseau hated the introduction of French plays in the same way that Cato hated the introduction of fine talkers from Greece. It was an innovation, and so habitual was it with Rousseau to look on all movement in the direction of what the French writers called taste and cultivation as depraving, that he cannot help taking for granted that any change in manners associated with taste must necessarily be a change for the worse. Thus the Letter to D'Alembert was essentially a supplement to the first Discourse; it was an application of its principles to a practical case. It was part of his general reactionary protest against philosophers, poets, men of letters, and all their works, without particular apprehension on the side of the drama. Hence its reasoning is much less interesting than its panegyric on the simplicity, robust courage, and manliness of the Genevese, and its invective against the effeminacy and frivolity of the Parisian. One of the most significant episodes in the discussion is the lengthy criticism on the immortal Misanthrope of Molière. Rousseau admits it for the masterpiece of the comic muse, though with characteristic perversity he insists that the hero is not misanthropic enough, nor truly misanthropic at all, because he flies into rage at small things affecting himself, instead of at the large follies of the race. Again, he says that Molière makes Alceste ridiculous, virtuous as he is, in order to win the applause of the pit. It is for the character of Philinte, however, that Rousseau reserves all his spleen. He takes care to describe him in terms which exactly hit Rousseau's own conception of his philosophic enemies, who find all going well because they have no interest in anything going better; who are content with everybody, because they do not care for anybody; who round a full table maintain that it is not true that the people are hungry. As criticism, one cannot value this kind of analysis. D'Alembert replied with a much more rational interpretation of the great comedy, but finding himself seized with the critic's besetting impertinence of improving masterpieces, he suddenly stopped with the becoming reflection—"But I perceive, sir, that I am giving lessons to Molière."[1]

The constant thought of Paris gave Rousseau an admirable occasion of painting two pictures in violent contrast, each as over-coloured as the other by his mixed conceptions of the Plutarchian antique and imaginary pastoral. We forget the depravation of the stage and the ill living of comedians in magnificent descriptions of the manly exercises and cheerful festivities of the free people on the shores of the Lake of

[1] *Lettre à M. J. J. Rousseau*, p. 258.

Geneva, and in scornful satire on the Parisian seraglios, where some woman assembles a number of men who are more like women than their entertainers. We see on the one side the rude sons of the republic, boxing, wrestling, running, in generous emulation, and on the other the coxcombs of cultivated Paris imprisoned in a drawing-room, "rising up, sitting down, incessantly going and coming to the fire-place, to the window, taking up a screen and putting it down again a hundred times, turning over books, flitting from picture to picture, turning and pirouetting about the room, while the idol stretched motionless on a couch all the time is only alive in her tongue and eyes" (p. 161). If the rough patriots of the Lake are less polished in speech, they are all the weightier in reason; they do not escape by a pleasantry or a compliment; each feeling himself attacked by all the forces of his adversary, he is obliged to employ all his own to defend himself, and this is how a mind acquires strength and precision. There may be here and there a licentious phrase, but there is no ground for alarm in that. It is not the least rude who are always the most pure, and even a rather clownish speech is better than that artificial style in which the two sexes seduce one another, and familiarise themselves decently with vice. 'Tis true our Swiss drinks too much, but after all let us not calumniate even vice; as a rule drinkers are cordial and frank, good, upright, just, loyal, brave, and worthy folk. Wherever people have most abhorrence of drunkenness, be sure they have most reason to fear lest its indiscretion should betray intrigue and treachery. In Switzerland it is almost thought well of, while at Naples they hold it in horror; but at bottom which is the more to be dreaded, the intemperance of the Swiss or the reserve of the Italian? It is hardly surprising to learn that the people of Geneva were as little gratified by this well-meant panegyric on their jollity as they had been by another writer's friendly eulogy on their Socinianism.[1]

The reader who was not moved to turn brute and walk on all fours by the pictures of the state of nature in the Discourses, may find it more difficult to resist the charm of the brotherly festivities and simple pastimes which in the Letter to D'Alembert the patriot holds up to the admiration of his countrymen and the envy of foreigners. The writer is in Sparta, but he tempers his Sparta with a something from Charmettes. Never before was there so attractive a combination of martial austerity with the grace of the idyll. And the interest of these pictures is much more than literary; it is historic also. They were the original version of those great gatherings in the Champ de Mars and strange suppers of fraternity during the progress of the Revolution in Paris, which have amused the cynical ever since, but which pointed to a not unworthy aspiration. The fine gentlemen whom Rousseau did so well to despise had then all fled, and

---

[1] D'Alembert's *Lettre à J. J. Rousseau*, p. 277. Rousseau has a passage to the same effect, that false people are always sober, in the *Nouv. Hél.*, Pt. I. xxiii. 123.

the common people under Rousseauite leaders were
doing the best they could to realise on the banks of
the Seine the imaginary joymaking and simple fellowship which had been first dreamed of for the banks of
Lake Leman, and commended with an eloquence that
struck new chords in minds satiated or untouched by
the brilliance of mere literature. There was no real
state of things in Geneva corresponding to the gracious
picture which Rousseau so generously painted, and
some of the citizens complained that his account of
their social joys was as little deserved as his ingenious
vindication of their hearty feeling for barrel or bottle
was little founded.[1]

The glorification of love of country did little for
the Genevese for whom it was meant, but it penetrated many a soul in the greater nation that lay sunk
in helpless indifference to its own ruin. Nowhere
else among the writers who are the glory of France
at this time, is any serious eulogy of patriotism.
Rousseau glows with it, and though he always speaks
in connection with Geneva, yet there is in his words
a generous breadth and fire which gave them an
irresistible contagiousness. There are many passages
of this fine persuasive force in the Letter to D'Alembert; perhaps this, referring to the citizens of Geneva
who had gone elsewhere in search of fortune, is as
good as another. Do you think that the opening of
a theatre, he asks, will bring them back to their

---

[1] Tronchin, for instance, in a letter to Rousseau, in M.
Streckeisen-Moultou's collection, i. 325.

mother city? No; "each of them must feel that
he can never find anywhere else what he has left
behind in his own land; an invincible charm must
call him back to the spot that he ought never to have
quitted; the recollection of their first exercises, their
first pleasures, their first sights, must remain deeply
graven in their hearts; the soft impressions made in
the days of their youth must abide and grow stronger
with advancing years, while a thousand others wax
dim; in the midst of the pomp of great cities and all
their cheerless magnificence, a secret voice must for
ever cry in the depth of the wanderer's soul, Ah,
where are the games and holidays of my youth?
Where is the concord of the townsmen, where the
public brotherhood? Where is pure joy and true
mirth? Where are peace, freedom, equity? Let us
hasten to seek all these. With the heart of a Genevese, with a city as smiling, a landscape as full of
delight, a government as just, with pleasures so true
and so pure, and all that is needed to be able to relish
them, how is it that we do not all adore our birth-
land? It was thus in old times that by modest feasts
and homely games her citizens were called back by
that Sparta which I can never quote often enough as
an example for us; thus in Athens in the midst of
fine art, thus in Susa in the very bosom of luxury and
soft delights, the wearied Spartan sighed after his
coarse pastimes and exhausting exercises" (p. 211).[1]

[1] A troop of comedians had been allowed to play for a short
time in Geneva, with many protests, during the mediation of

Any reference to this powerfully written, though most sophistical piece, would be imperfect which should omit its slightly virulent onslaught upon women and the passion which women inspire. The modern drama, he said, being too feeble to rise to high themes, has fallen back on love; and on this hint he proceeds to a censure of love as a poetic theme, and a bitter estimate of women as companions for men, which might have pleased Calvin or Knox in his sternest mood. The same eloquence which showed men the superior delights of the state of nature, now shows the superior fitness of the oriental seclusion of women; it makes a sympathetic reader tremble at the want of modesty, purity, and decency, in the part which women are allowed to take by the infatuated men of a modern community.

All this, again, is directed against "that philosophy of a day, which is born and dies in the corner of a city, and would fain stifle the cry of nature and the unanimous voice of the human race" (p. 131). The same intrepid spirits who had brought reason to bear upon the current notions of providence, inspiration, ecclesiastical tradition, and other unlighted spots in

1738. In 1766, eight years after Rousseau's letter, the government gave permission for the establishment of a theatre in the town. It was burnt down in 1768, and Voltaire spitefully hinted that the catastrophe was the result of design, instigated by Rousseau (*Corr.* v. 299, April 26, 1768). The theatre was not re-erected until 1783, when the oligarchic party regained the ascendancy and brought back with them the drama, which the democrats in their reign would not permit.

the human mind, had perceived that the subjection of
women to a secondary place belonged to the same
category, and could not any more successfully be defended by reason.   Instead of raging against women
for their boldness, their frivolousness, and the rest, as
our passionate sentimentalist did, the opposite school
insisted that all these evils were due to the folly of
treating women with gallantry instead of respect, and
to the blindness of refusing an equally vigorous and
masculine education to those who must be the closest
companions of educated man.   This was the view
forced upon the most rational observers of a society
where women were so powerful, and so absolutely
unfit by want of intellectual training for the right
use of social power.   D'Alembert expressed this view
in a few pages of forcible pleading in his reply to
Rousseau,[1] and some thirty-two years later, when all
questions had become political (1790), Condorcet ably
extended the same line of argument so as to make it
cover the claims of women to all the rights of citizenship.[2] From the nature of the case, however, it is
impossible to confute by reason a man who denies
that the matter in dispute is within the decision and
jurisdiction of reason, and who supposes that his own
opinion is placed out of the reach of attack when he
declares it to be the unanimous voice of the human
race.   We may remember that the author of this
philippic against love was at the very moment brood-

[1] *Lettre à J. J. Rousseau*, pp. 265-271.
[2] *Œuv.*, x. 121.

ing over the New Heloïsa, and was fresh from strange
transports at the feet of the Julie whom we know.

The Letter on the Stage was the definite mark of
Rousseau's schism from the philosophic congregation.
Has Jean Jacques turned a father of the church?
asked Voltaire. Deserters who fight against their
country ought to be hung. The little flock are
falling to devouring one another. This arch-madman,
who might have been something, if he would only
have been guided by his brethren of the Encyclopædia, takes it into his head to make a band of his
own. He writes against the stage, after writing a
bad play of his own. He finds four or five rotten
staves of Diogenes' tub, and instals himself therein
to bark at his friends.[1] D'Alembert was more tolerant,
but less clear-sighted. He insisted that the little
flock should do its best to heal divisions instead of
widening them. Jean Jacques, he said, "is a madman who is very clever, and who is only clever when
he is in a fever; it is best therefore neither to cure
nor to insult him."

Rousseau made the preface to the Letter on the
Stage an occasion for a proclamation of his final
breach with Diderot. "I once," he said, "possessed
a severe and judicious Aristarchus; I have him no
longer, and wish for him no longer." To this he
added in a footnote a passage from Ecclesiasticus, to
the effect that if you have drawn a sword on a friend

[1] To Thieriot, Sept. 17, 1758. To D'Alembert, Oct. 20,
1761. *Ib.* March 19, 1761.

there still remains a way open, and if you have spoken cheerless words to him concord is still possible, but malicious reproach and the betrayal of a secret—these things banish friendship beyond return. This was the end of his personal connection with the men whom he always contemptuously called the Holbachians. After 1760 the great stream divided into two; the rationalist and the emotional schools became visibly antipathetic, and the voice of the epoch was no longer single or undistracted.

END OF VOL. I.

Printed by R. & R. CLARK, LIMITED, *Edinburgh*

The Eversley Series.

Globe 8vo.   Cloth.   4s. net per volume.

The Eversley Series—*Continued.*

Globe 8vo. Cloth. 4s. net per volume.

French Poets and Novelists. By HENRY JAMES.

Partial Portraits. By HENRY JAMES.

Modern Greece. Two Lectures. By Sir RICHARD JEBB.

Letters of John Keats to his Family and Friends. Edited by SIDNEY COLVIN.

The Works of Charles Kingsley. 13 Vols.
WESTWARD HO! 2 Vols.
HYPATIA. 2 Vols.
YEAST. 1 Vol.
ALTON LOCKE. 2 Vols.
TWO YEARS AGO. 2 Vols.
HEREWARD THE WAKE. 2 Vols.
POEMS. 2 Vols.

The Works of Charles Lamb. Edited, with Introduction and Notes, by Canon AINGER. 6 Vols.
THE ESSAYS OF ELIA.
POEMS, PLAYS, AND MISCELLANEOUS ESSAYS.
MRS. LEICESTER'S SCHOOL, and other Writings.
TALES FROM SHAKESPEARE. By CHARLES and MARY LAMB.
THE LETTERS OF CHARLES LAMB. Newly arranged, with additions (1904). 2 Vols.

Life of Charles Lamb. By Canon AINGER.

Historical Essays. By J. B. LIGHTFOOT, D.D.

The Poetical Works of John Milton. Edited, with Memoir, Introduction, and Notes, by DAVID MASSON, M.A. 3 Vols.
Vol. 1. THE MINOR POEMS.
Vol. 2. PARADISE LOST.
Vol. 3. PARADISE REGAINED, AND SAMSON AGONISTES.

Collected Works of John Morley. 12 Vols.
VOLTAIRE. 1 Vol.
ROUSSEAU. 2 Vols.
DIDEROT AND THE ENCYCLOPÆDISTS. 2 Vols.
ON COMPROMISE. 1 Vol.
MISCELLANIES. 3 Vols.
BURKE. 1 Vol.
STUDIES IN LITERATURE. 1 Vol.
OLIVER CROMWELL. 1 Vol.

Essays by F. W. H. Myers. 3 Vols.
SCIENCE AND A FUTURE LIFE, AND OTHER ESSAYS.
CLASSICAL ESSAYS.
MODERN ESSAYS.

Records of Tennyson, Ruskin, and Browning. By ANNE THACKERAY RITCHIE.

The Works of Sir John R. Seeley K.C.M.G., Litt.D. 5 Vols.
THE EXPANSION OF ENGLAND. Two Courses of Lectures.
LECTURES AND ESSAYS.
ECCE HOMO. A Survey of the Life and Work of Jesus Christ.
NATURAL RELIGION.
LECTURES ON POLITICAL SCIENCE.

The Works of Shakespeare. 10 Vols. With short Introductions and Footnotes by Professor C. H. HERFORD.
Vol. 1. LOVE'S LABOUR'S LOST—COMEDY OF ERRORS—TWO GENTLEMEN OF VERONA—MIDSUMMER-NIGHT'S DREAM.
Vol. 2. TAMING OF THE SHREW—MERCHANT OF VENICE—MERRY WIVES OF WINDSOR—TWELFTH NIGHT—AS YOU LIKE IT.
Vol. 3. MUCH ADO ABOUT NOTHING—ALL'S WELL THAT ENDS WELL—MEASURE FOR MEASURE—TROILUS AND CRESSIDA.
Vol. 4. PERICLES—CYMBELINE—THE WINTER'S TALE—THE TEMPEST.
Vol. 5. HENRY VI.: First Part—HENRY VI.: Second Part—HENRY VI.: Third Part—RICHARD III.
Vol. 6. KING JOHN—RICHARD II.—HENRY IV.: First Part—HENRY IV. Second Part.
Vol. 7. HENRY V.—HENRY VIII.—TITUS ANDRONICUS—ROMEO AND JULIET.
Vol. 8. JULIUS CÆSAR—HAMLET—OTHELLO.
Vol. 9. KING LEAR—MACBETH—ANTONY AND CLEOPATRA.
Vol. 10. CORIOLANUS—TIMON OF ATHENS—POEMS.

The Works of James Smetham.
LETTERS. With an Introductory Memoir. Edited by SARAH SMETHAM and WILLIAM DAVIES. With a Portrait.
LITERARY WORKS. Edited by WILLIAM DAVIES.

Life of Swift. By Sir HENRY CRAIK, K.C.B. 2 Vols. New Edition.

Selections from the Writings of Thoreau. Edited by H. S. SALT.

Essays in the History of Religious Thought in the West. By Bishop WESTCOTT, D.D.

The Works of William Wordsworth. Edited by Professor KNIGHT. 10 Vols.
POETICAL WORKS. 8 Vols.
PROSE WORKS. 2 Vols.

The Journals of Dorothy Wordsworth. 2 Vols.

MACMILLAN AND CO., LTD., LONDON.